If you don't have a pension, you don't have a future.

If you're self-employed or outside a company pension scheme, you could be in serious trouble when it comes to retirement.

You could be dependent on a state pension, which today is £2260 per annum for a couple.

On the other hand, you could face the future secure in the knowledge that you and your family will be well taken care of. With an NPI personal pension.

And so you needn't worry about tying your money up, we offer a valuable additional facility called Loanback Plus. It not only lends you money, subject to security, but also pays your regular premiums if you're too ill to earn.

At NPI we've been specialising in life assurance and pensions for over 140 years. Planned Savings magazine has put us in the top four personal pension plans every year since they started their independent survey eight years ago. With a performance 40% better than the average for all the companies reviewed.

Ask your professional adviser about NPI.

Or write to John Fisher, National Provident Institution, 48 Gracechurch Street, London EC3V 0BB.

Because a future without a personal pension is really no future at all.

NPI
It pays to listen to experts.

WORKING FOR YOURSELF

IMAGINE

Starting your own business without any capital;

thorough training at no cost to you;

financial support until you are established;

the adult population for a self-renewing market;

remuneration for ten years on retained contracts;

the pleasure of being a professional adviser;

the high rewards of building a life-long clientele

and the deep satisfaction of being self-sufficient.

For the people who work with us, this is not imagination but reality. If you, too, have drive and integrity and enjoy helping people to help themselves, we would like to meet you. We offer what is probably the most demanding and rewarding sales career you could have — one that gives you the opportunity to earn the kind of income you thought only captains of industry enjoyed.

For further information, write to Richard Severn, Agency Director, ManuLife, ManuLife House, St. George's Way, Stevenage, Herts, SG1 1HP or telephone:

Stevenage (0438) 56101

ManuⁱLife

The Manufacturers Life Insurance Group

Working for Yourself

The *Daily Telegraph* Guide to Self-Employment

Godfrey Golzen

Kogan Page

First published 1975.
Reprinted 1976. Second edition
published 1978. Third edition published 1980.
Fourth edition published 1981 by Kogan Page Ltd,
120 Pentonville Road,
London N1 9JN.

British Library Cataloguing in Publication Data
Golzen, Godfrey
    Working for yourself. — 4th ed.
    1. Self-employed 2. Small business — Management
    I. Title
    658'.04   HD69.S6
ISBN 0 85038 455 9 (Hb)
ISBN 0 85038 456 7 (Pb)

Printed in Great Britain by
Richard Clay (The Chaucer Press) Ltd,
Bungay, Suffolk

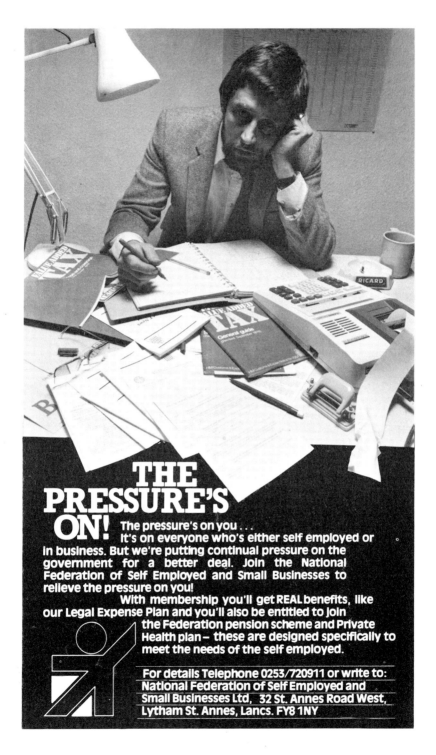
5

WORK FOR YOURSELF... AND PROFIT WITH US

Try the Prontaprint recipe for success – your own profitable business plus the expert advice, training, guidance and support that has helped over 130 successful franchisees build Europe's No. 1 chain of high speed printing and copying shops.

A Prontaprint franchise offers added freedom. The service you offer to the community is operated during normal office hours, you do not have the burden of regular late openings or unsocial hours which many franchises demand. This leaves you ample time for relaxation and leisure – two crucial ingredients in the making of any happy and successful businessman.

We offer nationwide

prontaprint ®
Europe's No.1 print & copy shop chain

opportunities, so if you consider yourself capable of meeting this challenge to join our highly successful team we would like to hear from you.

Franchise Director, Prontaprint Limited, Coniscliffe House, Darlington, DL3 7EX. Tel: 0325 55391/4.

Please quote reference W F Y 1

6

Contents

Acknowledgements

We should like to thank John Slade, R W Leff, John Forbes and W T Miller for their advice on accountancy and taxation; H F Armstrong of Development Capital Ltd for assistance with the chapter on raising capital; Dryden Gilling-Smith of Employee Benefit Services (Management) Ltd for his help on the financial advantages enjoyed by limited companies; John Blundell who read the whole book in manuscript; and the freelance and self-employed people who have contributed to Parts 2 and 3, particularly those who have answered questionnaires and allowed us to reproduce their comments.

We would be grateful for readers' comments and suggestions. There are as many ways of running small businesses as there are proprietors, and any advice on methods other than those we have indicated will be considered for inclusion in future editions of the book.

Preface

The scope of the book

The 'self-employed' are a very diverse group: they provide every conceivable type of product and service from tobacco tasting to golf course designing. This book mirrors that diversity. It is aimed at several different types of self-employed person. Part 1 deals with starting in business and offers advice on finance, taxation, bookkeeping, employment legislation, cash flow forecasting, marketing and so on. Part 2 concentrates on those who offer goods and services from business premises and property: farmers, retailers, franchise holders, restauranteurs, hoteliers, etc. Part 3 covers a wide range of freelance activities, which may be carried on full-time or part-time, from home or from an office or studio, individually or with staff.

For any enterprise Part 1, which covers the problems of raising capital, making financial projections and understanding commercial and employment law, will be useful. But it is particularly valuable as a crash course in basic business principles for those starting a small business. But the person (designer, typist, teacher, etc) who is simply supplementing his income by some freelance work will also find something of value in Part 1: how to assess himself for tax purposes, the importance of proper invoicing, the part played by professional advisers, the need to plan workload and meet schedules.

Though the reader should be aware of the several 'audiences' at which the book is aimed and should pay closest attention to the section which concerns him most directly, he may also profit from the other sections. And, who knows, today's freelance book designer may tomorrow have his own art studio, with staff to manage, creditors to satisfy and clients to cultivate. The section on business management will at least make you aware of the problems and pressures of expanding the scope of any business, and of the pleasures that come with success.

Not all the areas of self-employment are covered. However, although, for example, architects, accountants, doctors, lawyers, insurance brokers and management consultants are not dealt with, because they tend to have codes of conduct peculiar to their professions, much of the advice and information in this book is still applicable to their business concerns. Having decided to 'go it alone', of course, the advice given in Parts 1 and 2 will be as relevant to these as to other business enterprises.

The range of freelance activities covered, supplementing the general points made in Part 1 and the treatment of certain types of business management in Part 2, is sufficiently wide for the following principles of self-employment to emerge:

☐ Consider the drawbacks
☐ Be realistic about the risk you are taking
☐ Be aware of the competition to what you offer
☐ Be certain that your enterprise is financially sound
☐ Know and act within the law as it applies to you
☐ Use professional advice where necessary
☐ Fulfil commissions accurately and on time
☐ Commit yourself totally to a project.

These principles apply to the man with a medium-sized business as much as to the retailer or restaurateur, the part-time editor, typist or translator. If a service is required and completion is guaranteed to a satisfactory standard, people are prepared to pay for it. A reputation is established and customers return. An established group of clients provides a basis on which to expand and perhaps diversify, and, if this is achieved without standards falling, the process will be repeated. Whatever your area of interest and size of operation, we hope that our advice aids that process and enables you to avoid the pitfalls and enjoy the profits of self-employment.

Part 1:
Running Your Own Business

1: Going it Alone

Since the first edition of this book was published in 1975 the climate of political opinion towards the self-employed has changed dramatically for the better. Even under the last Labour Government important changes were enacted to make life easier for small businesses and this trend has been continued in the 1980 and 1981 Budgets, and through changes in employment law and company law. The present government favours a reduction in the administrative burdens on business, and the trend is therefore likely to continue, because both political parties seem to agree that the encouragement of small businesses may provide the answer to one of our most worrying problems: chronic unemployment. It has been demonstrated throughout the first half of the 1970s that creating jobs in the public sector — the solution favoured by the left — is vastly expensive and, in draining workers from potentially productive areas of the economy, carries the seeds of its own bankruptcy. From an ideological point of view there is also an increasing feeling that a highly bureaucratic corporate state, limiting people's choice about how they spend their money, or even ultimately where and at what they want to work, is a road down which we have travelled far enough. As for the belief that encouraging public and discouraging private ownership would lead to better industrial relations, that pious myth has been destroyed by the countless public sector strikes in the last 30 years.

Yet there is no doubt that unemployment is unacceptably high and that it is here to stay unless we do something about it. In fact it is here to increase, because automation of all kinds of processes, from controlling production lines to checking tins of groceries on supermarket shelves, will soon be within the financial reach of even the small firms. More automation may mean fewer jobs for people in the short term, and some readers of this book may already have fallen victim of this process. But it also means more uniformity, less flexibility and less choice and this is where the self-employed come into their own as a new kind of labour force, operating at every level from providing specialist consultancy to making goods and selling services which are still needed, but which the big firms with their colossal overheads no longer find it worthwhile to supply. Ironically, among the customers of many small independent companies are some of the big firms themselves, which find some service or part is unobtainable because of strikes, production hold-ups or because some other big firm has given up producing it. Not infrequently, they have to turn to some former employee who has gone into business for himself, having anticipated or had prior knowledge of exactly such a problem.

Often such a man might have been made redundant as a result of technological change. Here the person affected may find two kinds of opportunities for self-employment. The first arises because skills which are obsolete in one context may be greatly in demand in another; a case in point would be middle-level accounting experience, desperately needed by many small firms in the form of a consultancy service. The second because not everyone wants machine-made products off the assembly line. Indeed, all the indications are that as people become more affluent they want more, not less, individuality. The insatiable appetite for antiques does not arise simply because they are a good investment. They are also more individual and more human than mass-produced consumer items.

It is this human element in self-employment that is increasingly attracting the sort of thinkers who, a decade or so ago, might have been more interested in socialist solutions, and made even the Labour Government look on the self-employed with a kindlier eye. As people become less and less involved in what they produce and are consigned to the role of button-pushers on machines, they become alienated from their labour or in simpler terms, fed up — a situation of perpetual boredom which finds expression in strikes, absenteeism, general bloody-mindedness on the factory floor or total lack of interest in the office. There is no way, of course, that we can go back to a society of individual craftsmen without an unacceptable drop in our standards of living. But maybe, so the argument runs, we should leave to machines what machines do best and get human beings to cater to the individual taste, the quirky needs, the one-off problems and the sudden emergencies and breakdowns that machines cannot handle.

'And the next race will be the self-employed handicap'

You know what a dog race is like – however hard the greyhounds try, they never catch the hare. It must be a bit frustrating.

Inflation is a bit like that hare. Try as you might, you never seem to be able to keep up with it, particularly once you've retired. And if you're self-employed, you have an extra disadvantage – we call it the Self-Employed Handicap.

Because you're self-employed, you have to make your own pension arrangements. With most companies, however, the best you can get is a pension that increases at a fixed rate – say 5% or 8½%p.a. It may not increase at all.

Dynamic OPTION The Provident Mutual have a better solution. Our Dynamic pensions actually share in bonuses after retirement, which means that they do more than most to stave off inflation. This year, they will be increasing by 10.15%p.a. compound.

The Dynamic option is not the only thing our self-employed policies have going for them. They have one of the best track records in the market – our Personal Pension Plan has been one of the top four performers in each of the last five years.* And our high death benefits give your family an extra degree of protection in case the worst should happen.

You can find out more about our self-employed pensions by asking your insurance broker about us.

In the race against inflation, make sure you don't carry the biggest handicap.

*Planned Savings.

PROVIDENT MUTUAL
LIFE ASSURANCE ASSOCIATION · FOUNDED 1840
25-31 Moorgate, London EC2R 6BA   Tel 01-628 3232

This is certainly where the opportunities for the self-employed lie, and one of the objects of this preamble is to make an important practical point. The game the giants play has its limitations, but do not take them on direct. If, for instance, you are a skilled cabinetmaker, do not get into mass-produced furniture: you simply will not be able to get your prices down far enough to make a living, nor will you be able to handle distribution on the scale that mass production implies. Do something the giants do not do, such as making things to individual specifications. If you have always wanted to own a grocery shop, do not do the same thing as the supermarket round the corner. Bake your own bread or make your delicatessen or stay open round the clock — do something you can do better or differently.

How well prepared are you?

Having a sound idea is only part of the story. How prepared you are to take it further depends on the extent of your experience; not that it is absolutely essential at the 'thinking about it' stage to have all-round direct experience of the sort of self-employment opportunity you want to exploit. But you have to be aware of what you know and do not know about it. You may be a manager who is also a keen gardener and you want to set up a market gardening business. In that case you probably have a rather better knowledge of management essentials than that of a hypothetical competitor who is currently employed by a market gardener and wants to set up on his own. But on the finer points of growing techniques and hazards, and where to sell the products, your competitor is going to be much better equipped than you.

The first step, therefore, is to make a list of all the aspects you can think of about running the business: show it to someone who is already in the field to make sure nothing of importance has been missed out, and tick off the ones you think you can handle and consider how you are going to deal with the areas where your experience is limited. The best way may well be to gain practical first-hand experience. If you are thinking of buying a shop, for instance, working in one for a few weeks will teach you an amazing amount about the public's tastes — what sells and what does not — and you may save yourself hundreds of pounds in making the right buying decisions later on. As far as management principles are concerned, your library will provide you with lists for further reading.

You should also take advice from your regional Small Firms Centre. These provide consultancy services and a wide range of useful publications. Information is free and counselling incurs only a modest charge. The addresses of the regional centres are given in Appendix 1. In Scotland the service is operated through the Scottish Development Agency. In Wales the information service is provided by the Welsh Office and the counselling service is operated by the Welsh Development Agency. In Northern Ireland, the Department of Commerce provides an information service.

The importance of planning

If you are going to borrow money to get your firm off the ground, the lender (if he has any sense!) will want to know how you plan to use his money and if the operation you have in mind is going to give him an adequate return on his investment. This means that you must have a clear idea of how your business is going to develop, at least for the next year, where you see work coming from and whether you are going to have the future resources, human and financial, to handle it (see Chapter 7 on the importance of cash flow and financial forecasting).

Even if you do not need to borrow money, planning is vital. Landing a big contract or assignment for a new business is a heartening beginning, but well before work on it is completed you should be looking around for the next job. The completion dates you have given should take this into account, unless the amount of money you are going to get from it is so much that you will have plenty of time to look around for more work after this first job is done. But that, too, is a matter of planning.

Is self-employment right for you?

Let us leave aside Samuel Smiles-like homilies about having to be your own hardest taskmaster. We will take it for granted that you are not considering working for yourself as a soft option. But apart from the question of whether your health can stand the fairly demanding regime that full-time self-employment implies, there are also other questions you have to ask yourself about your aptitude − as opposed to a mere hankering − for going it alone. First of all, there are severely practical considerations: whether you have enough money or the means of raising it. And remember you will need money not only to finance your business or practice, but also for your own personal needs, including sickness and holiday periods.

Self-employment may mean a drop in your standard of living, possibly a permanent one, if things do not go as planned. Are you prepared for that? Is your family going to like it? Have you seriously considered the full price to be paid for independence? Is your wife (or husband) able and willing to lend a hand?

Insecurity, a necessary condition of self-employment, is not everyone's cup of tea. Neither are some of the implications of being your own master. One of the most important of them is the ability to make decisions and if you very much dislike doing this, self-employment is probably not the right channel for your abilities. You are constantly going to be called on to make decisions, some of them rather trivial, where it does not matter greatly what you do decide, so long as you decide *something*; but some of them will be fundamental policy decisions that could make or break your business.

You are also going to be called on to make decisions about people, and these are often the hardest of all. It is terribly difficult to sack someone with whom you have worked in the intimacy of a small office, but sooner or later that kind of situation will land in your lap. So another quality that is called for is toughness. This does not mean overbearing nastiness, but it does mean the readiness, for instance, to part company with a supplier, even if he is a personal friend, if his service starts to fall consistently below standard.

We have touched on the question of your aptitude for self-employment as such, but there remains the matter of your aptitude for the sphere of activity you have chosen. A management consultant friend of the writer's uses a basic precept in advising companies on personnel problems: staff are best employed doing what they are best at. The same applies to self-employment and most people go into it with that in mind. The problem with self-employment, however, is that at least at the outset you cannot absolutely avoid all the aspects of the work, such as bookkeeping, that in a bigger organisation you might have delegated or passed on to another department because you yourself do not much enjoy doing them. What you have to do is to maximise the number of tasks you are good at and minimise the others. This may mean taking a partner to complement your skills or employing an outside agency to

21

handle some things for you: selling, for instance, if you are good at making things but not so good at negotiating or dealing with people. That means less money for you, but at the risk of sounding moralistic, you are unlikely to succeed if making money is the only thing you have in mind and overrides considerations like job satisfaction.

At the same time, the costs of doing anything in business must always be taken into account. For example, if you take a partner, is there going to be enough money coming in to make a living for both of you? Unless you constantly quantify your business decisions in this way, you are unlikely to stay in business very long. In fact, you should not even start on your career as a self-employed person without investigating very carefully whether there is a big and lasting enough demand for the product or service you are proposing to offer, and whether it can be sold at a competitive price that will enable you to earn a living after meeting all the expenses of running a business.

In conclusion

If you have faced the issues we have touched on in the last paragraphs and feel confident about dealing with them, your chances of success in self-employment, whether full-time or part-time, are good. As for the opportunities, they are legion and later we examine what is involved in some areas. The list obviously cannot be comprehensive (though it should serve as a stimulus to looking in other directions as well) and neither can the coverage of basic management techniques in Part 1. But one of the essentials of effective management is to pick out no more from any topic than you need to know to accomplish the task in hand. We hope that these chapters give you the kind of technical information that you will be concerned with at this early stage of your career as a self-employed person.

Checklist: going it alone

1. Can you measure the demand for your product or service in terms of money?
2. Who are your competitors and what can you offer that they cannot?
3. Is the market local or national and how can you reach it? Can you measure the cost of doing so in financial terms?
4. How much capital have you got and how easy is it to realise?

5. How much money do you need for start-up costs and if it is more than your capital, how can you make up the difference?

6. How long is it likely to be before your income meets your outgoings and how do you propose to manage until then?

7. Do you have any established contacts who can give you business?

8. Is your proposed activity a one-off opportunity or a line for which there is a continuing demand?

9. What aspects of your proposed activity do you have first-hand experience in and how do you propose to fill in the gaps?

10. How good is your health?

11. What are you best at/worst at in your present job and how does this relate to your area of self-employment?

12. Is there any way you can combine your present job with self-employment for an experimental period while you see how it goes?

13. Have you made a realistic appraisal of your aptitude for going it alone, both generally and in the context of the line of work you have chosen?

14. Should you join up with someone else and, if so, is the net income you anticipate going to provide a livelihood for all the people involved?

2: Starting a Business

Before you start talking to bank managers, solicitors, accountants or tax inspectors you will have to start thinking about what sort of legal entity the business you are going to operate is to be. The kind of advice you seek from them will depend on this decision, and you have three choices. You can operate as a sole trader (ie a one-man business — it does not necessarily have to be a 'trade'), a partnership, or as a private limited company. Let us see what each of these options implies.

Sole trader

There is nothing — or at least very little — to stop you from starting a business under your own name, operating from a back room of your own house.* But if the place you live in is owned by someone else, you should get the landlord's permission. If the business you are starting in your home is one that involves a change of use of the premises, you will have to get planning permission from the local authority's planning officer. In that case you may also find that you are re-rated on a commercial basis. If you own your house, you should also check that there are no restrictive covenants in the deeds governing its use. On the whole, a business conducted unobtrusively from a private residence is unlikely to attract attention from the local authority but, to be perfectly safe, it is as well to have a word with the authority's planning department since any change of use, even of part of your residence, requires planning permission.

The next step is to inform your local tax inspector or to get your accountant to do so (see Chapter 4 on choosing professional advisers). This is always advisable if the nature of your earnings is changing and imperative if you are moving from employee to full-time self-employed status, because it changes

*If your business is likely to disturb neighbours or cause a nuisance (noise, smells, clients taking up parking space) or if it necessitates your building an extension, converting an attic, etc, you must apply for planning permission. Your property may then be given a higher, commercial rateable value.

Urgent advice to anyone about to enter a self-employed pension scheme.

Don't.

Don't, that is, until you and your advisers have checked out the new range of pension plans from Sun Life.

Because Sun Life now offer you a choice of schemes that is – to use an overworked phrase – quite literally unique.

More to the point, you can use the choice to save yourself money, to make your financial planning in the next few years a lot easier, and – most important of all – to provide a better retirement benefit.

Here are just some of the advantages Sun Life can offer you.

1. Loanback facilities

A special feature of Option Pension plans is the facility to obtain a loan from Sun Life Assurance Society Limited. Subject to adequate security being available, and to an equivalent sum being transferred to a Special Deposit Fund, this facility can provide a loan, on advantageous terms, for high-expenditure items such as, for example, school fees.

2. Private Pension Funds for Partners

Sun Life can offer groups such as partnerships their own private pension funds, where the total initial premiums amount to not less than £10,000.

3. A chance to maximise your own pension

Sun Life's Option Pension plans allow you to switch between a conventional insurance fund and unit-linked investment in response to changing markets.

4. Good investment performance

Ultimately, what will determine the size of your pension is the performance of the underlying fund.

Sun Life – managers of life assurance funds since 1810 – can offer you advantages here, too. For example, Sun Life's unit-linked funds have shown exceptional growth by any standards.

For full details of these and other benefits including the loanback facility, write to us (no stamp needed) – or consult your adviser.

**SUN LIFE ASSURANCE SOCIETY LTD
FREEPOST, BRISTOL BS1**

the basis on which you pay tax. The inspector will give you some indication of allowable business expenses to be set off against your earnings for tax purposes. These will not include entertainment of potential customers (unless they are overseas buyers) but will cover items 'wholly and exclusively incurred for the purposes of business'. These are spelt out in more detail in Chapter 11. Some things, of course, are used partly for private and partly for business purposes – your car or your telephone, for instance. In these cases only that proportion of expenditure that can definitely be attributed to business use is chargeable against tax. Careful records of such use must, therefore, be kept, and its extent must also be credible. If you are not exporting anything in the way of a product or service, you may be unable to convince the inspector that a weekend in Paris was in the course of business! But if you are, he is unlikely to quibble about a modest hotel bill, even if the business part of your visit only took a couple of hours.

The principal cautionary point to bear in mind about operating as a sole trader is that you are personally liable for the debts of your business. If you go bankrupt your creditors are entitled to seize and sell your *personal* possessions, not just equipment, cars and other items directly related to your business.

Partnerships

Most of the above points are also true if you are setting up in partnership with other people. Once again, there are very few restrictions against setting up in partnership with someone to carry on a business, but because all the members of a partnership are personally liable for its debts, even if these are incurred by a piece of mismanagement by one partner which was not known to his colleagues, the choice of partners is a step that requires very careful thought. So should you have a partner at all? Certainly it is not advisable to do so just for the sake of having company, because unless the partner can really contribute something to the business, you are giving away a part of what could in time be a very valuable asset to little purpose. A partner should be able to make an important contribution to running the business in an area which you are unable to take care of. He may have some range of specialised expertise that is vital to the business; or he may have a range of contacts to bring in work; or the work may be of such a nature that the executive tasks and decisions cannot be handled by one person. He may even be a 'sleeping partner' who is doing little else apart from putting up some money in return for a share of the eventual profits.

But whatever the reason for establishing a partnership as opposed to going it alone and owning the whole business may be, you should be sure that your partner (of course, there may be more than one, but for the sake of simplicity we will assume that only one person is involved) is someone you know well in a business, not just a social, capacity. Because of this, before formally establishing a partnership, it may be advisable to tackle, as an informal joint venture, one or two jobs with the person you are thinking of setting up with, carrying at the end of the day an agreed share of the costs and profits. That way you will learn about each other's strengths and weaknesses, and indeed whether you can work together harmoniously at all. It may turn out, for instance, that your prospective partner's expertise or contacts, while useful, do not justify giving him a share of the business and that in fact a consultancy fee is the right way of remunerating him.

Even if all goes well and you find that you can cooperate, it is vital that a formal partnership agreement should be drawn up by a solicitor. This is true even of husband-and-wife partnerships. The agreement should cover such points as the following:

1. Who is responsible for what aspects of the operation (eg production, marketing, etc)?
2. What constitutes a policy decision (eg whether or not to take on a contract) and how is it taken? By a majority vote, if there is an uneven number of partners? By the partner concerned with that aspect of things? Only if all partners agree?
3. How are the profits to be divided? According to the amount of capital put in? According to the amount of work done by each partner? Over the whole business done by the partnership over a year? On a job-by-job basis? How much money can be drawn, on what basis, and how often in the way of remuneration?
4. What items, like cars, not exclusively used for business can be charged to the partnership? And is there any limitation to the amount of money involved?
5. If one of the partners retires or withdraws how is his share of the business to be valued?

27

6. If one of the partners dies, what provision should the others make for his dependants?

There are obviously many kinds of eventualities that have to be provided for, depending on the kind of business that is going to be carried on. Some professional partnerships, for instance, may consist of little more than an agreement to pool office expenses like the services of typists and telephonists, with each partner drawing his own fees quite independently of the rest. The best way to prepare the ground for a solicitor to draw up an agreement is for each partner to make a list of possible points of dispute and to leave it to the legal adviser to produce a form of words to cover these and any other points he may come up with himself.

Private limited companies

Except when your business or freelance occupation is on a very small scale — something that brings in only a few extra pounds a week — it is generally advisable to set up as a private limited company, unless you are prevented from doing so for professional reasons or if you are under a legal disability such as applies to undischarged bankrupts. The advantage of a limited company is that, in law, it has an identity distinct from that of the shareholders who are its owners. Consequently, if a limited company goes bankrupt, the claims of the creditors are limited to the assets of the company. This includes any capital issued to shareholders which they have either paid for in full or in part. We shall return to the question of share capital in a moment, but the principle at work here is that when shares are issued the shareholders need not necessarily pay for them in full, though they have a legal obligation to do so if the company goes bankrupt. Shareholders are not, however, liable as individuals and their private assets outside the company may not be touched, unless their company has been trading fraudulently. On the other hand, if creditors ask for personal guarantees directors of limited companies are not protected and *personal* as well as business assets are at risk in the event of bankruptcy.

A limited company can be formed by two shareholders (who can be husband and wife), one of whom must be a director. It must also have a company secretary, who can be an outside person, such as your solicitor or accountant. Apart from this, the main requirements relate to documentation. Like sole traders or partnerships, a limited company must prepare a set of accounts annually for the inspector of taxes, but it has the further obligation that these have to be audited, normally by an accountant, who has to certify that they present 'a true and fair view' of the company's finances; and it must make an annual return to the Registrar of Companies, showing all the shareholders and directors, any changes of ownership that have taken place, a profit and loss account over the year and a balance sheet.

The cost of forming a company, including the capital duty which is based on the issued capital (we shall come to the distinction between this and nominal capital shortly), is likely to be around £100, depending on what method you use to go about it. The cheapest way is to buy a ready-made ('off the shelf') company from one of the registration agents who advertise their services in specialist financial journals. Such a company will not actually have been trading, but will be properly registered by the agents. All that has to be done is for the existing. 'shareholders' (who are probably the agent's nominees) to resign and for the purchasers to become the new shareholders and to appoint directors.

Alternatively you can start your own company from scratch, but whichever course you choose professional advice is vital at this stage. The technicalities are trickier than they sound, though simple enough to those versed in such transactions.

Registration of business names

One problem you may encounter with an 'off the shelf' company is when it has a name that does not relate meaningfully to the activity you are proposing to carry on. In that case there are two courses open to you:

1. You can apply to the Registrar of Companies (Companies Registration Office, Crown Way, Maindy, Cardiff CF4 3UZ) to change the name. A fee of £10 will be charged for this.

2. You can keep the name of the company, but apply to the Registrar of Business Names to *trade* under a name different from that of the company itself. The addresses of the Registrar of Business Names are: 55-71 City Road, London EC1Y 2DN (for England and Wales); 102 George Street, Edinburgh EH2 3DJ (for Scotland); and 43-47 Chichester Street, Belfast BT1 4RJ (for Northern Ireland).

The necessity to register the name, either of the company or the business (or both, if they are in any way different) does not only crop up in instances like the one we have just cited, however. If you intend to set up a company you will have to make application to use the name you have chosen to the Registrar of Companies. Permission will not be granted if it is too much like the name of an existing company, or if the Registrar considers the name is misleading (eg the use of the word 'international' when the firm is plainly not so). The fee for registering a company name is £50.

To use a *business* name you will have to apply to the Registrar of Business Names and you must do so within 14 days of starting to trade under the name you have chosen. You should apply well before you start trading, as registration takes time, your application may be refused (disastrous if your stationery is already printed!), and your bank manager may wish to see your RBN certificate before you open a business bank account. In the case of a limited company application has to be made to use a name other than its existing one or its full corporate one. For instance, your company may be called 'John Smith Ltd', but your business name might be 'Regency Antiques'. You will have to apply to use both the *company* name and the *business* name.

In the case of a sole trader or a partnership you will also have to apply to the Registrar of Business Names if the firm is to trade under any other name than that of the people or person concerned, without any qualification or description. (A somewhat sexist touch applies here to married women, who have to apply to the Registrar if they want to trade under their maiden name.) Thus, if you are proposing to trade as plain Tom Jones, it will not be necessary to register the name of your enterprise. But if you are calling your business 'Tom Jones, Design Consultant' you will have to apply to use this name within 14 days of starting to trade. The fee at present is £1. The government is currently considering important changes in this area. The two main points of interest are the proposal to abolish the Registry of Business Names and to create a new form of limited liability (the 'proprietary' company) especially suited to the needs of the smaller business.

It is worth giving a good deal of thought to the choice of a business name. Clever names are all very well, but if they do not clearly establish the nature of the business you are in, prospective customers leafing through a telephone or business directory may have trouble in finding you; or, if they do find you, they may not readily match your name to their needs. For instance, if you are a furniture repairer, it is far better to describe yourself as such in your business name than to call yourself something like 'Chippendale Restorations'. On the other hand if you already have a big reputation in some specialised sector, stick with it. Arguably, some of the Beatles' business ventures might have been more successful if they had traded on that name, instead of using the label 'Apple' for their other activities.

The rules governing the use of business names are like those for company names, except that the Registrar is less concerned about the fact that a similar trading name may already be in existence. Obviously, however, it is advisable in both cases to wait until the name you have put forward is accepted before having any stationery printed. When you do get to this stage the names of the proprietors (or, in the case of a limited company, the directors) have to be shown not only on letterheads, but also on catalogues and trade literature. Limited companies, in addition, have to show their registration number and the address of their registered office on such stationery.

This address may not necessarily be the same as the one at which business is normally transacted. Some firms use their accountant's or solicitor's premises as their registered office. You will probably see quite a number of registration certificates hanging in their office (they are required by law to be so displayed) when you go there. This is because it is to that address that all legal and official documents are sent. If you have placed complete responsibility for dealing with such matters in the hands of professional advisers, it is obviously convenient that the related correspondence should also be directed there. Bear in mind, though, that this does involve a certain loss of control on your part. Unless you at least first see these documents yourself, you will have no idea, for instance, whether the important ones are being handled with due dispatch.

Limited company documents

When you set up a limited company, your solicitor or accountant will be involved in drafting certain papers and documents which govern its structure and the way it is to be run. When this process has been completed you will receive copies of the company's Memorandum and Articles of Association, some share transfer forms, a Minute Book, the Company Seal and the Certificate of Incorporation. Let us explain briefly what these mean.

The Memorandum

This document sets out the main objects for which the company is formed and what it is allowed to do. There are standard clauses for this and your professional adviser will use these in drafting the document. The main thing to watch out for is that he should not be too specific in setting out the limits of the proposed operation, because if you change tack somewhere along the line — for instance if you move from mail order to making goods for the customers you have built up — you may lose the protection of your limited liability unless the Memorandum provides for this. There are, however, catch-all clauses which allow you to trade in pretty much anything or in any manner you like. Furthermore, the 'objects' clauses can be changed by a special resolution, passed by 75 per cent of the shareholders.

The Memorandum also sets out the company's nominal or authorised share capital and the par value per share. This is a point about which many newcomers to this aspect of business get very confused. The thing to remember is that in this context the value of share capital is a purely *nominal* value. You can have a company operating with thousands of pounds' worth of nominal share capital. This sounds very impressive, but what counts is the *issued* share capital, because this represents what the shareholders have actually put into the business or pledged themselves so to do. It is quite possible to have a company with a nominal capital of £1000, but with only two issued shares of £1 each to the two shareholders that are required by law.

The issued share capital also determines the ownership of a company. In the case we have just quoted, the two shareholders would own the company jointly. But if they then issue a third £1 share to another person without issuing any more to themselves they would now only own two-thirds of the company. This is a vital point to remember when raising capital by means of selling shares.

Apart from determining proportions of ownership, issued share capital also signifies how much of their own money the shareholders have put into the company or are prepared to accept liability for. Therefore in raising money from a bank or finance house, the manager there will look closely at the issued share capital. To the extent that he is not satisfied that the liability for the amount he is being asked to put up is adequately backed by issued share capital, he is likely to ask the shareholders to guarantee a loan or overdraft with their own personal assets — for instance by depositing shares they privately hold in a public quoted company or unit trust as security. In the case of a new company without a track record this would, in fact, be the usual procedure.

The nominal share capital of a new small-scale business is usually £100. It can be increased later on, as business grows, on application to the Registrar of Companies. The point of such a move would be to increase the *issued* share capital, for instance, if a new shareholder were to put money into the company. But, once again, it should be borne in mind that if the issued share capital was increased from £100 to £1000, and a backer were to buy £900 worth of shares at par value, the original shareholders would only own one-tenth of the business; the fact that they got the whole thing going is quite beside the point.

One last question about issued share capital which sometimes puzzles people. Must you actually hand over money for the shares when you start your own company, as is the case when you buy shares on the stock market, and what happens to it? The answer is yes. You pay it into the company's bank account because, remember, it has a separate legal identity from the shareholders who own it. However, you need not pay for your shares in full. You can, for instance, pay 50p per share for a hundred £1 shares. The balance of £50 represents your liability if the company goes bankrupt and you only actually have to hand over the money if that happens or if a majority at a shareholders' meeting requires you to do so. The fact that you have not paid in full for shares issued to you does not, however, diminish your entitlement to share in the profits, these being distributed as dividends according to the proportion of share capital issued. The same applies to outside shareholders, so if you are raising money by selling shares to people outside the firm, you should normally ensure that they pay in full for any capital that is issued to them.

The Articles of Association

These are coupled together with the Memorandum, and set out the rules under which the company is run. They govern matters like issue of the share capital, the appointment and powers of directors and the proceedings at general meetings. As in the case of the Memorandum the clauses are largely standard ones, but those relating to the issue of shares should be read carefully. It is most important that there should be a proviso under which any new shares that are issued should be offered first of all to the existing shareholders in the proportion in which they already hold shares. This is particularly so when three or more shareholders are involved, or when you are buying into a company; otherwise the other shareholders can vote to water down your holding in the company whenever they see fit by issuing further shares. For the same reason, there should be a clause under which any shareholder who wants to transfer shares should offer them first of all to the existing shareholders. The Articles of Association also state how the value of the shares is to be determined, the point here being that if the company is successful and makes large profits, the true value of the shares will be much greater than their 'par' value of £1, 50p or whatever. It should be noted, though, that the market valuation of the shares does not increase the liability of shareholders accordingly. In other words, if your £1 'par' shares are actually valued at, say, £50, your liability still remains at £1.

Table A of the Companies Act of 1948, which can be purchased at any HMSO branch, sets out a specimen Memorandum and Articles.

The Minute Book

Company law requires that a record be kept of the proceedings at both shareholders' and directors' meetings. These proceedings are recorded in the minute book, which is held at the company's registered office. Decisions made at company meetings are signed by the chairman and are legally binding on the directors if they are agreed by a majority. Therefore, any points of procedure that are not covered by the Memorandum and Articles of Association can be written into the minutes and have the force of law, provided that they do not conflict with the former two documents. Thus, the various responsibilities of the directors can be defined and minuted at the first company meeting; so can important matters such as who signs the cheques. It is generally a good idea for these to carry two signatures to be valid.

The Company Seal

The company seal is a metal disc bearing the name of the company in raised letters. The disc is pressed into all official documents and its use on any occasion must be authorised by the directors.

The Certificate of Incorporation

When the wording of the Memorandum and Articles of Association has been agreed and the names of the directors and the size of the nominal capital have been settled, your professional adviser will send the documents concerned to the Registrar of Companies. He will issue a Certificate of Incorporation which is, as it were, the birth certificate of your company.

Company directors

When your Certificate of Incorporation arrives you and your fellow shareholders are the owners of a fully fledged private limited company. You will almost certainly also be the directors. This title in fact means very little. A director is merely an employee of the company, who is entrusted by the shareholders with the running of it. He need not himself be a shareholder at all; and he can be removed by a vote of the shareholders which, since each share normally carries one vote, is a good reason for not losing control of your company by issuing a majority shareholding to outsiders.

Another good reason is that since the ownership of the company is in proportion to the issued share capital, so also is the allocation of profits, when you come to make them. If you let control pass to an outsider for the sake of raising a few hundred pounds now — there are other means of raising capital than the sale of shares, as we shall show in Chapter 3 — you will have had all the problems of getting things going, while only receiving a small part of the rewards. Remember, furthermore, that without control you are only an employee, even if you are called 'managing director'.

Checklist: setting up in business

Sole trader

1. Do you need planning permission to operate from your own home?

2. Does your lease allow you to carry on a trade from the premises you intend to use?
3. If you own the premises, whether or not they are your home as well, are there any restrictive covenants which might prevent you from using them for the purpose intended?
4. Have you notified your tax inspector that the nature of your earnings is changing?
5. Are you aware of the implications of being a sole trader if your business fails?
6. Have you taken steps to register a business name?

Partnerships

1. Points 1 to 6 above also apply to partnerships. Have you taken care of them?
2. How well do you know your partners — personally and as people to work with?
3. If you do not know them well what evidence do you have about their personal and business qualities?
4. What skills, contacts or other assets (like capital) can they bring into the business?
5. Have you asked your solicitor to draw up a deed of partnership and does it cover all the eventualities you can think of?
6. Have you talked to anybody who is in, or has tried, partnership in the same line of business, to see what the snags are?

Private limited companies

1. Do you have the requisite minimum number of shareholders (2)?
2. Do you have a competent company secretary, who can carry out the legal duties required under the Companies Acts?
3. Are you yourself reasonably conversant with those duties?
4. Have you registered, if this is required, a company name and a business name?
5. Has permission been granted to use the names chosen?
6. Have the necessary documents been deposited with the Registrar of Companies? (Memorandum and Articles of Agreement, a statutory declaration of compliance with registration requirements, a statement of nominal share capital.)
7. Have you read and understood the Memorandum and Articles? Do they enable you to carry out all present and

any possible future objects for which the company is formed?

8. Do your stationery, catalogues, letterheads, etc show all the details required by the Companies Acts?

9. Is the Registration Certificate displayed in the company's registered office, as required by law?

10. Do you understand the wide range of benefits — company cars, other business expenses, limited liability, self-administered pension schemes, etc — enjoyed by limited companies?

11. Clauses 1 to 3 of the 'Sole Trader' checklist may also apply to you. If so, have you taken care of them?

3: Raising Capital

There are many methods of raising money. Some of these are direct forms of borrowing or obtaining loans, others are ways in which you can spin out your cash resources. But for most small businesses, and many large ones, bank borrowing is the one most widely used.

Approaching your bank

Banks make money by using the funds deposited with them to lend out at rates of interest which vary according to government policy. During periods of economic expansion that rate will be lower — and money easier to get — than during the 'stop' parts of the 'stop and go cycle' which has characterised the British economy since the war. But banks, like everybody else, have to continue to trade even through less prosperous times. You will find, therefore, that the bank manager will be willing to discuss making money available to you, because potentially you are a source of income to him. How much that will be depends somewhat on the size of the branch you are approaching. This is an argument in favour of going to a large branch if you need a sizeable sum; on the other hand in a smaller community, where personal contacts still matter, your professional adviser may well have a shrewd idea of what the bank manager's lending limits are.

Whether you can convince him that your business is a good risk depends on how well you have thought out your approach. To some extent he will go on personal impressions and on what he can gather of your previous business experience. If you have already been running your own firm for a year or two he will have some hard evidence to go on in the shape of your profit and loss account and your balance sheet. He will look at the financial position of your firm, particularly the relationship of current assets to current liabilities and of debtors to creditors (see Chapter 5). He will want to be satisfied that you are valuing your stock realistically and he will want to know how much money you (and your partners, if you have any) have put into the business from your own resources. In the case of a limited company he will want to know what the issued share capital is. Proposals for lending to a new business will need to be fully worked out and have realistic and thorough cash flow protection.

The bank will be looking to see whether your business satisfies three criteria. First, that its money is secure, and in the case of new business will probably ask for security to be in the shape of tangible items like fixed assets within the business or shares and other assets belonging to the owners in their private capacity in a ratio which may be as high as $1:1$. Second, that your firm is likely to have an inflow of enough liquid assets to enable it to recall its money, if necessary. Third, that you will be able to make profitable use of it and pay the interest without difficulty.

There is a saying that banks will only lend you money if you do not need it and reading these requirements you may be coming to the conclusion that there is an element of truth in it. But what it really means is that it is no use going to a bank to bail you out of trouble. A business in trouble generally requires assistance on the management side at the very least and banks are just not in a position to provide such assistance, no matter how glowing the prospects might be if the firm could be brought back on track. So the bank manager is only going to be looking at present and quantifiable situations. He will not be very interested in often vague assets like goodwill and even less in your hopes for the future.

If you have only just set up in business you may not have much more than hopes for the future to offer, and the bank manager will obviously be cautious in such cases. But can these hopes can be quantified, and have you outlined a thorough cash flow budget? If you are opening, say, a new restaurant facts such as that you and your wife are excellent cooks, have attended courses in catering and have established that there would be a demand for a good place to eat in a particular locality are relevant. But what the bank also wants to know is what your start-up costs are going to be, whether you have fully worked out what your overheads and direct costs are (ie items like rent, rates, gas and electricity, depreciation on equipment, staff wages and the cost of food), what relation these are going to bear to your charges for meals, and what levels of seat occupancy you need to achieve to make a profit. This may take quite a lot of working out and it is advisable that you consult closely with your accountant in preparing your case for the bank. Indeed it may be a good idea to take your accountant along with you when you are approaching the bank for financial help.

The commonest form of help, as far as the small business is concerned, is an overdraft, rather than a bank loan. You will be given facilities to overdraw up to a certain amount, but the advantage of an overdraft, as opposed to a loan, is that interest (usually 2 to 3 per cent above base lending rate) is paid only on the actual amount by which you are overdrawn. Overdrafts are particularly useful, therefore, for the firm whose pattern of business fluctuates, such as the market gardener whose income is higher in spring than in winter, or a business which needs money to finance a large contract until the first progress payments are received. The disadvantage of an overdraft is that it can be called in. Though in practice this rarely happens, it is unwise to use money raised in this way to finance medium- and long-term requirements, particularly those which make no immediate contribution to profits, like having your office done up! A more likely peril than the overdraft being called in, however, is the fluctuation of interest rates. If these go up sharply because of some economic crisis, you want to be in a position where you are keeping the facility you are using down to a minimum.

If you do need to finance the cost of purchasing plant or equipment, however, you might sleep more easily if you have negotiated a bank loan. This would normally run for between two and five years, would have repayment periods built into it and would carry a somewhat higher rate of interest than an overdraft. Alternatively, you may need a mixed package – both overdraft facilities and a term loan. Your bank manager and your accountant should be able to advise you on your requirements, provided you have worked out a clear plan for the course of your business over the period during which you need financial help. For larger sums you might consider, with the help of your trusty financial adviser, an approach to the Industrial and Commercial Finance Corporation (ICFC). Its London office is at 91 Waterloo Road, London SE1 8XP, but it also has local offices in other cities. The advantage of ICFC is that although it is a commercial body (it was in fact founded by the clearing banks and the Bank of England), it is rather less aggressive than some of its competitors in its approach to participation in the equity and management of the companies to which it lends money; but it is not, on the whole, interested in getting involved in businesses that are not yet established, especially small ones.

In the case of a limited company, the bank is likely to call on individual directors to guarantee any overdrafts or loans against their personal resources. There are certain pitfalls about some forms of guarantee and it is vital that you check with your solicitor when entering into such an arrangement. If you find the terms under which your bank is offering finance unacceptable, it is worth shopping around to see if you can get a better deal elsewhere.

Alternatively you might try one of the growing number of foreign banks now located in London. The American ones are reported to combine the highest degree of reputability with adventurousness in advancing risk capital.

Private loans

You may have friends or relatives who are prepared to lend you money, but private loans are a rich source of misunderstanding, so you should be clear about all the implications of such an arrangement. The best plan is to get a solicitor to draw up the terms of the loan, covering the rate of interest, the period over which the loan is repayable and the circumstances under which it can be withdrawn. It must also be made clear to what extent, if any, the lender has any say in the running of the business and what the nature of this control is. Normally, however, the lender should not be entitled to participation in management matters; nor does the existence of his loan entitle him to a share of the profits, no matter how strong a moral claim he thinks he might have once your business starts making real money. In the case of a limited company, you must explain to the lender that a loan is not the same thing as a shareholding, though of course the offer of a loan might be conditional on acquiring shares or the option to acquire them. You should be clear about the implications of this: it entitles the shareholder to a percentage of profits in proportion to his holdings; and though loans can be repaid it is virtually impossible to dismantle issued share capital in this way.

Often private loans are not offered directly; but in the form of guaranteeing an overdraft on the basis that, if the recipient of the overdraft is unable to repay it, then the guarantor is liable for that amount. In the 1978 Budget an important concession was made in relation to such arrangements. Losses incurred by the guarantor of a business loan can now be treated as a capital loss, which can be offset against capital gains. This principle was extended in the 1980 Budget, and tax relief can now be claimed by private investors on investment losses.

The 1981 Budget proposes to take matters even further, although the Chancellor's ideas have yet to be approved by Parliament. His key proposals are as follows:

1. *The business start-up scheme.* This is a new income tax incentive for individuals who invest in certain business start-ups. The purpose is to encourage outside investors (that is, individuals other than the proprietor and his associates) to take up equity in new small companies starting up certain kinds of new trading venture.

   Relief will be available on up to £10,000 per person in each year (but not for any investment of less than £1000 in any single company), provided that the investor is not connected with the company in which he invests. The scheme will run for three years, so the relief will be available for shares issued in the years 1981-82 to 1983-84 (inclusive), and will be given by repayment of tax when the conditions are satisfied. To qualify, the investment must be in a new, single company (ie one not connected with other companies) which is starting up a genuinely new business venture in certain kinds of trade requiring risk capital, or which has done so up to three years previously. The capital must remain in the company for a period of at least five years. The relief will be given at the investor's marginal rate of income tax.

   Unfortunately, however, it looks as though the Finance Bill before Parliament at the time of going to press has hedged the scheme about with so many conditions that its value is being questioned by a number of commentators. Not only is the definition of trades which can qualify very narrow — retailing and wholesaling would seem to be excluded altogether — but no more than 30 per cent of the company's total capital can be subscribed in this way. The logic of this situation is that a company would not be helped very far on its way if it has to raise 70 per cent of its capital from other sources. As it stands the Bill does not appear to be the spur to adventurous private investment that it was presented by the Chancellor as being. The Bill may, however, be amended in such a way that some of these limitations are overcome.

2. *The loan guarantee scheme.* Agreement in principle has been reached with the major clearing banks and the ICFC on the introduction of a pilot loan guarantee scheme. Its purpose is to discover whether there is a need for term loans, at market rates of interest, which is at present unsatisfied for reasons other than inherent risk. It has been suggested that some worthwhile projects fail to find adequate finance because, for example, of the potential borrower's lack of a track record or his unwillingness to provide personal guarantees. To test whether this financing gap exists, government guarantees will be made available to participating financial institutions to encourage additional lending.

The scheme is designed to run for three years, subject to an overall maximum commitment of £50 million to be lent in each year, and will be administered by the Department of Industry. Individual term loans of up to £75,000 will be available for periods of between two and seven years. The government guarantee will apply to 80 per cent of each loan. Borrowers will pay a full commercial charge for the loan, part as an interest payment to the lender and part as a guarantee premium to the Department of Industry. Premia will be set at a level designed to cover the cost of claims under the guarantee provision.

It is possible in the case of a limited company for the shareholders to lend money to the company. This does not increase their liability in the same way as taking up issued share capital. However, outside lenders like banks do not take kindly to such arrangements because it indicates a certain reluctance by the shareholders to put their money where their mouth is!

Money from the government

One of the problems of excessive government legislation is that it becomes increasingly difficult to sort out the useful bits from the others, so that there is a tendency to shove the whole lot to one side. This is certainly true of the Industry Act of 1972, which in fact includes provision for financial help to businesses, large and small.* The government has millions of pounds available for this purpose, the money being offered in the form of cash grants and special rate loans. In particular, they are trying to promote industrial development in the so-called special

* Note that these provisions will change when the new Industry Bill is passed.

development areas, which in the main are those areas where traditional industries, like shipbuilding, are on the decline and where unemployment is therefore apt to be high. The minimum project values go as low as £10,000 to £50,000 and though the authorities tend to look more favourably at established businesses who are relocating in development areas, the prospects are certainly worth investigating if you are in or are thinking of moving to such an area. Development areas have the further advantage of usually having a large pool of local labour, and though the spectre of unemployment is no longer a guarantee for getting a cooperative labour force together, unions in such areas are often fairly realistic in their demands. Application forms for assistance in moving to a development area can be obtained from the Department of Industry, 1 Victoria Street, London SW1.

If your proposed enterprise is in a small town or a rural area in England or Wales, you should contact the Council for Small Industries in Rural Areas (CoSIRA). Its head office is Queen's House, Fish Row, Salisbury, Wiltshire SP1 1EX (tel: 0772-24411). As the name implies, it concentrates on industries, including tourism, and cannot offer assistance in the spheres of agriculture, horticulture or retail shops.

A number of similar regional bodies also exists. These include the Welsh Development Office, the Scottish Development Office, the Highlands and Islands Development Board, and the Northern Ireland Development Office. Your regional Small Firms Centre should be able to advise you whether you have a case for approaching them. Addresses are given in Appendix 1.

A good deal of encouragement is now being given to small firms setting up in run-down urban areas and this can take the form of actual risk-funding. Details are available from one of the Department of Industry's regional Small Firms Centres, or from the Department's Small Firms Division, Abell House, John Islip Street, London SW1P 4LN (tel: 01-211 3000).

But what about the marvellous invention that nobody will finance? Is the government prepared to sponsor British initiatives in new technology? The answer is a guarded yes. There is such a body, but it is reputed to take an extremely cautious view of approaches made to it. Perhaps for this reason and because it demands a 50:50 share of the action if the idea works, it has been financially very successful. The body in question is the National Research Development Corporation, 66 Victoria Street, London SW1.

Finance houses and merchant banks

Though many business success stories one reads about in the financial sections of the press begin with the owners getting a loan from a merchant bank, this is not usually a viable source of finance for the small business (ie one with an existing or rapidly foreseeable turnover of much under £100,000). These banks — and in this context we are using the term to include finance companies acting on behalf of institutional and other clients with risk capital to invest — are set up to fund medium- and large-scale enterprises and do not usually involve themselves with smaller firms, even if they are profitable and soundly run.

A typical example of such a finance house is Development Capital Ltd. It looks for investment opportunities in businesses with a turnover of between £100,000 and £3 to £4 million which are funded largely from insurance companies and pension funds. They are interested in expansions, acquisitions, managers buying the equity of an established company back from a corporate holding body or promising new ventures, etc. They expect to be represented on the board in a non-executive capacity, to have a minority equity stake, to provide loan funds over a 10 tò 15 year period and, of course, to receive a return on their investment. The sort of investment criteria they look for can be summarised as follows:

1. *Management.* Must have proven expertise in the field in which it is seeking to start up or to expand.
2. *Market.* Must be expanding and provide the opportunity for substantial growth over the next few years.
3. *Product or service.* Should possess advantages over other products in the same market and use the latest technology available in that field.
4. *Duration of investment.* Normally 5 to 15 years; but both shorter and longer periods are considered.
5. *Area of operation.* All UK companies including those with overseas subsidiaries or branches.
6. *Return on capital.* Must be attractive over the medium-term.

These are fairly characteristic funding prerequisites for finance companies, though there are considerable variations on such important details as the amount of the equity stake they require, the degree of involvement in management matters, the length of time over which they are prepared to lend and whether or not they are prepared to consider new and untried ventures.

If you feel that your firm offers prospects that are likely to interest a merchant bank or similar financial institution, it is certainly worth talking to them. The regional Chambers of Commerce or Small Firms Centre, or your accountant or bank manager may be able to advise you on suitable houses to approach. Before meeting them you should be careful to prepare your case for financial help. Development Capital Ltd, for instance, look for the following basic information from applicants.

1. *The business.* A short description of the company, its history, its products or services mentioning any 'bull points' and patent protection if applicable. Trade brochures and catalogues are also useful if available.
2. *Management.* Brief details giving age, business experience and background of the full-time directors and senior executives.
3. *Market.* An outline of the opportunity for substantial growth accompanied by a forecast of sales and profits over the next two to three years, assuming the company is adequately financed.
4. *Finance.* An estimate of the total development capital required with an indication of how it is intended to be used and a copy of the company's audited accounts for the last two years (if applicable).

Hire purchase arrangements can also be made with the help of a finance company. This is a useful way of financing medium- to longer-term commitments, such as the purchase of machinery, equipment and vehicles. The arrangements are basically similar to a private hire purchase contract, in that the buyer asks the finance company to buy the asset. He then hires it for a specific period, paying hiring charges and interest as he goes along; and can then exercise an option to buy goods at the end of an agreed period. Until that point they remain the property of the finance company, and there is thus no need, as a rule, for the hirer to provide security as is the case with a loan. On the other hand, the finance company will require him to maintain the asset in good order, to insure it and possibly to fulfil other special conditions such as providing satisfactory evidence that the money earned from it will at least cover the high interest charges (around 20 per cent at present) involved.

The periods over which a hire purchase agreement may run

vary with the nature of the asset, but in general terms the Finance Houses Association lays down that 'the goods should have a useful life greater than the period of the hire purchase agreement'.

It is worth calculating the true rate of interest reflected in leasing or hire purchase charges over the given period of time. As in every other form of business, there are sharks around who turn out to charge astronomical rates of interest. It is worth getting more than one quote if there are several possible sources from which to obtain equipment on lease or hire purchase.

Other sources of finance

A rather helpful and significant concession to private investors in small businesses was made in the 1980 Budget. Henceforth, investors who buy shares in small unquoted companies will be able to offset losses incurred in the disposal of such shares against taxable income, not just against capital gains. The problem, of course, is how do you find private individuals with risk capital? Surprisingly enough they do exist and, equally surprisingly, one way of getting at them is through stockbrokers. Stockbrokers have, in the past, been very coy about recommending investments of this kind, but the new legislation might, as it is intended to do, make them change their policy.

One is reluctant to suggest names of brokers because, as in the case of finance houses, there are horses for courses; but here again discreet inquiries by your accountant or bank manager might bear fruit.

Another source of information on private individuals with money to invest are solicitors and accountants in rural areas and small towns. They are often much more in touch with the situation on the availability of such funds than their brethren in larger, more imposing metropolitan offices.

Private Company, a private fortnightly subscription only magazine published by Duke Street Brokers, 35 Thayer Street, London W1, contains a regular eight-page 'marketplace' supplement which often carries information about private investors. LENTA, the London Enterprise Agency, publishes a monthly list of business propositions which occasionally includes details of a private investor.

If you are in a bigger league you might also think about talking to your advisers about going into the Unlisted Securities Market. This is a method of offering shares without the huge expense of 'going public'. However, your annual profit would have to be in the £100,000 pre-tax class for this option to be feasible.

Table 3.1 gives a comprehensive survey of sources of finance other than clearing banks, of the type of deal they offer, the criteria you must meet and the terms of the arrangement.

Using your own money

Inevitably you will have to put up at least some money of your own. Even if your form of business involves selling an intangible skill, as in the case of consultancy, you are going to need some basic equipment, not to mention the fact that you have to have enough money to live on until your business income builds up. You should bear in mind that any money of your own that you put into your firm should be earning a rate of interest comparable to what you could get outside (ie greater than its opportunity cost), and this must be reflected in your costing and estimating. This topic is dealt with in more detail in Chapter 7.

Apart from ready cash in the form of savings, jewellery and other liquid and saleable personal assets you will also have other, less immediate resources to turn to. The most obvious is your house and if you bought it before the huge rise in property prices which took place in the early 1970s its current value may be far in excess of your mortgage. You could take out a second mortgage on this basis, but interest rates on second mortgages are very high. Moreover, taking out a second mortgage will involve your spouse, since one person cannot obtain a second mortgage on the marital home without the other's permission. A better approach would be to take out a mortgage on anther house and sell the one you are in.

Life insurance policies are also worth bearing in mind because companies will generally be prepared to lend money against up to 90 per cent of their surrender value. Whether this yields a worthwhile amount of cash obviously varies from case to case. Interest rates on these loans, however, are generally less than on bank overdrafts.

Raising money by effective cash management

Any method of raising money from the outside costs money. In a period of high interest rates, borrowing can be so costly as to swallow up the entire profits of a business that is over reliant on it. There are instances where borrowing huge amounts of money has made sense, for instance in the property market, where the value of assets in the early 1970s increased much faster than the value of the money borrowed to acquire them. But subsequent events showed that this is dependent on the assumption that the asset does go on appreciating in value at a very rapid rate, and certainly from the point of view of the smaller business one could state as golden rules the following: never borrow more than you have to, never buy until you need to. And when you need to, consider whether hire purchase or even leasing might not make more sense for you than committing cash to an outright purchase. Remember it is cash that pays the bills, not assets or paper profits.

A surprising amount of borrowing can be avoided by effective cash management. It is not dishonest to take the maximum period of payment allowed by your suppliers, and though you do not want to get the reputation of being a slow payer once you have established a reputation of being a reliable account your suppliers may give you quite a bit of leeway before they start pressing you for payment even on an overdue sum. Nor is it dishonest to take note that some suppliers press for payment fairly quickly, whereas others are more lax. The former get paid first.

The reverse is true in the case of the customers you supply. Send out invoices as soon as the work is done. You are more likely to get paid at that point than some weeks later when the novelty has worn off and maybe quibbles have arisen. Send out statements punctually and make sure that your terms of payment are observed.

Take one simple example of how money can work for your business. If your VAT quarter is January to March you have to pay over the VAT you have billed to your customers minus the VAT you have been billed by your suppliers by the end of April. Thus, if you can send a lot of invoices out to customers on 1 January and get the money in quickly all your VAT can sit in a deposit account for nearly four months. Equally, if you are planning to buy a large piece of equipment (say, a van) on which there is many hundreds of pounds VAT for you to claim back, juggling with the precise date on which you make the purchase can minimise the damage to your cash flow.

Vehicle for capital	Backers	Capital earmarked	Type of client or situation	Min/Max funds injected	Start up capital
Abingworth Ltd Tel: (01) 839 6745	Leading UK and European institutions	Open	Usually established/ profitable companies	£100,000– £500,000	Possibly, if management of proven calibre
Barclays Development Capital Tel: (01) 600 9234	Barclays Bank Group	Open	Established growth companies earning £100,000+ pre-tax	£100,000 minimum, but may syndicate large investments	No
Brown Shipley Developments Tel: (01) 606 9833	Brown, Shipley & Co	Open	Quality of individuals of prime importance and above average growth sectors	£25,000–£250,000 equity preference shares, may syndicate larger investments and provide loans	Yes, if individuals have previous experience
Capital Partners International Tel: (01) 629 9928	Private European investors	Open	Companies with overseas expansion potential	£10,000–£350,000. Would form syndicate for larger investments and is interested in participating in such deals	Yes, if very convincing management and exceptional investment potential
Castle Finance Tel: Norwich (0603) 22200	Norwich Union Insurance	Open	Profitable private companies requiring capital for expansion	£30,000–£500,000	Exceptionally
Charterhouse Development Tel: (01) 248 3999	Charterhouse Group	Not disclosed	Mature and/or swiftly growing companies	£50,000–£5m	Exceptionally
CIN Industrial Finance Tel: (01) 353 1500	National Coal Board Pension Funds	£35m–£40m per annum	Small and medium sized companies, public or private with growth potential. Equity subscription, loan and equity packages, development capital and project finance are undertaken	£½m–£2m— amounts below £½m are referred to our small companies investment fund	Yes, this is also referred to our small companies investment fund

Table 3.1 *Sources of finance: where to go when the bank manager says 'no'*

Rescue capital	Equity stake	Seat on Board	Term of funding	Exit criteria	Special features	Portfolio
Occasionally	Always minority	Usually	Open	Flexible, but happy to take long-term view	Extensive overseas contacts, particularly in the US, Europe and the Far East	£20m+ in UK and the US
Exceptionally	Yes, 10–40%	Yes	Open	Flexible	Able to formulate equity/loan packages in co-operation with Barclays branches	8 companies —£4m
Exceptionally	Yes, usually 10–30%	Frequently, in active non-executive capacity	Equity: open Loans: up to 8 years	Flexible. Aim to capitalise by flotation or sale or require running yield if little prospect of realising capital gain at outset	Other merchant banking facilities available. Aim to establish a close relationship and provide continuing financial support	24 companies
By backing and/ or introducing new management	Yes	Yes	Open	Flexible, to suit company and other shareholders but willing to stay involved long-term	Management support and overseas marketing development	15 companies —£1·6m
No	Yes up to 30%	No	Medium and long term loans—fixed or variable interest	Looking for dividends: sale of equity when convenient to all shareholders	Supplementary financial services of the Norwich Union Group	Group holdings 42 companies —£4m
Only within portfolio	Yes	Yes	Open	To suit company and shareholders	Non-executive director with financial skills and experience advising and helping the company but no interference with day-to-day management	Over 125 companies in UK, France, USA and Canada— £20m
Yes, viable subsidiaries or divisions sometimes in the form of management takeouts	Yes, 10–49%	Yes, when a significant stake is taken in a company; panel of experienced non-executive directors available	Medium and long term loans available only with some form of equity participation	Flexible to suit the company and and the shareholders	Individual equity/loan packages formulated to match needs of company. Support given for acquisitions and developments. Close working relationship with senior management encouraged	£100m in 100 investments

(continued)

This table is reproduced by kind permission of *Investors Chronicle*

Vehicle for capital	Backers	Capital earmarked	Type of client or situation	Min/Max funds injected	Start up capital
Commercial Bank of the Near East Tel: (01) 283 4041	Range of shareholders predominantly Greek	Open	Small and medium sized companies, public & private	Up to £250,000	Yes
Common-wealth Development Finance Company Tel: (01) 407 9711	Several Commonwealth central banks and 160 major UK companies	£40m or equivalent in foreign exchange	Investment in UK where there is strong overseas involvement, in main involvement in overseas companies	£200,000–£1m equivalent	Yes, with good short-term prospects
Council for Small Industries in Rural Areas (CoSIRA) Tel: Salisbury (0722) 6255	HM Government plus financial institutions including ICFC under new scheme	£20m	Companies with no more than 20 skilled employees in countryside or in towns with less than 10,000 population	£250–£50,000	Loans are available for new starters
County Bank Tel: (01) 638 6000	National Westminster Bank	Open	Any growing company with proven management: finance for the company, to enable shareholders to realise part of their investment, or to assist management in buying an equity stake	£50,000+	Yes, for sound projects where the individuals can make a financial contribution
Development Capital Tel: (01) 486 5021	Co-operative Insurance, Commercial Union, Electra Investment Trust, NCB Pension Fund	Open	Proven management with prospects of growth. Both unquoted and quoted situations	£100,000–£½m	Yes, with proven expertise
Development Capital (NCDC) Tel: (01) 486 5021	Institutional funds	Open	Good track record £100.000 pre-tax profits potential	Up to £1m	No
Estate Duties Investment Trust (EDITH) Tel: (01) 928 7822	Listed authorised investment trust, (managed by ICFC)	£22m issued share capital	Established private and unlisted public companies and smaller listed companies	£5,000–£1m	No
Equity Capital for Industry Tel: (01) 606 8513	City institutions	Initially £42m	Industrial companies with capitalisation of £1m–£40m or similar unquoted	£200,000–£4m	Exceptionally

Rescue capital	Equity stake	Seat on Board	Term of funding	Exit criteria	Special features	Portfolio
Exceptionally	No	Not under normal circumstances	Open	Flexible. Good performance would encourage continuing contact	Closeworking relationship with senior management to promote trust and without unnecessary involvement. No bank charges	Cannot be differentiated from total bank holdings
No	Yes, 10–49%	Not usually in UK, occasionally in overseas companies	Up to 10 years	Through local flotation or sale to partners. Looks for dividends. Discussed fully at outset	Highly flexible. All overseas expansions, mergers and takeovers considered	89 worldwide investments— £21·7m
Working capital loans are available	No	No	Building loans—20 yrs. Working capital—5 yrs. Equipment loans—20 yrs.	Repayment of loan	Availability of long term building loans. Local representatives throughout the country. Technical and business advice available	2,500 "live" loans—£16m committed
Exceptionally	If appropriate; often 10–15%; usually less than 25%	Rarely	Loans up to 15 years; equity open	Prefers running dividend; realisation indeterminate	Informal advice on financial and other matters; further substantial funds available if company is successful	£60m provided in equity linked funding to over 100 companies
Yes	Yes, to 40%	Yes, in participating non-executive capacity	5-10 years, including permanent capacity	When appropriate to company's development programme or when convenient	Directors all ex-industry	15 companies —£6m
No	Participation in profits but not necessarily direct equity	Yes	Up to 12 years	Repayment	Own experienced directors on board	14 companies —£3m
No	Yes—minority, enabling shareholders to realise investment	No	Provision of cash or exchange of shares for personal shareholders or family trusts	No time limit on duration of investment	Roll-over relief on CGT	200 companies —£20m (by cost)
Yes	Yes, usually 5–25%	Usually, but depends on circumstances	Long term: Equity/ convertible/ loan package; tailored to circumstances	Flexible	Long term relationship with undertaking not to deal in shares	12 companies —£14m

(continued)

Vehicle for capital	Backers	Capital earmarked	Type of client or situation	Min/Max funds injected	Start up capital
European Investment Bank (European Community's long term bank) Tel: (01) 222 2933	1) Scheme operated by DoI and Scottish, Welsh and Northern Ireland offices 2) Scheme operated by ICFC	1) At least £20m for 1980–1981 2) Initially £5m	1) For small and medium sized ventures in UK assisted areas to create or preserve employment 2) As for 1)	1) £15,000— £2·5m. Maximum contribution is 50% of fixed asset cost of project 2) £15,000– £50,000 also up to 50% of fixed asset costs	1) Loans can be made for sound projects by new companies with adequate equity 2) As for 1)
Federation Pension Fund Tel: (01) 639 3828	The National Federation of Self Employed and Small Business, City of Westminster Assurance, Matthew Boys Group	Open	Established self employed/small business; 3 year record; must be a member of the Federation	£10,000–£25,000	No
Gresham Trust Tel: (01) 606 6474	Gresham Investment Trust	Open	Profitable private companies looking for expansion, realisation of shareholders' interests, help for management in buying equity	Up to £500,000 May syndicate larger amounts	Exceptionally
Hambros Bank Tel: (01) 588 2851	Hambros and institutional clients	Open	Good management track record either in proposed investment or previous companies	£250,000—£5m	Exceptionally
Highlands and Islands Developments Tel: Inverness (0463) 34171	HM Government (Scottish Office)	£15m per annum	Manufacturing tourist, agriculture, fisheries and other industries in the Scottish Highlands and Islands	Up to £400,000	Yes
Industrial and Commercial Finance Corporation (ICFC) Tel: (01) 928 7822	Finance for Industry (Bank of England and clearing banks)	Open	Small and medium sized companies public and private	£5,000–£2m	Yes
Local Enterprise Development Unit Tel: Belfast (0232) 691031	Dept of Commerce (Northern Ireland)	£5½m	Mainly manufacturing and service companies employing up to 50 people in Northern Ireland	£1,500+	Loans, guarantees and grants available

54

Rescue capital	Equity stake	Seat on Board	Term of funding	Exit criteria	Special features	Portfolio
1) No 2) No	1) No 2) No	1) No 2) No	1) 7 years including 2 year capital repayment moratorium. Fixed rate in region of 10% 2) Up to 8 years including 2 year capital repayment moratorium	1) Not applicable 2) As for 1)	1) Priority to small and medium sized companies. EIB disburses in foreign currency but UK Government covers exchange risk for small premium 2) As for 1)	1) Over £50m lent since 1978 to about 150 companies 2) New scheme
No	No	No	Up to 20 years	Repayment of loan	Available to Federation members only. Linked with competitive retirement benefit scheme. Available from Federation member brokers	First applications to be processed soon
Exceptionally	Usually	Yes	Preference shares or loans: 5–10 years Equity: Open	Looking for dividends	Gresham director on board. Other merchant banking services available	60 companies —£5m
No	Yes	Yes	3–5 years	Looking for dividends	Panel of outside businessmen to take directorships	Cannot be differentiated from total bank holdings
Yes	Up to 40%	Exceptionally	5–10 years. 20 years for building loans	Equity by sale	Supplementary advisory and support services. Recent tie-up with Bank of Scotland and ICFC to form Highlands Venture Capital	3,000 businesses assisted
Exceptionally	Yes, minority	Not under normal circumstances. Nominee director only with mutual agreement	Fixed interest loans medium and long term	Redemption negotiated individually, no requirement to sell shares	18 branch offices, leasing and hire purchase corporate advisory services, sale and leaseback facilities management consultancy	3,240 companies— £347m
"Maintenance packages" are provided	Yes	Not usually	Grants/loans/ guarantees average 5 years	Repayment of loan or grants as required under terms and conditions of offer	Financial package tailored to requirements. Business, technical, marketing, accountancy and design advice	Variable

(continued)

Vehicle for capital	Backers	Capital earmarked	Type of client or situation	Min/Max funds injected	Start up capital
Lovat Enterprise Fund Tel: (01) 621 1212	National Coal Board Pension Funds, Legal & General Assurance Society Limited, Prudential Assurance Company Limited, Electra Investment Trust Limited, The Equitable Life Assurance Society	Initially £7·5 million	Small and medium sized companies with potential for growth and current pre-tax profits of £100,000 plus	£100,000–£500,000 typically, but may participate in or syndicate larger investment	No
Melville Street Investments Tel: Edinburgh (031) 226 4071	British Linen Bank and other financial institutions	£7m	Profitable companies with good financial discipline	£50,000–£500,000 May syndicate larger investments	Yes
Meritor Investments Tel: (01) 638 8861	Midland Bank, Rolls Royce Pension Fund	£4m	Development situations and shareholders' needs	£100,000–£250,000	No
Midland Bank Industrial Equity Holdings Group Tel: (01) 638 8861	Midland Bank	Open	Development situations and shareholders' needs	£5,000–£2m	Yes
Minster Trust Tel: (01) 623 1050	Minster Assets	Open	Small and medium sized companies, public and private. Profitable private companies looking for expansion, realisation of shareholders' interests, help for management for buying equity	£50,000–£250,000	Exceptionally, where entrepreneurs have previous experience
Moracrest Investments Tel: (01) 638 8861	Midland Bank, Prudential & British Gas Pension Fund	£15m	Development situations and shareholders' needs	£200,000+	No
National Enterprise Board (NEB) Tel: (01) 730 9600	Public corporation financed by Parliament, dividends and National Loans Fund	Open	Manufacturing concerns as per statutory guidelines	As appropriate	Exceptionally
National Research Development Corporation (NRDC) Tel: (01) 828 3400	HM Government	£28m retained earnings plus up to £50m available borrowing	Technological innovation with business potential	Open	Yes. provided innovatory

* NRDC has recently launched the Small Company Innovation Fund (SCIF) for fast response Balance Sheet funding for small innovating companies requiring injections of up to £60,000

Rescue capital	Equity stake	Seat on Board	Term of funding	Exit criteria	Special features	Portfolio
No	Yes 5–40%	Not usually but reserves the right to nominate one member to the Board	Open	Listing on The Stock Exchange or quotation on The Over-the-Counter Market, operated by M.J.H. Nightingale & Co. Limited	Independent investment board. Fund managed by M.J.H. Nightingale & Co. Limited, specialists in small and medium sized company financing	Fund formed in June 1980 1 company £500,000
Exceptionally	Minority	If asked	Long term capital	Flexible. Building up investment portfolio and does not seek to realise investments	Other merchant banking facilities available through British Linen Bank	25 companies —£4m
No	Yes	Yes	Open	Dividend flow: sale when convenient to majority shareholders	Adaptability	New company
Only in takeover situations or restructuring for capital transfer tax. Would back a new management	Yes	Usual	Open	Dividend flow: sale when convenient to majority shareholders	Adaptability	61 companies —£11·8m
Exceptionally	Yes—minority	Not under normal circumstances	Open	Flexible	Complementary advisory and support services	Approx. £½m
No	Yes	Yes	Open	Dividend flow: sale when convenient to majority shareholders	Adaptability	9 companies —£5·1m
Exceptionally with long-term prospects	Yes	Reserve right to appoint non-executive director	Longer-term equity/loan package with maximum private sector involvement	Flexible	Small companies, regions, advanced technology and catalytic investments	Shareholdings 61 companies —£1·41bn Loans 28 companies —£50·5m
No	Yes, if requested by company and usually with buy back arrangements	Not normally	Variable, depending on sales success	When convenient to company. Usually when agreed sales levies recovered	No obligation to repay in event of failure. Flexible. Availability of science, engineering, patent, legal, management specialists *	290 current industrial development projects. £30m plus other development work

(continued)

Vehicle for capital	Backers	Capital earmarked	Type of client or situation	Min/Max funds injected	Start up capital
Noble Grossart Investments Tel: Edinburgh (031) 226 7011	Noble Grossart and Scottish institutional shareholders	£10m+	Good management in growth or turnround situations	£50,000–£1m	Yes, if the management has good track record in previous business
Rainford Venture Capital Tel: St Helens (0744) 28882	Pilkington Brothers, Community of St Helens Trust, Prudential, Nat West, B.P. and ICFC	£2m	Entrepreneurs; primarily start-ups in St Helens	£50,000+	Primarily
Safeguard Industrial Investments Tel: (01) 235 9693	Over 83% of shares held by 17 major insurance cos. or pension funds	Open	Small or medium sized UK companies	£50,000–£300,000	Exceptionally
Scottish Allied Investors Tel: (041) 204 1321 (041) 226 3551	James Finlay, Royal Bank Development Ltd., Scottish Western Trust Co. Ltd.	£3m	Profitable private companies looking for expansion capital	£100,000– £500,000	No
Scottish Development Agency (SDA) Tel: Glasgow (041) 248 2700	UK Government	Open	Manufacturing & Service companies in Scotland	Open Up to £250,000	Yes
Scottish Offshore Investors Tel: (041) 204 1321	James Finlay & other financial institutions	£1m	Energy related service companies with growth prospects	£50,000– £250,000	No
Sharp Unquoted Midland Investment Tel: (021) 236 5801	Legal & General, Royal Insurance, Sun Life Assurance Society and others	£5m	Successful private companies and management buyouts	£20,000– £500,000	No
Smithdown Investments Tel: (01) 629 9891	Private individuals	Open	Start-up situations and very small companies	£5,000–£50,000	Yes
Technical Development Capital (TDC) Tel: (01) 928 7822	ICFC	Not limited	Technology-based companies	£5,000–£2m	Yes
Venture Founders Tel: (0295) 65881	British Investment Trust	Open	Small–Medium size growth Companies	£50,000– £350,000	Yes
Welsh Development Agency Tel: Treforest (044 385) 2666	UK Government	Open	Manufacturing and service industries in in Wales	£2,000–£1m	Yes

58

Rescue capital	Equity stake	Seat on Board	Term of funding	Exit criteria	Special features	Portfolio
No	Yes, usually 20–40%	Yes with active non-executive participation	Open	Flexible but no requirement to sell	Emphasis on close working relationship with senior management	14 companies —£7·5m
No	Yes but preferably not control	If appropriate	Primarily equity. Loans where appropriate to agreed term	Equity— according to circumstances. Loan repayment	Advice on premises, accounting, training, marketing and local services through Trust	New company
No	Yes	Not usually	Medium to long	Flexible	Continuing financial advice available	200 + Listed and Unlisted investments —£13·4m
No	Yes usually	Yes	Medium or long term investment in equity or loan/equity package	Flexible—building up portfolio and not seeking to realise investment	Adaptability together with a management consultancy service	New company
Exceptionally	Where appropriate. Loans and guarantees	If equity taken— right to appoint non-executive director	2-20 yrs. Equity open	By agreement with other share-holders	Management and technical advisory services. Special interest rates available	453 companies —£27·4m
No	Yes usually	Yes	Medium or long term. Equity or loan/equity package	Flexible—not seeking to realise investments	Other merchant banking facilities in U.K. and U.S.A.	4 companies —£1m
No	10–35%	Negotiable	Open	Looking for earnings; no pressure to sell	Based in Midlands, quick decisions in principle	6 companies £1·5m+
No	Yes	By agreement	Open	Open	Financial management advice etc.	5 companies —around £200,000
Possibly	Yes, minority	When appropriate	Fixed interest long term loans and preference shares	Redemption negotiated individually	Assistance with strategy from TDC Developments	110 companies —£7m
Exceptionally	Yes. Prefer minority position	Yes	Open	Flexible	Seek out start-ups. Strong equity orientation	—
Only by supporting new management in takeover situation	Yes	Reserve right. Exercised for larger investments	5-15 years— equity open	Sales by agreement with other shareholders	Range of advisory services. Outside businessmen appointed directors	153 companies —£11·5m

Progress payments

In the case of work done on contract — say a design or consultancy job involving sizeable sums of money over a longer period of time like three or four months — it is worth trying to persuade your customer to make advance and/or progress payments. After all, you are going to be involved in considerable expenditure before the final sum becomes due. Whether an approach of this kind should be made depends of course on how well you know the customer and how badly you think he needs you. If you need his work more than he needs your services, you should consider a bank overdraft, though the cost of this should be reflected in your charges.

Credit factoring

Credit management is a tricky business which has sunk more than one promising new enterprise which, hungry for business, too inexperienced or simply too busy to pay attention to time-consuming detail, has let its credit index — the length of time money is outstanding — get out of control. A possible solution is to have a credit factor to look after this aspect for you. The firm using their services continues to send out its own invoices but the factor, who, of course, gets copies of the invoices, takes over the whole business of collecting the receivables. He will also generally give advice on credit limits and, if required to do so, may be able to discount the invoices, ie allow you to draw cash from him against a percentage of the amounts he is due to collect. Naturally a fairly substantial fee is charged for this service, varying with turnover, and on the whole they are not interested in firms whose annual turnover is less than £100,000, nor in those invoicing too many small amounts to small customers. Your bank should be able to advise you on the choice of a factor. Indeed a number of banks have subsidiaries who offer a factoring service. There is also now an Association of British Factors, made up of some of the largest firms in the business.

Coping with expansion

A recent British Prime Minister came in for some derisive criticism when he described the dire state of the British economy at that time as 'suffering from the problems of success'. It is, nevertheless, a phrase which would ring a bell with many a businessman caught unprepared on a tide of expansion, even though at the level of the firm the symptoms are somewhat different. They may emerge as problems with people, when the staff who were in at the beginning find it difficult to handle a larger-scale operation; or as mistakes made in interviewing and selecting people for new jobs in an expanding company; or simply when the owners are stretched in too many different directions to look at individual trouble spots in enough detail.

Most frequently these trouble spots turn out to be connected, directly or indirectly, with finance. You are producing something for which there is a demand; the world starts beating a path to your door; you appear to be selling your product profitably, and suddenly, in the midst of apparent plenty, you start running out of cash. In that case what has probably happened is that you have forgotten that in general you do not get paid until you have delivered the goods, but your suppliers and the additional staff you have taken on have to be paid out of cash flow generated by a previous and smaller scale of operations.

The way to avoid this situation is to make complete budgeting and cash flow forecasts (see Chapter 7) because you will then be able to select the financial package that is appropriate: short-term loans and overdrafts to meet seasonal or fluctuating demands, such as the materials to supply a big contract; long-term finance for plant, machinery or vehicles, or to make a tempting acquisition; and finance from within by tighter controls and better cash management to keep the ordinary course of expansion on an even keel. In other words, the trick is to find the right mixture, not just to grab the first jar of financial medicine on the shelf. It may not contain anything like the cure you need.

Checklist: raising capital

1. How much do you need? Have you made an initial cash flow projection?
2. Is it to finance short- or long-term financial facilities?
3. Should you be looking to your bank for overdraft facilities? If so, to what limit?
4. Should you be looking for a loan from your bank or some other commercial or official body? If so, how much and over what period?
5. Have you considered leasing or hire purchase as an alternative to raising a lump sum? If this option is open to you, have you worked out the cost of leasing and credit finance as compared to interest charges on loans?
6. If your need for cash is related to difficulties with credit control, have you considered invoice factoring?
7. Have you considered liquidating personal assets to raise cash?
8. Assuming options 5, 6 and 7 have been considered and rejected, have you worked out how to repay the loan and interest charges?
9. What security can you offer a lender, and has it been independently valued?
10. Exactly how do you propose to use the money?
11. Have you prepared a written description of your firm, what skills the key people in it have to offer, what your objectives are, how your product or service compares with the competition, what firm orders you have secured and what your realistic expectations, opportunities and goals are?
12. Do you have supporting evidence on orders you have obtained or are likely to obtain?
13. Have you (and your associates, if any) made as full a commitment to your enterprise in terms of time and money as

can reasonably be expected of you?

14. Have you previously obtained financial help for this or any other business? Have you repaid it within the period due?

15. If you have any loans outstanding on the business, how much are they for, for what purpose and how are they secured?

16. Can you produce an up-to-date balance sheet showing the present financial state of your company?

17. Do you have a detailed cash flow projection, monthly over the first two years and quarterly thereafter, showing cash flow over the period of the loan?

18. Do you have annual projected profit and loss accounts and balance sheets over the period of the loan?

19. If you are approaching a merchant bank or private individual for venture capital have you considered how much of the equity in and control of your company you are prepared to let go?

20. If you are raising money to enable you to fulfil a large contract, have you talked to your customer about the possibility of his paying you in stages?

4: Professional and Other Outside Advisers

We have already touched on the importance of the role that professional advisers, particularly accountants and solicitors, are going to play in the formation of your business, whether it is to be a limited company or some other kind of entity. You are going to be using their advice quite frequently, not only at the beginning but also later, in matters such as acquiring premises, suing a customer for payment, preparing a set of accounts or finding out what items are allowable against your or your company's tax bill. Obviously, therefore, how you choose and use these advisers is a matter for careful thought.

Making the right choice

Many people think that there is some kind of special mystique attached to membership of a profession and that any lawyer or accountant is going to do a good job for them. The fact is, though, that while they do have useful specialist knowledge the competence with which they apply it can be very variable. A high proportion of people who have bought a house, for instance, can tell you of errors and delays in the conveyancing process; and some accountants entrusted with their client's tax affairs have been known to send in large bills for their services, while overlooking claims for legitimate expenses that were the object of employing them in the first place.

So do not just go to the solicitor or accountant who happens to be nearest; nor should you go to someone you only know in a social capacity. Ask friends who are already in business on a similar scale, and if possible of a similar nature to your own, for recommendations. (If you already have a bank manager you know well, he may also be able to offer useful advice.) The kind of professional adviser you should be looking for at this stage is not a big office in a central location. He will have bigger fish to fry and after the initial interview you may well be fobbed off with an articled clerk. Apart from that he will be expensive, for he has big office overheads to meet. On the other hand, a one-man operation can create a problem if the one man is ill or on holiday. The ideal office will be a suburban one, preferably close to where you intend to set up business because knowledge of local conditions and personalities can be invaluable, with two or three partners. Apart from that, personal impressions do count. You will probably not want to take on an adviser who immediately exudes gloomy caution, or one who appears to be a wide boy, or somebody with whom you have no rapport. Some people recommend that you should make a short list of two or three possibles and go and talk to them before making your choice.

What questions do you ask?

Obviously later on you will be approaching your adviser about specific problems, but at the outset you and he will be exploring potential help he can give you. Begin by outlining the kind of business or service you intend to set up, how much money you have available, what you think your financial needs are going to be over the first year of operation, how many people are going to be involved as partners or shareholders and what your plans are for the future. An accountant will want to know the range of your experience in handling accounting problems, how much help you are going to need in writing up the books and he will advise you on the basic records you should set up. Remember to ask his advice on your year end/year start; this does not have to be April 5 to April 6, and there may be sound tax reasons for choosing other dates. He may even be able to recommend the services of a part-time bookkeeper to handle the mechanics; but, as we shall show in Chapter 5, this does not absolve you from keeping a close watch on what money is coming in and going out. It should be stressed at this point that certainly in the case of a private limited company the accountant you are talking to should be qualified, either through membership of the Institute of Chartered Accountants or of the Association of Certified and Corporate Accountants. Someone who advertises his services as a bookkeeper or merely as an 'accountant' is not qualified to give professional advice in the true meaning of that term, though a good unqualified man can do a very adequate job in preparing tax returns for something like a small freelance business.

A solicitor will also want to know the kind of business you are in and your plans for the future. But he will concentrate, obviously, on legal rather than financial aspects (so do not go on about money) — he is a busy man, and this is only an exploratory visit). He is interested in what structure the operation is going to have and, in the case of a partnership or limited company, whether you and your colleagues have made any tentative agreements between yourselves regarding the running of the firm and the division of profits. He will want to get some idea of what kind of property you want to buy or lease and whether any planning permissions have to be sought.

How much is he going to charge?

This is rather like asking how long is a piece of string. It depends on how often you have to consult your adviser, so it is no use asking him to quote a price at the outset, though if you are lucky enough to have a very clear idea of what you want done — say, in the case of an accountant, a monthly or weekly supervision of your books, plus the preparation and auditing of your accounts — he may give you a rough idea of what his charges will be. Alternatively he may suggest an annual retainer for these services and any advice directly concerned with them, plus extra charges for anything that falls outside them, like a complicated wrangle with the inspector of taxes about allowable items. When calculating the likely cost of using an accountant remember that his fees are tax deductible.

An annual retainer is a less suitable way of dealing with your solicitor because your problems are likely to be less predictable than those connected with accounting and bookkeeping. A lot of your queries may be raised, and settled, on the telephone: the 'Can I do this?' type. Explaining that kind of problem on the telephone is usually quicker and points can be more readily clarified than by writing a letter setting out the facts of the case (though you should ask for confirmation in writing in matters where you could be legally liable in acting on the advice you have been given!). However, asking advice on the telephone can be embarrassing for both parties. You will be wondering whether your solicitor is charging you for it and either way it could inhibit you from discussing the matter fully. You should, therefore, check at the outset what the procedure is for telephone inquiries and how these are accounted for on your bill.

A guide – not a crutch

For someone starting in business on their own, facing for the first time 'the loneliness of thought and the agony of decision', there is a temptation to lean on professional advisers too much. Apart from the fact that this can be very expensive, it is a bad way to run a business. Before you lift the telephone or write a letter, think. Is this clause in a contract something you could figure out for yourself if you sat down and concentrated on reading it carefully? Would it not be better to check through the ledger yourself to find out where to put some item of expenditure that is not immediately classifiable? Only get in touch with your advisers when you are genuinely stumped for an answer, not just because you cannot be bothered to think it out for yourself. Remember, too, that nobody can make up your mind for you on matters of policy. If you feel, for example, that you cannot work with your partner, the only thing your solicitor can or should do for you is to tell you how to dissolve the partnership, not whether it should be done at all.

Your bank manager

The other person with whom you should make contact when you start up in business is your bank manager. The importance of picking a unit of the right size which we have mentioned in connection with professional advice also holds true in this case. A smaller local branch is more likely to be helpful towards the problems of a small business than one in a central urban location with a lot of big accounts among its customers. You might also discuss, with your accountant, the possibility of going outside the 'big five'. It is necessary to be careful here because there have been some notorious failures of 'fringe banks', but there are a number of solid smaller banking houses who are more accommodating about charges on handling your account and loans. If you are changing banks, as opposed to merely switching branches, it will be difficult for you to get a sizeable overdraft until the manager has seen something of your track record.

You must inform your bank manager of your intention to set up in business, providing him with much the same information as you gave to your accountant. Indeed, it is quite a good idea to ask your accountant to come along to this first meeting, so that he can explain any technicalities.

You may be operating a small-scale freelance business that

does not call for bank finance. It is very important, in that case, to keep your personal and business accounts separate, with separate cheque and paying in books for each one. Mixing up private and business transactions can only lead to confusion, for you as well as your accountant. Even if you are simply, say, a one-man freelance consultancy it is worth keeping your bank manager well-informed about your business. Your cash flow as a freelance might well be highly erratic and unless he knows you and your business well he will be firing off letters about your unauthorised overdraft.

Insurance

If you are setting up a photographic studio and an electrical fault on the first day destroys some of your equipment you are in trouble before you have really begun. If you are a decorator and a pot of paint falling from a window sill causes injury to someone passing below you could face a suit for damages that will clean you out of the funds you have accumulated to start your business. Insurance coverage is, therefore, essential from the start for almost all kinds of business.

Insurance companies vary a good deal in the premiums they charge for different kinds of cover, and in the promptness with which they pay out on claims. The best plan is not to go direct to a company, even if you already transact your car or life insurance with them, but to an insurance broker. Brokers receive their income from commissions from the insurance companies they represent, but they are generally independent of individual companies and thus reasonably impartial. Here again, your accountant or solicitor can advise you of a suitable choice, which would be a firm that is big enough to have contacts in all the fields for which you need cover (and big enough to exert pressure on your behalf when it comes to making a claim), but not so big that the relatively modest amounts of commission they will earn from you initially are not worth their while taking too much trouble over, for instance, when it comes to reminding you about renewals. Apart from these general points you will have to consider what kinds of cover you need and this will vary somewhat with the kind of business you are in. The main kinds are:

1. Insurance of your premises.
2. Insurance of the contents of your premises.

3. Insurance of your stock.
(The above three kinds of cover should also extend to 'consequential loss'. For instance, you may lose in a fire a list of all your customers. This list has no value in itself but the 'consequent' loss of business could be disastrous. The same is true of stock losses. If a publisher loses all his books in a fire it is not only their value that affects him, but the consequent loss of business while they are being reprinted, by which time the demand for them may have diminished.)
4. Employer's liability if you employ staff on the premises, even on a part-time basis.
5. Public liability in case you cause injury to a member of the public or his premises in the course of business. You will also need third-party public liability if you employ staff or work with partners.
6. Legal insurance policies cover you against prosecution under Acts of Parliament which relate to your business (eg those covering unfair dismissal and fair trading).
7. Insurance against losing your driving licence, important if your business depends on your being able to drive.

Your broker will advise you on other items of cover you will need. Some professions, for instance, need professional liability cover, but do not leave the whole business of insurance in his hands. Read your policies carefully when you get them and make sure that the small print does not exclude any essential item.

Insurance is expensive (though the premiums are allowable against tax inasmuch as they are incurred wholly in respect of your business), and you may find that in the course of time you have paid out thousands of pounds without ever making a claim. However, it is a vital precaution, because one fire or legal action against you can wipe out the work of years if you are not insured. For this reason you must check each year that items like contents insurance represent current replacement values and that your premiums are paid on the due date. Your broker should remind you about this, but if he overlooks it, it is you who carries the can.

The National Federation of Self-employed and Small Businesses now includes automatic legal insurance in its membership subscription. This covers professional and legal fees of up to £10,000 for appeals to VAT Tribunals, defence of Health and Safety at Work prosecutions, 90 per cent of the cost of an

Industrial Tribunal Award and defence of private and business motoring prosecutions. The NFSE also runs a voluntary top-up scheme to supplement this basic legal cover.

Other advisers and suppliers

In the course of transacting your business, you will probably need the services of other types of people: builders, to maintain and perhaps refurbish your premises; printers, to produce letterhead, advertising material, etc; surveyors and valuers to assess your property; and so on. You should apply the same criteria to these as to your professional advisers. Their services should be reasonably priced, and the service performed to the required standard. If the service is of a professional nature, the consultant should be a member of the relevant professional body. If this does not apply, it may be worth asking for recommendations from the local Chamber of Commerce or Small Firms Centre.

Checklist: professional advisers

Solicitors

1. How well do you know the firm concerned?
2. What do you know of their ability to handle the kind of transactions you have in mind?
3. Is their office convenient to the place of work you intend to establish?
4. Do they know local conditions and personalities?
5. Are they the right size to handle your business affairs over the foreseeable future?
6. Have you prepared an exhaustive list of the points on which you want legal advice at the setting-up stage?

Accountants

1. Have they been recommended by someone whose judgement you trust and who has actually used their services?
2. Are the partners members of one of the official accountants' bodies? If not, are you satisfied that they can handle business on the scale envisaged?
3. Is their office reasonably close by?
4. Does it create a good and organised impression?

71

5. Can they guarantee that a member of the firm will give you personal and reasonably prompt attention when required?
6. Have you thought out what sort of help you are going to need?
7. Have you prepared an outline of your present financial position and future needs?
8. Have you considered, in consultation with your solicitor, whether you want to set up as a sole trader, a partnership or a limited company?

Bank manager

1. Is your present bank likely to be the right one for you to deal with in this context?
2. Have you informed your bank manager of your intention to set up a business?
3. Have you established a separate bank account for your business?
4. Have you discussed with your bank manager the possibility of switching your account to a local, smaller branch?

Insurance

1. Do you have a reliable reference on the broker you intend to use?
2. Is he efficient, according to the reports you receive, about reminding you when policies come up for renewal?
3. Has he any track record of paying promptly on claims?
4. Have you prepared a list of the aspects of your proposed business which require insurance cover?
5. Are you fully insured for replacement value and consequential loss?
6. Have you read the small print on your policies or checked them out with your solicitors?

5: Simple Accounting Systems and Their Uses

Any bank manager will tell you that at least 80 per cent of all business failures are caused by inadequate record keeping. Unfortunately this fault is by no means uncommon in small businesses because the entrepreneurial person who tends to set up on his own is often temperamentally different from the patient administrative type who enjoys paperwork and charting information in the form of business records. He is apt to feel what really keeps the show on the road is obtaining and doing the work, or being in the shop to look after customers. However, unless you record money coming in and going out, owed and owing, you will never have more than the haziest idea of how much to charge for your products or services, where your most profitable areas of activity are (and indeed whether you are making a profit at all), how much you can afford to pay yourself and whether there is enough coming in to cover immediate commitments in the way of wages, trade debts, tax or professional fees, rent, rates, etc.

Legally, in fact, only a limited company is obliged to keep proper books of account: the definition is that they have to do so 'with respect to all receipts and expenses, sales and purchases, assets and liabilities and they must be sufficient to give a true and fair picture of the state of the company's affairs and to explain its transactions'. This is actually no bad objective for anyone carrying on a business on a full-time basis; the only trouble is that keeping and entering up a full set of books is very time-consuming, and, though not inherently difficult, does require a certain amount of training and some natural aptitude for organising facts and figures if you are to avoid getting into a muddle.

As a rule of thumb, if your scale of operations is big enough to come within the orbit of VAT (that is, if your turnover is, or is likely to be, over £15,000 a year) we suggest you get qualified help with bookkeeping. But first of all, let us look at the very basic records you ought to keep if you are in business for yourself at all, even as a part-time freelance.

Two starting points

At the small scale sole trader end, one reason why you need to keep records is to justify your expenditure claims to the tax inspector. For this purpose you may find that your most useful investment is a spike on which incoming receipts, invoices, statements and delivery notes can be placed. This ensures that essential documentary evidence of expenditure is retained and kept together, not used to put cups on or carried around in your wallet for making odd notes on the back. As your business grows you may find that the spike should be supplemented by a spring loaded box file in which all such items should be placed in date order.

However, not all expenditure can be accounted for in this way. Fares, for instance, are not generally receipted, nor is postage, or you may be buying items for personal use at the same time as others that are directly connected with your business. Thus it is a good idea to carry a notebook around with you and enter up any expenses that you have incurred that are not documented. You will find that the taxman will accept a certain level of claims of this kind provided they bear a credible relationship to the business you are in. For example, if you are earning income from travelling round the country giving lectures he will accept a fairly high level of claims for fares, but not if the nature of your business is carrying out a local building repair service.

For larger outlays you may find credit cards a useful record keeping aid. Apart from the fact that when card companies render their account for payment they provide a breakdown of where, when, and how items were purchased they also, in effect, give you six weeks' credit. With inflation currently running at some 10 - 15 per cent per annum this is a real consideration.

Keeping a cash book

The next stage is to keep a cash book. It does not have to be anything elaborate. The object of the exercise is to provide a record from which an accountant or bookkeeper can write up a proper set of books and to save him the time and trouble (which you have to pay for) of slogging through dozens or possibly hundreds of pieces of paper in order to do this. Since your professional adviser will have to work off your records it is a good idea to ask him what the most convenient way of setting them out is. He may suggest that you buy one of the ready-made books of account like the *Complete Traders Account Book* or the *Self-employed Account Book*, though such books are not suitable for every kind of self-employment. If you find it difficult to follow his instructions, or you are using a ready-made book and are having trouble with it, here is something very simple you can do (see Table 5.1).

Buy a large (A4) rule notebook and open it up at the first double page. Allocate the left-hand page to sales and the right-hand page to expenditure. If sales and expenditure fall into further categories which you want to keep track of, say if you want to keep travel costs separate from the cost of materials, or if you are registered for VAT, divide up the page accordingly. You should also rule up columns for the date, the invoice number and the details of the invoice. Enter these details up at the end of each day's trading and you will find that it works both as a discipline in checking that all your sales and purchases are logged and that you now have a further record in addition to the documents on your spike or in your box file.

More elaborate systems

This sort of record is fine as far as it goes and in a small business engaged mainly in cash transactions your accountant may not need very much more than this to produce a set of accounts. In a larger concern, or one that operates extensively on taking and giving credit, it has some obvious limitations. For example, keeping track of when payments are made or received can become rather messy and difficult, and you will need to have a separate record, called a ledger, of the customers and suppliers with whom you do business so that you can see at a glance how much you owe or are owed in the case of individual accounts. Such details will be taken from further books — purchases and sales day books and a more elaborate kind of cash book than the simplified one we have described above. Though we have recommended that you leave the details of this kind of book-keeping to a qualified person, let us look briefly at what is involved.

1. *Cash book.* Shows all payments received and made, with separate columns for cash transactions and those made through the bank (ie payments by cheque). Amounts received from customers are credited to their account in

INCOME

Date	Invoice No	Date paid	Details	Amount (£)	VAT (£)
1.5.80	8061		Six tables	112	16.80
5.5.80	cash		Desk	200	30.00
9.5.80	8062		Dining table	162	24.30
11.5.80	cash		Repair of wooden chest	83	12.45

EXPENDITURE

Date	Invoice No	Cheque/Credit card	Details	Amount (£)	VAT (£)
2.5.80	–	911112	Wooden Top timber yard	425	63.75
3.5.80	Petty cash voucher 23	cash	Stamps	3	–
4.5.80	Petty cash voucher 24	cash	Expenses: trip to Harwich to inspect timber	20	3
12.5.80	–	911113	Electricity bill	44	6.60

Table 5.1 *Sample entries from the cash book of a cabinet maker*

the ledger (see below). Payments made to suppliers are debited to their account in the ledger.

2. *Petty cash book.* Shows expenditure on minor items — postage, fares, entertainment and so forth, with a column for VAT.

3. *Sales day book.* Records invoices sent out to customers in date order, with some analysis of the goods or service supplied and a column for VAT.

4. *Purchases day book.* Records similar information about purchases.

5. *Ledger.* Sets out details, taken from sales and purchases day books, of individual customers' and suppliers' accounts and serves as a record of amounts owed and owing. Details from the analysis columns of the sales and purchases day books are also transcribed, usually monthly, under corresponding headings in the ledger. This enables you to see at a glance where your sales are coming from and where your money is going.

6. *Capital goods ledger.* If you own expensive capital equipment — cars, lorries, machine tools, high class film or photographic equipment, etc — you should have separate accounts for them in the ledger because the method of accounting for them is somewhat different. Capital items depreciate over a period of time (as you will know if you have ever sold a car) and this fact must be reflected both in your balance sheet and profit and loss account, and in the way you price your goods and services.

Writing down capital goods affects your tax liability. With some items you can write down the full value in the year of purchase, but it may not pay you to take advantage of this concession. How you deal with depreciation is very much an area where you are dependent on your accountant's expert advice.

Trading account

From the books described above, your accountant can draw together the information needed to compile the trading account and profit and loss account (see Table 5.2). The function of the trading account is to tell you whether you have been making a gross profit on your trading. It must be compiled annually and preferably more often than that, quarterly for instance, to enable you to measure your progress and make your VAT return.

Trading Account for Year Ended 31.12.80			
	£		£
Opening stock at 1.1.80	2000	Sales	20,000
Net purchases (less		Closing stock at	
credits, etc)	12,000	31.12.80	3000
Gross profit	9000		
	23,000		23,000

Profit and Loss Account for Year Ended 31.12.80			
	£		£
Rent and rates	1000	Gross profit	9000
Salaries	2750		
Heat, light	200		
Phone	120		
Travel	300		
Repairs	200		
Depreciation	650		
Professional advice	150		
	5370		
Net profit	3630		
	9000		9000

Table 5.2 *Examples of trading account and profit and loss account*

To put together a trading account he begins by identifying the period you want to cover. He then totals up the value of all sales, whether paid for or not, adds them to the value of your stock (based on cost or market value, whichever is the lower) at the end of the period you want to cover. Then he takes your opening stock and adds it to the purchases (but not expenditure like rent or repayment of interest on loans). Deducting the value of opening stock plus purchases from the value of closing stock plus sales will give him your gross trading profit (or loss) over the period.

Profit and loss account

From this information he can compile the net profit and loss account over the same period. The gross profit figure from your trading account appears in the right-hand column and he sets against it all the items from the various expenditure accounts in the ledger. He also includes in this figure the depreciation on capital equipment, but not its actual cost (even if you purchased it during the period in question) because that crops up later, in the balance sheet.

Deducting the left-hand total from the right-hand total gives you your profit over the period. If the total expenditure exceeds the gross profit you have obviously incurred a loss.

The balance sheet

We have mentioned in the previous section that capital equipment does not figure in the profit and loss account, but goes into the balance sheet. The balance sheet is a picture, taken at a particular point in the year (usually the end of a company's financial year) of what the firm *owes* and what it *owns* (see Table 5.3). (This is not the same as a profit and loss account, which covers a period of time.) Indeed it is quite possible for a firm to have been making a loss on its profit and loss account, but for what it owns (its assets) to exceed what it owes (its liabilities).

In a balance sheet the assets of the firm usually go on the right and the liabilities on the left. However, all the assets and all the liabilities are generally not lumped together, but distinguished qualitatively by the words 'fixed' and 'current'.

'Fixed assets' are items which are permanently necessary for the business to function, such as machinery, cars, fixtures and fittings, your premises or the lease on them. 'Current assets' on the other hand are things from which cash will be realised in the course of your trading activities. These include amounts owed

Balance Sheet as at 31.12.80					
Liabilities			**Assets**		
Capital			*Fixed assets*		
500 Shares of £1 each	£500		Vehicle less	£1600	
Profit	£3630		depreciation	£400	£1200
		£4130	Fixtures and fittings	£1000	
			less		
Fixed liabilities			depreciation	£250	£750
Loan repayable 1980	£1000				£1950
Current liabilities			*Current assets*		
Trade creditors	£795		Stock	£3000	
			Debtors	£900	
		£1795	Cash	£75	£3975
		£5925			£5925

Table 5.3 *An example of a balance sheet*

to you by your debtors (from the customers' accounts in the ledger), and the value of your stock (from the trading account). It also, of course, includes cash at the bank (from the cash book).

With liabilities, the position is reversed. 'Fixed liabilities' are those which you do not have to repay immediately, like a long-term loan from a kindly relative. What you do have to repay promptly, however, is the interest on that loan and this goes under current liabilities if it is due, but has not been paid at the time the balance sheet has been prepared. The same is true of any amounts you owe to your suppliers' accounts in the ledger. Another item that goes on the 'liabilities' side is the share capital in the business and the profit from the trading account because both these amounts are ultimately owed by the company to the shareholders. Where, on the other hand, the company has been making a loss, the amount is deducted either from profits retained from earlier periods or from the shareholder's capital.

What should you be looking for in your records?

You will want to know whether you are making or losing money, but there are many other useful bits of information to be gleaned as well. If you are making a profit, what relationship does it bear to the capital employed in the business? You can calculate this by subtracting total liabilities from total assets. If you are making less than a 15 per cent return on capital, you are not, on the face of things, making much progress, though, of course, you could be paying yourself a very handsome salary before the profit figure was arrived at.

The percentage return on capital can be calculated by the following sum:

$$\frac{\text{profit}}{\text{capital employed}} \times 100$$

Another thing you can work out from your balance sheet is whether you are maintaining sufficient working capital to meet your requirements for new stock or materials or to pay for wages and rent. Here you look at current assets and current liabilities. The calculation:

$$\frac{\text{current assets}}{\text{current liabilities}}$$

gives you your *current* ratio. If you have, say, £1000 of each you are said to have a current ratio of $1:1$. Clearly in that case you would be in trouble if a major debtor were to go bankrupt. So it may be that you should cut back on some item of expenditure you were planning on. Furthermore, the current ratio includes certain items, like stocks, which may not be immediately realisable. If your current ratio is low, and you are still in two minds whether or not to buy that new machine you might apply what is known as the *acid test ratio*, which shows your ability to meet liabilities quickly if the need arises. Here you simply deduct stock from your figure for current assets to give you a figure for liquid assets, ie debtors and cash. If the ratio liquid assets : current liabilities is too low you may have more money tied up in stock than you should have.

Even the acid test ratio assumes that your debtors are going to pay you in a reasonable period of time: most likely within the terms of trade you are allowing. But is this assumption really correct? Look at the annual sum:

$$\frac{\text{debtors}}{\text{sales}} \times 365$$

If your sales are £10,000 and your debtors owe £1000, they are near enough to meeting net monthly terms for you not to worry about it. But if your debtors, on the same sales turnover, are running to £3000, there is something wrong with your credit control and you are probably heading for serious trouble.

Another important ratio is profit to sales. What this should be depends on the sort of business you are in. Your accountant should be able to advise you here on the basis of his knowledge of similar traders. If your percentage is on the low side you may be buying badly, failing to pass on cost increases, or possibly incurring losses from pilferage.

There are other ratios to look out for, but we hope that you will now be clear that the balance sheet and trading and profit and loss accounts are not just a financial rigmarole you have to go through, but very valuable indicators of the way your business is going, or some other business you are thinking of buying. They are also useful for:

1. Assisting the bank manager to determine the terms of an overdraft.
2. Selling your business to a proposed purchaser.
3. Agreeing tax liabilities with the inspector of taxes.

Checklist: simple accounting systems

1. Do you carry a notebook to record smaller items of business expenditure, such as taxi fares, as soon as they are incurred?
2. Have you considered using credit cards for larger outlays?
3. Do you have a system for filing incoming invoices as soon as they are received?
4. Have you asked your accountant what books and records he advises you to keep?
5. Do you know and understand the procedures involved?
   If not, have you asked your accountant to recommend someone who can help you on a regular basis – at least once a week or once a month, depending on your scale of operations?
6. Do you have any idea of the ratios current in your type of business, so that you can measure your performance against the norm?

6: Invoicing and Credit Control

Time is money, as an old saying goes. It ought to be written large in the minds of anyone giving credit, that is, any business that supplies goods and services which are not on a strictly cash-on-the-nail basis.

In these days of tight money there is a tendency for many customers, including large and reputable firms, to delay payment as long as possible; because, as noted in Chapter 3, taking credit long — and preferably giving it short — is one way to maintain a flow of cash in the business. The supplier who does not demonstrate that he is in a hurry for payment, therefore, is the one who comes last in the queue.

Sending out invoices and statements

The first step towards ensuring that you are not in this position is to issue an invoice for work done or goods supplied as soon as possible after you deliver. On the invoice you should give the customer's order number. If it was a telephone order and you forgot to get an order number, you should at least give the date of the order. You should also state when you expect to receive payment. The usual period is between seven and 30 days after delivery. Many private individuals, in fact, pay on receipt of an invoice. Business firms, on the other hand, expect to receive a statement of their account at the end of the month, setting out invoices due or sent during this period: their dates, invoice number, the nature of the goods and the amount. You can have statement forms printed, but if you are not a limited company you can use your letterheads for this purpose, simply typing the word STATEMENT at the top. Every customer who has received an invoice and not paid at the end of the month when it is due should get a statement, which should repeat your payment terms.

The particulars of the invoice(s) are drawn from your customers' ledger, though it is essential to keep copies of the actual invoices as well, filed in date order. You are going to need them for VAT purposes, or to check queries. When you receive payment, check that it tallies with the amount due on the customer's ledger entry, mark off the details against each individual item as shown in the previous chapter and enter the amount in the cash book. If the customer requires a receipt, ask him to return the statement (or the invoice if he has paid on that) with his remittance — otherwise you will be involved in time-consuming typing — tick off the items paid, and attach a receipt form or bang on a rubber stamp, 'Paid'. Be uniform about your systems. If you have two different ones for the same part of your operation you are going to waste a lot of time looking in the wrong place when you come to check a document.

Do not neglect the process of checking payments because any amounts unpaid must go into next month's statement. Some invoices which have appeared on your statement will not be paid because they are not yet due for payment. For example, if your terms are 30 days and you have invoiced an item on the 20th of the month, a business customer is unlikely to pay you until the month following. Quite often he only activates payments at the end of the month, unless he is unusually punctilious, efficient or being offered extra discount for quick settlement.

What happens if payment becomes overdue? This is extremely annoying, because at best it is going to involve you in extra correspondence. You must be tactful and patient if you want more business from your clients, and remember that some large organisations are slow in paying, not by choice but because they are dictated to by their computer accounting systems. But if your patience is exhausted, there are usually three stages. The first is a polite reminder of the amount due, how long it has been due and of your terms of supply. This should be coupled with asking the customer whether he has any queries on any of the invoices which might explain the delay. If there is not a reply by the end of that month, write again, referring to your first reminder and setting a deadline for payment. A telephone call to the customer is often opportune at this stage. If that deadline is not met, you will have to write again, referring to your previous reminders and threatening legal action unless a new and final deadline is met. (If you have a large number of credit accounts, it may pay you to have sets of blank letters for each stage prepared in advance.)

In most cases the threat of legal action will do the trick, but whether you actually carry out your threat will depend on the amount involved. Sums under £75 are not really worth pursuing because your solicitor's services are going to cost you money; and it is not worth taking matters to court – that is, to the stage beyond a solicitor's letter – unless quite a sizeable sum is involved. Your solicitor will advise you on the best course of action. Alternatively, there are firms of debt collectors who are geared to this kind of work and who will endeavour to collect debts for a percentage of the amount due. Five per cent is the norm. But there are some doubtful operators and a good deal of tricky legislation in debt collecting, and you would be well advised to check out any agency that has not been personally recommended with the National Association of Trade Protection Societies, 8 New Street, Leicester LE1 5NF.

You can, of course, ask for references before giving credit though this is a matter which has to be approached with some delicacy; but if you receive a sizeable order out of the blue from some business firm with whom you have not previously dealt, it is advisable to ask for a couple of references in acknowledging the order. Ask the referees to what amount they give credit to this particular customer, how long they have been doing business with him and whether he pays promptly.

If your business consists of making or repairing goods to order – tailoring, for instance – it is not unusual to ask the customer to pay up to 50 per cent on account where an estimate of over £50 or so has been given. This helps cash flow as well as protecting you against possible default. Equally, if goods of resaleable value are left with you for repair you should display a notice reserving the right to dispose of them if the customer does not come to collect them within a reasonable time of completion of the work.

A common delaying tactic, or it may be a perfectly legitimate query, is for the customer to ask for copy invoices on receipt of your statement. Do not part with your file copy. You will have to send a photocopy if you do not keep duplicates for this purpose.

Credit cards

For larger personal transactions and for items such as the settlement of restaurant bills credit cards are becoming an increasingly popular method of making payment. A typical scheme is the one operated by the Joint Credit Card Companies, which include Access. A business which wants to offer credit card payment facilities to its customers has to make application to join the scheme to the Joint Credit Card Companies, General Sales Office, 30-31 Newman Street, London W1P 4LJ. The Joint Credit Card Companies then set a money limit to the transaction per customer for which the business in question can accept payment on the cards of JCC member companies. Above that limit, which is based roughly on the applicant's average transaction per customer, the sale has to be referred back to JCC. This can be done over the telephone.

Each sale, as it is made, is entered up on a voucher supplied by the credit card company. The voucher is paid into the bank by the seller and the amount is debited to the card holder's bank account. The advantage of credit cards from the seller's point of view is that he gets guaranteed payment. Against this, he has to pay a small percentage on every transaction to the bank, the amount of this percentage being negotiated at the time he joins the scheme.

Most credit card companies operate on lines very similar to the scheme we have just outlined. Diner's Club vouchers, for instance, though not paid into a bank are sent to the Club organisation on certain specified dates, whereupon payment is made to the seller.

Checking incoming invoices and statements

Unless you transact your business by paying in cash or by cheque on the spot (which is likely in only a few business spheres), you will also be at the receiving end of invoices and statements from your suppliers. The moment they come in, put them on the spike. Then, daily if possible, enter the details in the supplier's ledger, as described in Chapter 5. File incoming invoices in date order, for you will need them for VAT purposes.

When you receive your statement make sure it tallies with the amounts and details which you have entered in the suppliers' ledger, mark off all the items paid and write up the amount in the cash book.

If you are paying by cheque there is no need to ask for a receipt (which only adds to the paperwork) since an honoured cheque is itself a receipt. Make sure, though, that you enter up the stubs, unless you write up the cash book at the same time as you draw the cheques.

Checklist: invoicing and credit control

Invoicing

1. Are you invoicing promptly, on or with delivery?
2. Do your invoices clearly state your terms?
3. Do you ensure that the customer's name, address and order number (if any) or date is correctly stated on your invoice?
4. Are your statements sent out promptly at the end of the month? Do they state your payment terms?
5. Are they clear and easy to follow? Would they make sense to you if you were the recipient?
6. Are you checking payments received against ledger entries?

Credit control

1. Does every account have a credit limit?
2. Is it based on first-hand knowledge of the customer as a credit risk or personally, his track record as a payer with you or others in your line of business, on representatives' reports or reliable trade references, or on bankers' references, in that order of usefulness?
3. Do you exercise special vigilance on new accounts?
4. Do your statements show the age of outstanding balances and do you or your credit controller look at outgoing statements to check on customers whose payments situation seems to be deteriorating?
5. Do you have a system for dealing with customers who exceed their credit limit?
6. Do you have a sequence of reminder procedures for dealing with overdue accounts by telephone calls and/or letters?
7. Do you check orders received against a list of customers who have exceeded their credit limit or who are proving to be reluctant or non-payers?
8. Does the person in charge of credit control liaise with those responsible for supplying the account in question to make sure that there are no special reasons for non-payment before sharper warnings are delivered?
9. Do you regularly check on the debtor : sales ratio to make sure you are not heading for a liquidity problem by being too generous about extending credit?

7: Budgeting and Cash Flow Forecasting

One principle that it is vital to grasp is the importance of liquid cash in running a business. This should not be confused with profitability. Because of the way the profit figure is arrived at on the trading account (see Chapter 5), it is perfectly possible for a business to be trading profitably and yet be quite unable to pay the tax bill or the rent because its resources are tied up in stock or, even worse, in equipment.

Failure to understand the distinction between profit and cash flow is not uncommon and it can be disastrous. For example, you may be offered very persuasive financial inducements to carry or manufacture additional stock. If it is a good product and one for which there is a consistent demand you may say to yourself that you are going to need more anyway in six months' time, so why not stock up for a whole year at a bargain price? This can be a valid argument, but before you accept it consider that when the bills come in they have to be paid with money, not with stock. Profitability means very little unless cash is there when it is needed.

This is true even for businesses that do not carry stocks, like a photographic studio producing goods only to order, or a design consultancy selling more or less intangible skills. You are still going to have outgoings on travel or materials; and even if your premises are a back room in your own house there are still rate demands to be met, apart from the matter of needing money to live on.

Planning your cash requirements

Planning your cash requirements is crucial from the outset of your career as a self-employed person. It will determine much of your policy towards what kinds of work you take on. It is far better, if you are short of liquid capital, to take on a number of small jobs which will keep money coming in than one big, tempting, potentially profitable one where you might run out of cash three-quarters of the way through. For, unless you make provision to get progress payments from your customer backed up, possibly by a bank overdraft, your suppliers are going to be pressing you for payment before you are in a position to send your bills to the customer. Even at best, in most businesses which are not taking cash across the counter there is going to be a lag between the time you are being asked for payment and when your customer pays you.

In order to estimate what your needs for cash are going to be you should set up and revise at three- or six-monthly intervals, a cash flow budget; and in order to refine it, you should also check it back against what actually happened. Indeed, before you begin you should have (and the bank manager will want to see) a fully worked out cash flow projection for the first 12-18 months.

The words 'cash flow budget' sound intimidatingly technical, but mean simply that you should make a realistic forecast of money coming in and going out over the period. Again, how accurate you can be depends somewhat on the circumstances and the type of business you are in. If you have bought a going concern there may be regular contracts that you hope to maintain, or in the case of a retail business or a restaurant some kind of predictable pattern of trade which can be established from the cash book or general ledger. If you have started a new business of your own, on the other hand, you may not have much to go on in the way of facts on cash coming in. You might only have enough certain information on the next two or three months, though if you have asked yourself the questions we outlined in Chapter 1 you will have ensured, as far as possible, that there is a continuing demand for your product so that orders will go on arriving while you are completing the work you have already lined up. But even in cases where you do not know where the penny after next is coming from, at the very least the cash flow budget will tell you what commitments you have to meet and, therefore, what volume of sales should be your target to this end. You can include this sales target in your budget, but do not forget that in order to achieve it costs of materials and additional overheads will also be involved. Moreover, both in cases where income is firmly expected and where it is only a forecast of expectations the cost of materials and wages will have to be met before you actually get paid.

Let us take a hypothetical case here to illustrate a cash flow budget in operation over the first four months of the year, for a small offset printing business with two partners and one employee. Over these months they have a contract to print the spring catalogue from a local firm of nurserymen, a monthly list from a firm selling militaria by mail order and a booklet on the town for the Chamber of Commerce. They also have some orders for what is known as 'jobbing' — small jobs such as wedding invitations, brochures, printed labels and the like — with the prospect that a regular flow of such work can be picked up. Against this, they have to meet wages, rent, PAYE, VAT, telephone, the running of a van, the purchase of materials, rates, electricity, National Insurance contributions, etc.

As you will see from the forecast (see Table 7.1) the partners budgeted for a deficit in the first two months, but they were not worried because they knew that in March and April they could expect a couple of big payments from Rosebud Nurseries and from the Chamber of Commerce. However, in order to keep solvent they had to borrow £2000 from the bank, interest payments on which had to be paid at intervals. They also had to plan the purchase of their most costly item, paper, as close as possible to the month in which they would actually be using it for their two big jobs. There is no point in holding expensive stock which cannot be used at an early date. Even though, with inflation, it might actually have been cheaper for them to have ordered all their paper for the first four months back in January, their bank overdraft would not have been sufficient to meet the bill.

In March they had to allow for three quarterly items, electricity, telephone and their VAT return, and as the year progresses they will have to make plans to meet such major items as rates and taxes. Note also that expenditure which is central to the activities of the business, in this case paper, has to be forecast more carefully than incidentals such as postage where a monthly average has been extended. If postage was a more crucial factor, as might be the case with a mail-order firm, this part of the cash flow budget would have to be worked out in more detail.

Regarding the revenue part of the forecast, the partners had enough orders for jobbing work to budget fairly accurately for the first two months. For March and April they guessed a figure, hoping spring weddings and a general upturn of business after the winter would lead to a modest growth in incoming funds after that point.

The overall March and April figures look quite rosy, but after that it was clear that they would have to turn up some more

	January	February	March	April
Income (£)				
	From December Statement	From January Statement	From February Statement	From March Statement
	Militaria Ltd 500	Militaria Ltd 500	Rosebud Nurseries Ltd 5300	Chamber of Commerce 2000
	Other work 400	Other work 250	Militaria Ltd 500	Militaria Ltd 500
			Other work 500	Other work 500
	900	750	6300	3000
Expenditure (£)				
	Wages, salaries, PAYE, National Insurance 750	Wages, etc 750	Wages, etc 750	Wages, etc 750
	Rent 100	Rent 100	Rent 100	Rent 100
	Maintenance contract 20	Maintenance 20	Maintenance 20	Maintenance 20
	Petrol 40	Petrol 40	Petrol 40	Petrol 40
	Postage 20	Postage 20	Postage 20	Postage 20
	Travel and Entertainment 40	Travel, etc 40	Travel, etc 40	Travel, etc 40
	Paper 1500	Materials 100	Materials 150	Materials 100
	Other materials 200	Bank Interest 60	Electricity 70	Paper 1500
			Telephone 40	
			VAT 300	
			Paper 1000	
	2670	1130	2530	2570
Cash surplus (deficit)	(1770)	(380)	3770	430

Table 7.1 *An example of a cash flow budget*

jobs like Rosebud Nurseries and the Chamber of Commerce booklet because the overheads — wages, rent, the maintenance contract on their machines, bank interest — plus the cost of paper and materials needed to fill forecast work were running slightly above the expected income. So even though they are running well ahead of the game at the end of April, they would be unwise to start reducing that bank overdraft just yet.

There are many other lessons to be learned from your cash flow budget. They vary from business to business, but the essential points are that it is an indispensable indicator in making your buying decisions both of stock and materials, that it helps you decide your priorities between getting work (and what sort of work) and devoting all your energies to executing it and points to the importance of getting the maximum credit and allowing the minimum!

Checklist: budgeting and cash flow

1. Is the forecast of money coming in based on firm orders or at least reasonable expectations or does it include an element of fond hope?
2. Are the customers concerned likely to pay you at the times forecast?
3. Can you persuade any large customers to offer you progress payments to help you over difficult months?
4. Have you included everything in the outgoings section of the budget, including allowing for things like VAT and the heating of premises in winter months?
5. Do you have the resources to see you through deficit months, or have you secured finance to this end?
6. Is there any way you can cut down on the expenditure element by delaying or staggering buying decisions of stock or leasing rather than buying equipment?

8: Costing, Pricing and Estimating

How much should you charge your customers? Or, to put it more searchingly, on what factors should your charges be based? It is surprising that many self-employed people would be hard put to it to give a clear answer to that question. There are such things as 'going rates' and 'recommended' (or generally accepted) prices, but often these are in the nature of broad guidelines and unless you know what all your costs are, not just the cost of materials, or how long the job took you, you are sooner or later going to be in the position of either undercharging or making an actual loss.

There are some self-employed occupations where the scope for how much you can charge is either narrow or non-existent. This applies particularly to many areas of the retail trade, where goods tend to have recommended prices printed on them by the suppliers; but even there you may want to consider *reducing* some prices in order to undercut a competitor and the question arises whether you can afford to do so. This depends on your overall costs — rent, rates, power supplies and many other factors. Equally, some freelance jobs are subject to generally accepted 'going rates' and the more commonplace such jobs are (ie the smaller the degree of service or expertise that is involved) the more strictly you have to keep within that rate. But the corollary of this statement is also true: the more unique your product or service, the more you can afford to charge for it.

This can apply even in the ordinary retail trade where, on the face of things, the prospect of getting away with charging more than the competition is not promising. Recently a small supermarket opened near my house. It is open late at night, on Sundays and on public holidays and, quite rightly, it charges for that extra time. Most things cost a penny or two above what they do in the larger shops down the High Street, but it is offering something more than they are, and meets competition not by charging less, but by providing more — a much-needed neighbourhood service for out-of-hours shopping.

The same principle can be applied to even rather routine

freelance jobs. Provide a straightforward typing service and you will have to stick pretty much to the going rate; but offer something special, like accurately typing mathematical material or unusually high turnround speeds, and you can move into a different price bracket.

Determining your costs

You could say to yourself: 'I'm going to charge as much as I can get away with' or, 'I'm going to charge the standard rate for the job'. These are quite sensible guidelines to be going on with, but at some point you are probably going to be in the situation of wondering whether you should be charging a little more, or perhaps whether you can afford to reduce your price in order to land some work that you badly want. It is then that you have to get to grips with what your costs really are.

The most obvious one is your own time, and curiously enough it is an element that self-employed people are often confused about, because they tend to regard it as being somehow different from the time taken by employees. If a job involves your working flat out for a 100-hour week, you are underpricing the product of that work if your remuneration is less than that of an employed person doing the same kind of work at full overtime rates. There may be a reason why you *should* be undercharging: you may want a 'loss-leader' introduction to a particular customer, or to undercut a competitor, or you may simply need the money that week. But if you undercharge, you should be clear in your mind why you are doing so.

Another factor that is sometimes overlooked is that in most cases there are overhead costs incurred in running your business, irrespective of whether you have work coming in or not. We will deal with these overheads in more detail in a moment, but the point to be made here is to correct any misconception that the margin between what you charge and your basic costs in time and/or materials represents your profit. True, it is a profit of a kind — gross profit. But the real profit element in a job, the net profit, only emerges when the overhead costs have been met. So the right way to work out your price to the customer, or to determine whether a job is worth taking on, is to establish whether it will pay for materials, overheads, wages (if you employ others) and still leave you with a margin of net profit that adequately reflects the time and skill you are putting into it.

Once you have been in business for a few months you should have accumulated enough facts and figures to establish what your overhead costs are. To what extent you can control the situation beyond that depends, again, on what sort of business you are in. If you are running an ordinary retail shop, operating on margins that are more or less fixed by the supplier, there is not much you can do about pricing your goods, but at least you will know whether you can afford to spend more on extra fittings or take on more staff, or whether you should be staying open longer to attract extra trade. But if you are manufacturing something, then you can work out a rule-of-thumb method in the form of a percentage to add on to your materials costs in quoting prices; or in the case of a service, an average hourly rate. It is important, though, to keep on monitoring these rule-of-thumb procedures against what actually happened, so you should keep a record detailing the specification of each job, in which actual costs can be compared against your original estimate. Over a period of time you should in this way be able to build up a reliable set of costs which can be referred to when an assignment which sounds similar comes up.

At the beginning, though, you will have very little to go on, so let us look in more detail at the factors you will have to take into account.

Costs connected with your premises

Rent, heat, light, telephone, rates, insurance, finance (if you own or have bought a lease of the premises), cleaning and maintenance contracts.

Costs of finance

Interest charged on overdrafts or loans. You should include in this calculation interest on any money you yourself have put into the business, because it should be earning a rate of return equivalent to what you could get on the open market.

Costs of equipment

If you are renting equipment or buying it on hire purchase this item of expenditure presents no problems. The issue is more complicated if you have bought equipment outright, because you have to figure out some way of recovering the purchase price and this is done by bringing in the concept of 'depreciation'. What this means is that you gradually write off, over a period of time based on the item's useful life, most of the amount you paid initially; not all, because it will have some resale value at the end of the depreciation period.

Supposing you bought a van for £3000 and you think it will last you for four years, at the end of which time you could expect to get £1000 for it. This leaves you with £2000 to depreciate over four years − £500 per annum. There are also a number of other ways to calculate depreciation and your accountant will advise you on the method most advantageous to your kind of business. The important point to bear in mind, though, is that depreciation is a real factor, not just an accountancy device. Assets like motor cars and equipment do wear out and have to be replaced. Reserves should be built up to enable you to do this.

Administrative costs

Running your business will involve general expenditure which cannot be directly related to particular assignments: stationery, publicity, travel, postage, entertainment of clients, fees to professional advisers, and so forth.

Salaries and welfare

Salaries are best calculated as an hourly rate, based on an average working week. In the case of employees these rates are usually determined by the market for that particular kind of employment. The problem is deciding how much you should pay to yourself. Again, this obviously varies with the kind of business you are in, but as a rough guideline you should, after meeting all your expenses, be earning at least as much as an employed person with the same degree of skill and responsibility. It is most important to cost your time properly; let us, therefore, look at a worked example of what might be involved in the case of a person in full-time self-employment.

Supposing you were aiming to earn £10,000 a year. To start with you would want to take into account four weeks' annual paid holiday (three weeks, plus statutory holidays) and you would assume an eight-hour day and a five-day working week. However, not all your time would be directly productive: some of it would be spent travelling, on administration and on getting work. So let us say your productive time is 32 hours a week. That would give you an hourly rate based on 32 x 48 hours a year: 1536 hours. Divided into £10,000 that means a rate of about £6.51 per hour. On top of that you have to allow for welfare items: your National Insurance stamp, possible contributions to a retirement pension scheme and certainly insurance against sickness or death. Let us assume this comes to another £800 a year. Divided by 1536 working hours, this adds another 52 pence to your hourly rate.

Similarly, when costing the time of any full-time staff working for you, it is not just a question of calculating basic rates of pay. You have to allow for holidays, the employer's contribution to National Insurance stamps and to the graduated pension scheme. These items can add 6 to 8 per cent to the cost of wages.

Variable costs

All the costs we have just described are fixed costs. You incur them whether you have work coming in or not. Variable costs are items like materials which can be attributed to specific jobs. There are circumstances in which what we have described as fixed costs can vary slightly. If you are running a lot of overtime, this will mean an increase in your fuel bills and extra payments to your staff or to yourself. But the benefit of achieving properly costed increases in productivity, for example, in the case of a shop staying open late to attract more trade, is that, provided you are able to keep fixed overheads stable, this element will form a smaller proportion relative to your turnover; and that means a more profitable business.

Establishing your prices

You now have a set of basic data on costs which can be applied to your prices when you are asked to quote for a job or in making up your invoice. If you are supplying a service, the best way to do this is to take all your fixed costs, establish an hourly rate based on your usual working week and then estimate how long the job will take you. The effect of this is that if jobs do not materialise in the way the 'usual working week' concept implies you yourself are going to be carrying the can for the fixed overheads which are being incurred during all the hours in that week when you are not working. And if you only get

20 hours' work during a week in which you had budgeted for 40, loading your charges to the customer to make up for the shortfall could mean that you will come up with an unacceptable quotation or a price that will discourage your customer in the future.

The other lesson to be learned is that fixed overheads should be kept as low as possible. For instance, if you are planning a freelance design service to earn extra money in the evenings you should be chary of acquiring expensive equipment. In the limited hours of work which a part-time freelance operation implies you may never be able to charge enough money to do more than pay the overheads. As far as possible, keep your costs in the variable category by hiring or renting equipment only when and for as long as you need it.

This is also true of businesses that produce manufactured articles (and activities which operate on lines similar to manufacturing like a restaurant, where the product is created in the form of a meal), though in these cases some machinery and equipment are usually essential. The price here will be based on a unit per item rather than on an hourly rate, but the principle is the same. Instead of fixing an hourly rate based on an expected working week, calculations should be made on a projected volume of costs spread over the number of units sold. Thus, if you aimed to sell in a week 20 chairs which cost you £5 each in materials your variable costs would be £100. If your fixed overheads, including your own remuneration, came to £300 a week, you would have to charge £20 per chair. And do not forget that even if your object is only to make a living wage out of your business, you should still be putting aside reserves to replace equipment as it wears out, and that the cost of doing so will, in periods of inflation, be a great deal higher than its original cost.

Preparing quotations

With many jobs, whether they are a service or a commission to manufacture something, you will be asked to supply a quotation before a firm order is placed. Once that quotation has been accepted it is legally binding on both parties, so it is important not only to get your sums right but to make it clear in the wording attached to them what exactly you are providing for the money. In the case of a decorating job, for example, you should specify who is providing the materials and, if you are, to what standards they are going to be. Consider also whether any out-of-pocket expenses will be involved (travel, subsistence) and whether these are to be met by your customer or whether they have been allowed for in your quotation.

Apart from variable factors such as these, every quotation should set out the conditions of sale under which it is being offered. Different businesses will involve different kinds of conditions, but here are some basic points to bear in mind:

1. Particularly in times of inflation, you should make it clear that the prices quoted are current ones and may have to go up if costs rise during the course of the job.
2. Terms of payment should be set out, for example 30 days net.
3. You will have to cover the not uncommon situation of the customer changing his mind about the way he wants the job done subsequent to his accepting your quotation. You should leave yourself free to charge extra in such circumstances.
4. If you have agreed to complete a job within a certain length of time, set out the factors beyond your control which would prevent you from meeting the agreed date.
5. You should make it clear what circumstances of error, loss or damage will be your responsibility and what would fall outside it.
6. You should stipulate that, once the quotation is accepted, the order cannot be cancelled except by mutual consent and that the customer will be liable for all charges up to that point.
7. You should mention that the total is subject to VAT at the rate ruling at the date of invoice. This is particularly important when the customer is a private person who is unable to claim back his VAT inputs. (See Chapter 11 for details of VAT.)

Having gone to all the trouble to set out the quotation and conditions of sale, you should not neglect to check, before you start work, that the customer has actually accepted it in writing! It is all too easy to forget this or to imagine that an amicable verbal OK is sufficient. If a dispute arises, however, you will be very thankful to have carried out all the formal steps of documentation.

Every few months sit back for half an hour and consider your pricing policy. If you have set up as a consulting engineer and have no wish to get involved with renting offices and employing others, then your workload capacity is limited to the number of hours you put in. To start with you will probably be glad of work at any price but as your business builds up to the point where you are working all hours the only way you will be able to increase your real income is to increase your prices. So if you have a reliable supply of work coming in which is giving you a reasonable income, do not be afraid to put in some highish quotes for new work. It is not always the case that the lowest tender wins the job, particularly in the field of consultancy.

Checklist: costing, pricing and estimating

1. How unique is your product or service? If it is not particularly uncommon, how can you make it more so?
2. How essential is it to the customer?
3. What is the competition charging for the same or similar product or service?
4. How badly do you need the job or order?
5. Is your customer likely to come back for more if the price is right, or is it a one-off?
6. Will doing business with this customer enable you to break into a wider market, and thus enable you to reduce your unit costs?
7. What is the element of risk involved (ie is the customer, to your knowledge, a quick and certain payer)?
8. Do you have any idea how long the job will take you?
9. Can you relate the time element to your fixed costs?
10. Have you made a full assessment of all your fixed costs?
11. Do you have any idea what your materials are going to cost you?
12. Have you costed your own time properly?
13. Will the job leave you a margin of net profit? Or should you forgo this in the interest of meeting fixed costs?
14. Have you prepared a quote, specifying exactly what you are going to provide or do, including terms of payment?
15. Has the customer accepted your quotation?
16. Are you keeping records of what the job cost you so that you can adjust your prices or quote more accurately next time?

9: Marketing Your Work

Good ideas, it is sometimes dismissively said, are ten a penny; the implication being that the really difficult part is putting them into effect. Apart from the obvious virtues of persistence, hard work and technical know-how, this also requires a modicum of marketing skill. In other words, you will have to know whether there is a big enough demand for your product or service at the price you need to charge to make a living and how to identify and reach your potential customers.

Manufacturers

You may be the world's most skilful maker of hand-carved model sailing ships, but unless enough people want them, you are going to have a hard time trying to make a living out of producing them commercially. So before you start in business, look around. Go to gift shops, luxury stores or wherever it is that the kind of item you are aiming to produce is being sold and find out about prices, quality standards and the extent of the demand. Any intelligent shop manager or assistant will be glad to give you such information, provided you do not buttonhole them at a busy time of the day. It may be that by modifying your idea in quite a minor way, you will come up with a much more saleable article than the one that was originally in your mind.

Another point to watch out for is whether there is a long-term future for your product. This is particularly true with regard to fashion goods. There may be a craze for some particular kind of accessory and for a while you will be able to sell everything you produce. But before long some large manufacturer will come along and make the same thing much more cheaply and distribute it more effectively than you can. When the craze dies down he will get off the bandwagon and on to something else. Are you going to be able to keep a step ahead of him by being in a position to meet the next craze before the big manufacturers become aware of it?

You also have to keep an eye on competitors of your own size. If you are making and selling pottery, consider how many other craft potters are active in your area and whether your work is so good and so competitively priced that it does not matter how many there are; or whether you can produce something commercially viable that they are not doing.

But no matter how good or unique your product may be, the ultimate key to success lies in effective sales and distribution. At the smallest level you might be selling direct to the public through your own shop, as is the case with many craft goods, but you have to bear in mind that you need to achieve a considerable turnover for a shop in a good location to be viable. This is difficult if the range of specialisation is very narrow, and many small-scale manufacturers, therefore, combine having their own shop with direct mail and mail order (which we shall come to in a moment) and with marketing to other retail outlets. Shop and workshop premises can be combined in the same floor area, so that you can switch readily from the sales counter to the workbench when the shop is empty. This requires permission from the local planning authority if a 'change of use' of what were originally shop premises is involved.

Starting-up costs will eat deeply into your capital, so unless you have enough experience of the marketing (as opposed to the manufacturing) end of your specialty to be absolutely convinced that you can sell it, it is a good idea to begin by making a few prototypes of the product and its packaging and by trying to get orders from retailers. Though your friends and family may think your idea is wonderful, the acid test is whether it will survive in the marketplace. In the course of investigating this, the natural conservatism of most branches of the retail trade may at times depress or irritate you, but it is worth listening to what people who are involved in it have to say. If the same criticisms keep on cropping up you should think seriously of modifying your prototype to take them into account.

Distribution can be another big headache and your premises should be big enough to enable you to hold roughly as many days' or weeks' supply of stock as it takes to replace it at its rate of demand. If a business is selling 10 chairs a week and it takes two weeks to get that number of replacements there should, ideally, be space for something like 20 chairs. A customer might be prepared to wait a week for delivery, but he is unlikely to wait a month.

Accessibility of non-selling areas is important too. Adequate entry for goods and materials at the rear or side of the premises is often essential and will always save time and energy.

Shops and service industries

The first large shopping centre built in Britain was a flop because, among other disadvantages, it had no parking facilities and was situated in a working class area a few minutes' walk away from a large, long-established and very popular street market. The developers, for all their vast financial resources, had ignored hotel magnate Conrad Hilton's three factors in siting a business serving the public: location, location and location. If you are thinking of setting up a shop, restaurant or some other service outlet, find out as much as possible about the area. What sort of people live there? Is the area declining economically or on the up and up? What is the range of competitors? How efficient do they look and how well are they doing? If you are thinking of opening a high-class restaurant and there are nothing but fish and chip establishments in the neighbourhood, does this mean that there is no demand for a good restaurant or a crying need for one?

Taking the case of a bookshop. You would want to conduct some rule-of-thumb market research about the area before going any further. For example, you would want to know whether there were enough people in the area to support such a venture, whether they were the sort of people who regularly bought books, and how good the local library was. You would also want to know what impact the result of your market investigations might have on your trading policies. Thus, if there were a lot of families with young children around, you should be considering getting to know, and stocking, children's books; or, if there were a lot of students in the neighbourhood, it would be worth your while finding out what textbooks were being used in local educational institutions. Alternatively, if your bookshop is highly specialised — medicine, academic history, chess, or some other specific activity — an expensive High Street location is likely to be wholly inappropriate. You will want to be near the centre of that activity, or, more likely, will want to sell to your well-defined audience through direct mail.

The same broad principles apply to almost every kind of retail or service outlet and you will have to conduct this kind of research, which is really just plain commonsense — whatever

Introducing
The CML Personal Pension Plan

*   Excellent Pension + substantial TAX FREE cash sum at retirement.

*   Highly attractive tax savings.

*   Flexibility in contributions and benefits.

*   Valuable death benefits before retirement now available under our Executive Life Plan.

For further details contact James D. Urwin at the address shown below.

P.O. BOX 60   24 LUDGATE HILL LONDON EC4P 4BD

your venture. Do not be tempted to overlook it just because you are buying what is supposed to be a 'going concern'. One reason why it is up for sale may be that, despite the owner's or agent's protestations to the contrary, it was doing badly. If that was because the previous owner was a poor manager or stocked the wrong kind of goods for the neighbourhood, you might be able to turn the business around; but if there was simply too much competition in the area from similar shops and there is no chance of trading viably in something else from the same address, you would be well advised to forget about those premises, however good a buy they may seem from a purely cost point of view. You will also be able to check on the vendor's assertions by looking, preferably with your accountant, at his profit and loss accounts, not just for the past year's but the previous three to five years', to get a picture of the general trend of things. On the whole, buying a going concern has to be approached with great caution, particularly by the inexperienced, because of the difficulties of valuing stock and goodwill with any accuracy. See Chapters 15 and 17 for more detailed treatment of these points.

Freelance services

Most freelances agree that the way you get work is by knowing people who are in a position to give it to you. That sounds rather like a chicken and egg situation, and to begin with, so it is. You would be ill-advised to launch into freelance work, certainly on a full-time basis, until you have built up a range of contacts who can provide you with enough work to produce some sort of living for at least the first few months. Often these are people whom you have got to know in the course of a full-time job, or while doing temporary work. Many advertising agencies, for instance, have been started by a breakaway group taking a batch of clients with them when they start up.* And it may even be that your employer, having been compelled to make you redundant, will still be willing to put work out to you on a freelance basis.

Once you have got going and established a reputation for doing good, reliable work, things get much easier. For one thing, word-of-mouth recommendations have a strong effect in

---

* To combat this trend many firms now include clauses in their employment contract expressly stating that it is not permissible to work for a client of the employer for two years after leaving that employer.

the freelance world. Moreover, you will be able to produce examples of work sold, or be able to refer prospects to other clients who have engaged you successfully. Evidence, for instance, that your fashion photographs have actually been used by national magazines generally impresses more than a folder of prints, no matter how good they are. In freelance work, as in other spheres, nothing succeeds like success.

One problem with freelance work, though, is that clients often want something done in a hurry — over a weekend or even overnight. This can be highly inconvenient at times, but it is generally a bad idea to turn work down simply for this reason. If you have to be selective, turn away the smaller, less remunerative jobs or commissions from people who are slow to pay their bills. One thing you should never do, though, is to let a client down. If you cannot, or do not want, to take on an assignment, say so immediately.

Press advertising

Advertising is a marketing tool and like any other tool you have to use it in the right place, at the right time and for the right job if it is going to be of any use to you. If you are a local building contractor, there is no point advertising in national newspapers, because most of the circulation, which is what you are paying for in the rates charged, will be outside the geographical area you are working in. On the other hand, if you are making a product to sell by mail order, the bigger the circulation the better. There are, however, still provisos: there is, for example, no point in advertising a product aimed at 'top people' in a mass-circulation tabloid.

The first rule is to pick the right medium for the product or service you have to sell. Do not be dazzled by circulation figures. What matters is the *quality* of the circulation in relation to your marketing needs, and a trade or local paper may often provide the best value for money. A few years ago the author was responsible for marketing a very expensive American book on Japanese flower arranging. It turned out that there was a small journal with a circulation of a few hundred copies to devotees of this arcane hobby and a full-page advertisement (which then cost a mere £15), combined with an order coupon, produced a quite extraordinary response. Of course, full-page advertisements normally cost a good deal more than that and in the nationals they can run to thousands of pounds. A small, regular insertion in a local or specialist paper is what you should be thinking of; and the keyword is 'regular'. People's needs change from week to week, and unless you happen to hit them in the week they need your product, you will not hit them at all.

Regular advertising need not be expensive. An advertisement in the 'classified' section (but be sure to specify the right classification!) costs only a few pounds, and there may be bulk rates for regular insertions. You can also have a display advertisement. These are charged by column inches (or centimetres) rather than by line as is the case with classified. It costs more, but the advantage is that you may be able to control the position in which your advertisement is to appear. The top and outside edges are more eye-catching than, say, the inside corners. 'Facing matter' advertisements, particularly when they are facing a feature article relating to your kind of product, can also be very effective. It is a good idea to get a graphic designer — you will find plenty of addresses in Yellow Pages or your Thomson local directory — to do a layout for you. It will only cost you a few pounds and the result will be infinitely more attractive and eyecatching than if you leave it to the printer's typesetter.

Some days are reckoned by admen to produce a better response than others, although there are divided opinions on what these days are. The best advice is to experiment with different days. It is worth experimenting with the wording, too. Try several variations on the same theme and use the one that brings you the best response. But avoid trying to cram in too many words. People do not, on the whole, respond to over-crowded ads.

One important feature is that your advertisement should be very specific about how the goods and services advertised can be obtained. Your address should be prominent and if you are only available at certain times of the day or in the evenings this should be stated. If you are selling a product, an order coupon (stating price *and* postage) reinforces this point. It will also enable you to measure the extent of the response. You should, in fact, keep a close eye on where most of your sales or assignments come from: the type of customer and how he is getting to hear about you. This will enable you to concentrate future marketing efforts in the most rewarding sectors.

Public relations

It may be possible, particularly if you have a specialist line of business, to obtain free coverage in trade journals and local newspapers by sending them press releases to mark events such as the opening of an extension or the provision of some unique service. You simply type the information on a slip marked PRESS RELEASE; 'embargo' it — ie prohibit its use — until a date that suits you, and send it to newspapers and magazines you choose as the likeliest to use it. Newspapers and other news media — don't forget about local radio and even local TV — are, however, only interested in *news* and the mere fact that you have opened a business may not interest them much. Try to find a news angle, for instance, that you have obtained a large export order, or are reviving a local craft or are giving employment to school leavers. If you have any friends who are journalists ask their advice on the sort of information that is likely to get the attention of editors. Better still, ask them if they will draft your press release for you.

There are many other PR activities — sponsorship, stunts, celebrity appearances at your premises, public speaking, and so on. All are designed to publicise who you are and what you do, and suggest to the public that you provide a worthwhile and reliable service. PR for the small business is covered throughly in Michael Bland's *Be Your Own PR Man* (published by Kogan Page).

Direct mail and direct response promotion

Direct mail selling is a considerable subject in its own right. It differs from mail order in that the latter consists of mailing goods direct to the customer from orders engendered by general press advertising, whereas in the case of direct mail selling the advertising is a brochure or sales letter specifically directed at the customer. Direct response promotion consists of an ad plus coupon placed in a newspaper or journal, to be posted to the manufacturer as an order. If you use these methods, remember to allow for postage in your pricing and since the response to direct mail averages around 2 per cent, the postage cost per sale is quite a considerable factor. It can, however, be a very effective way of selling specialised, high-priced items (£8 is around the viable minimum these days) or of identifying people who are likely to buy from you regularly if you are selling variations on the same product. Unless you are very skilful at writing brochures or sales letters you should get this done for you by an expert. Such people are employed by mailing list brokers (you will find those in the Yellow Pages) who will often provide a complete package: they will sell to you, or compile for you, specialised lists, address and stuff envelopes and produce sales literature.

Their services are not cheap and before you plunge into a direct mail campaign there are relatively inexpensive ways of testing the market for yourself. Pick 100 specialist addresses of the type you want to reach on a bigger scale – again, you may find them in the Yellow Pages. A small want ad in one of the advertising industry's trade papers will soon raise the services of freelance copywriters and designers if you need such help. From the percentage reply to the sample mailing you will be able to gauge whether a bigger campaign is worth mounting and you will also get some idea of how to price the product to take into account the likely mailing costs per sale. It is generally essential, by the way, with direct mail advertising, to include a reply paid card or envelope with your sales literature. Details of how to apply for reply paid and Freepost facilities are available from the Post Office.

Checklist: marketing your work

Manufacturers

1. Have you tested your idea by discussing your proposed product with potential customers? Or, better still, showing it to them?
2. Is the market for it big enough? How accessible is it?
3. Can the customers you have in mind afford a price that will produce a profit for you?
4. Have you studied the competition from the point of view of price, design quality, reliability, delivery dates, etc?
5. Should you modify your produce in some way so as to get the edge on the competition? Have you worked out what this will do to your costs?
6. Is there a long-term future for your product? If not, do you have any ideas for a follow-up?
7. Can you handle distribution? Do you have access to a van if the market is local? Do you have adequate parking facilities if it requires despatching?

Selectaplan Ltd.

Planning To Acquire Your Own Business, Expand, Or Have Cash-Flow Problems?

Contact us to help you raise the money you need, point out the tax advantages of borrowing, and show you how best to set up your business now.

17 Nottingham Street,
London W1M 3RD
Tel. (01) 486-4887/8.

8. In the latter case, have you taken post and packing costs into account in working out how much the product will cost the customer?
9. Do you have adequate space to hold stock, taking into account production time?
10. Do you have someone who can deal with customer queries and complaints? Or have you allowed for the fact that you will have to take time out yourself to deal with them?

Shops and service industries

1. How much do you know about the area?
2. Is the location good from the point of view of attracting the kind of trade you are looking for?
3. What competitors do you have?
4. How are they doing?
5. Based on your study of the area, and the people who live in it, how does this affect the type of goods or the nature of the service you are going to offer?
6. If you are buying a going concern, have you checked it out thoroughly with your professional advisers?

111

Freelance services

1. Do you have any contacts who can give you work?
2. Have you made a realistic appraisal of how much you can expect to earn over the first six months?
3. Have you allowed for the fact that you will need a good deal of spare time to go around looking for more business?
4. What evidence can you produce of your competence to do freelance work in your proposed field?
5. Have you shown that evidence to the sort of person who might be a customer to get his reaction on whether it is likely to impress?
6. Who are your competitors, what do they charge and what can you offer that is superior to their services?

Advertising and promotion

1. Have you chosen the right medium to promote your product or service?
2. Do you have any idea of the circulation and how this is broken down, geographically or by type of reader?
3. Have you worked out any way of monitoring results, for instance by including a coupon?
4. Have you included the cost of advertising and promotion in your cash flow budget and in costing your product?
5. Have you worked out how many orders you need to get from your advertising/promotion campaign to show a profit?
6. In the case of a display advertisement, have you specified a position in which it is to appear?
7. Again, in the case of a display ad or a brochure have you had it properly designed?
8. Does your advertising/promotion material state where your product or service can be obtained and, if relevant, the price?
9. Is the wording compelling? Does it clearly describe the product or service and does it motivate the customer? Would you buy it, if you were a customer?
10. In the case of a classified advertisement, have you specified under which classification it is to appear?
11. Are all the statements and claims you are making about your product or service true to the best of your knowledge and belief, bearing in mind that untruths can leave you open to prosecution under the Trade Descriptions Act?

10: Employing People

A fairly common observation about employing people has always been to say that this is when your troubles begin. Today this is truer than ever, because apart from the difficulty of finding Mr or Ms Right — a task which even experienced personnel people admit, in their more candid moments, is something of a lottery — a mass of legislation has been enacted in recent years which, it is thought by some, favours the rights of employees at the expense of employers. Though the aim of this legislation has mainly been to protect the workforce of larger companies from arbitrary hiring and firing, it embraces even the smallest employer and to a large extent it covers part-time as well as full-time employees. Whole books could be and have been written about the legal technicalities involved, but all we can do in this section is to draw the reader's attention to some of the major pitfalls you should look out for when you start employing people.

The contract of employment

The contract of employment statement which has to be issued in writing to every employee who is going to work for you for 16 hours or more per week within 13 weeks of joining is in fact not a pitfall, but a rather sensible document which clarifies right from the outset what the terms of employment are. From the employer's point of view, the necessity of drafting a contract of employment statement should concentrate the mind wonderfully on issues about which it is all too easy to be sloppy at the expense of subsequent aggravation, such as hours of work, holidays and, above all, exactly what it is the employee is supposed to be doing. The following points have to be covered in the contract, and you must say if you have not covered one or other of them:

☐ The rate of pay and how it is calculated
☐ Whether it is paid weekly or monthly

☐ The normal hours of work and the terms and conditions relating to them
☐ Holidays and holiday pay
☐ Provision for sick pay
☐ Pension and pension schemes
☐ Notice required by both parties
☐ The job title
☐ Any disciplinary rules relating to the job
☐ Grievance producedures.

Unfair dismissal

Probably the area of legislation which it is easiest and most common to fall foul of is that relating to unfair dismissal. Every employee, including part-timers if they work for you in other than a freelance capacity for more than 16 hours a week, who has been on your staff continuously for 52 weeks or more (104 weeks or more in the case of a new business) must be given a written statement of your reason if you want to dismiss him. You must also give him one week's notice (or payment in lieu) if he has been with you continuously for four weeks or more and, after two years, one week's notice for every year of continuous employment. Fair enough, you might say, particularly as, on the face of things, what the law regards as fair grounds for dismissal are perfectly reasonable: incompetence, misconduct or genuine redundancy. The problem is that the employee is at liberty to disagree with you on the fairness issue and to take his case to an industrial tribunal, which stipulates that the employment grounds for dismissal must be *reasonable*.

The 1980 Employment Act made four changes of particular relevance to small businesses employing staff:

1. The qualifying period for alleged unfair dismissal claims was extended from six months to 12. For firms with 20 employees or less it has been extended to two years in respect of new employees; an important simplification since redundancy has a similar two-year qualifying period.
2. Industrial tribunals are directed to take account of the size and resources of employer. For example where an employee proves unsatisfactory in one job, a large employer might be able to offer him another position, but a small employer would find this more difficult in most cases.
3. Post-maternity reinstatement is waived for firms of five employees or less, if re-instatement is not practicable.

4. Frivolous claims are to be deterred by a liability to costs.

If the employee has been guilty of gross misconduct, such as persistent lateness, you will probably win your case, provided you warned him in writing to mend his ways well before you dismissed him. The point here is that you must not only have good reasons for dismissing him, but you must also have acted reasonably in the dismissal situation. This means that you have got to follow a proper sequence of written warnings, not less than three is the number generally recommended, stating his inadequacies, telling him what he has to do to put them right and spelling out the consequences if he fails to do so.

When it comes to matters of competence, though, things are rather less clear-cut, particularly if the task involved is not one where performance can be readily quantified or where there are many imponderables. It would be relatively easy to argue a case against a machine operator who was consistently turning out less work than his colleagues on similar machines, but far more difficult in the case of a salesman who could plead that a poor call-rate was the result of difficulties in finding car parking or inefficient back-up from the office.

The fact is that in all matters affecting competence you really have to do your homework very carefully before dismissing someone. The inexperienced employer may unwittingly contribute to a judgement by the Tribunal going against him by such steps as including the person concerned in a general salary rise not long before informing him he is not up to the job.

There may be cases where you, as the employer, are satisfied that dismissal is fair, but where the law does not agree with you. One where you have to be very careful is dismissal on medical grounds. No reasonable employer would dismiss anyone in such circumstances if he could help it, but if you get stuck with someone who is persistently off sick and is able to provide satisfactory medical evidence you would have to show proof that the absences were of such a nature as to cause disruption to your business before you could discharge him. Even more tricky is the case of employees who are engaged in public duties, such as being on the local council. You have to give them reasonable time off to attend those duties, though not necessarily with pay.

We have used the word 'he' of employees so far (in the interests of brevity, not for sexist reasons) but, of course, all these provisions extend to women as well. The Sex Discrimination Act and the Equal Pay Act mean that women have in all respects to be treated on an equal footing with men.

There are some additional hazards to employing women of child-bearing age. Provided she works until 11 weeks before her confinement a women who has been continuously in your employ for two years or more is entitled to take 40 weeks off if she becomes pregnant and to return to her original job, without loss of seniority, at the end of that time. Furthermore, she is entitled to remuneration at nine-tenths her normal salary less NI maternity allowance, for the first six weeks of her absence, though the employer can recover the money from the Department of Employment. And if you bring in a replacement for her, or any other employee who is off for any longer period of time, be very careful. Her replacement could sue you for unlawful dismissal unless you notify him or her in writing that the appointment is a temporary one and give notice when it is coming to an end.

The penalties for losing an unfair dismissals case can be ruinous for a small firm. In the most extreme instances you could be in for a compensation award of £6250, plus any redundancy pay to which the employee is entitled, plus a basic award related to age and length of service of up to £3900. On top of all this, in the most aggravated cases, there is a further additional award of £6760. Thus if you are in any doubt at all about a dismissal you should consult a solicitor who is versed in this aspect of the law.

Redundancy

Redundancy is a ripe area for misunderstanding. Redundancy occurs when a job disappears, for example, because a firm ceases trading or has to cut down on staff. It does not have the same restrictions as dismissal, but nevertheless does involve some financial penalties for employers if the employee has been continuously employed by the firm concerned for two years or more. In that case he will be entitled to redundancy pay on a formula based on length of service and rate of pay. About half of this can be recovered from the Department of Employment, which you should notify if you intend to make anyone redundant. As usual, there is a good deal of form filling involved. The law also requires you to give advance warning to the relevant unions if any of their members are to be made redundant.

What happens if you buy a business, lock, stock and barrel, together with the staff? You may find that you do not like some of the people the previous owner took on, or that you want to change or drop some of the things he was doing, with the result that staff will be made redundant. Irrespective of the fact that you did not hire the people concerned, you are still stuck with your responsibility towards them as their current employer, so that being the proverbial new broom can be a very costly exercise. Before buying a business, therefore, it is very important to look at the staff and at the extent of any redundancy payments or dismissals situations you could get involved in.

In the same context, another Act of Parliament you should keep an eye open for when buying a business is the Health and Safety at Work Act which lays down standards to which working premises have to conform. Before putting down your money you should check with the inspectors of the Health and Safety Executive that any premises you are buying or leasing as part of the deal meet those standards.

Recruitment

The cost of discharging staff, whether because of redundancy or by dismissal, makes it imperative that you should make the right decisions in picking people to work for you in the first place. We have said that the sphere of personnel selection is something of a lottery. It could equally be described as a gamble and there are ways in which you could cut down on the odds against you.

The most obvious question to ask yourself is whether you really do need to take someone on permanently at all. The principle we have put forward for the purchase of equipment — never buy anything outright unless you are sure you have a continuing use for it and that it will pay for itself over a reasonable interval of time — also applies to personnel. The legal constraints that cover part-time or full-time employees do not extend to freelances, personnel from agencies or outside work done on contract, and this could well be the best way of tackling a particular problem such as an upward bump in demand until you are sure that it is going to last.* It is worth remembering, too, that when you take on staff you take on a good many payroll and administrative overheads in addition to their salary.

*However, in some cases freelances have successfully argued retrospectively that since they were subject to the same conditions as the ordinary employees of a firm, they were covered by employment law. It is not enough to say that 'A' is a freelance and 'B' is not; there must be recognisable differences in the way they work. The freelance must not be under your direct supervision and control, or he will be likely to be classified (for the purposes of redundancy pay, etc) as an employee.

These can add quite significantly to your costs.

Sooner or later, though, if you want your business to grow (and growth of some kind seems to be an inevitable concomitant of success) you are going to need people. But even then you should ask yourself what exactly you need them for and how much you can afford to pay. Clarifying these two issues is not only important for itself, but it will also give you the basis of a job description which you can use in your press advertising or approach to a recruitment agency, at the interview and, finally, in the contract of employment. Around it you should also build a series of questions to ask the interviewee that should give you some indication of his competence to do the job. Such questions should call for a detailed response rather than a 'yes' or 'no' type of answer. For example, if you are interviewing a sales representative, asking him how long he has been in the business will tell you something, but not nearly as much as the answer to a question that tries to elicit which buyers he knows and how well he knows them.

Competence is part of the story. Equally important is the interviewee's track record: how many previous employers he has had and whether his progress has been up, down or steady. Too many job changes at frequent intervals can be a bad sign and it is fair to ask searching questions about this if it is part of the employment pattern. It is also wise to be cautious about people who are willing to take a large drop in salary. In these days when good jobs are hard to come by there can be a perfectly good reason for this, but you ought to tactfully find out what it is.

Possibly the references will give you a clue and you should always ask for and check references. They are not always reliable — most employers are reasonable people and they will not speak ill of an ex-employee if they can help it (though they should be aware that it is illegal to misrepresent the abilities or overstate the capability of an employee or ex-employee to another employer) — but they will generally alert you to real disaster areas. Telephone reference checks are widely reckoned to be more reliable than written ones because referees are nearly always more forthcoming in conversation than in a letter, since the law of libel and industrial relations law looms large in any written deposition.

Conditions of work

Numerous regulations affect working conditions and you should be conversant with those relevant to your area, particularly if it is a potentially dangerous trade. Length of hours, minimum wages, employment of young persons, etc will tend to apply to all businesses, and, though you may escape persecution for a while, to fall foul of the law is likely to be embarrassing and expensive.

Checklist: employing people

1. Do you really need to take on staff? Will there be enough to keep them busy a year from now?
2. Have you worked out a job description which sets out the purpose of the job, the duties involved and who the person appointed will report to?
3. Have you decided how much you can afford to pay?
4. Do your advertisements or approach to a recruiting agency spell out the job description, the salary and the approximate age of the person you are looking for?
5. Does it in any way contravene the Sex Discrimination Act or the Race Relations Act?
6. Have you prepared a series of questions that will throw some light on the interviewee's competence, personality and previous record of employment?
7. Have you taken up and checked references?
8. Are you satisfied, before making the appointment, that you have seen enough applicants to give you an idea of the quality of staff available for this particular job?
9. Do you have a procedure for reviewing the employee's progress before the expiry of the 52-week (or, in the case of small firms, 104-week) period after which he can claim unfair dismissal if you decide he is not suitable?

11: Taxation

How you are affected by taxation depends on the nature of the commercial activity in which you are engaged. Virtually everyone pays tax on income from some source, whether this be from full-time employment, from dividends or interest or from self-employment or from a combination of several of these elements. The various kinds of income are assessed under several headings or schedules and the ones we will be particularly concerned with are:

1. Schedule D. Case I and Case II: Income from trades, professions or vocations. (In the interests of simplicity we will refer to this as Schedule D, though there are four other 'Cases' of Schedule D income.)
2. Schedule E: Wages and salaries from employment.

There are also other ways in which you may be involved in tax matters. You may be paying capital gains tax on the disposal of capital assets. If you are employing people full-time, you will be responsible for administering their PAYE payments; also, in certain circumstances, your own PAYE. If you are a shareholder in a limited company, it will be paying corporation tax on its profits. Lastly, you may — and if your turnover exceeds £15,000 a year, you must — for the supply of certain goods and services collect VAT from your customers and pay it over to Customs and Excise, less any VAT on goods and services supplied to you in the course of business.

One cannot, in a book of this nature, deal with a subject as complex as taxation exhaustively. But, with this proviso, let us look in broad outline at some of its principal implications. There are certain income tax advantages in working for yourself, or even in earning a supplementary income from part-time self-employment. To some extent these advantages were eroded by the National Insurance contributions for the self-employed (Class 4) which came into force in April 1975 and imposed what was, in effect, an additional 8 per cent tax on self-employed people's taxable income between £1600 and £3600 a year.

In 1978, though, this burden was somewhat lightened. For one thing the levy is now only payable by men under 65 and women under 60; more important, the Class 4 levy has been reduced and currently stands at 5.75 per cent on profits/gains between £3150 and £10,000.

There have also been some changes in real terms in the flat-rate weekly (Class 2) National Insurance contribution additionally payable by people who have an income from self-employment as well as a salary from another source. The earnings rate from self-employment above which this additional contribution has to be paid has been raised from £1250 to £1475 a year and the weekly contributions have been raised from £2.50 for 1980-81 to £3.40 for 1981-82. There is, however, a maximum on the total contributions due and if your contributions exceed that maximum then the excess is refunded. Alternatively you can apply to defer your weekly contribution until the end of the year when your total potential contribution is known. Your accountant should be able to advise you on the best course of action to take. Details of what you have to do to get deferment are given in a government leaflet, NP 18.

The reasoning behind what remains a somewhat doctrinaire piece of legislation appears to be that self-employed people are obtaining tax concessions that are not offered to the rest of the community. There is therefore a correspondingly strong case for taking the fullest possible advantage of these concessions in so far as they are indeed available.

Like the income of employed persons, the income from self-employment in its various forms is subject to an ascending rate of tax, starting at a flat 30 per cent up to the first £11,250 per annum and rising to a maximum of 60 per cent. These figures are subject to certain personal tax reliefs, such as allowances for dependent relatives, for part of the premiums on life assurance policies, etc, which you can deduct from your total income in arriving at the rate at which you pay tax.

Where income from self-employment or even part-time employment differs from ordinary wage- or salary-earning status is that you are allowed, in assessing your earnings, to deduct from your profits any revenue expenditure 'wholly and exclusively incurred' in carrying on your trade or profession. Under the heading of revenue expenditure comes business expenses, and since your profits and your earnings will be either synonymous or closely related, the first point to observe is that you must claim all the business expenses to which the taxman entitles you.

Principal allowable business expenses

1. *The cost of goods bought for resale and materials bought in manufacturing.* This does not include capital expenditure like cars or machinery, though certain minor items like small tools or typewriters may be allowed under this heading.

2. *The running costs of the business or practice.* Under this concession come heating, lighting, rent, rates, telephone, postage, advertising, cleaning, repairs (but not improvements of a capital nature), insurance, the use of special clothing. If you are using your home as office you can claim up to two-thirds of the running costs of the premises as a business expense – provided you can convince the taxman that you are indeed using as high a proportion of your house as this exclusively for business purposes. In the past some people have been advised not to make this type of claim at all, because of the probability that, on selling, they might have to pay Capital Gains Tax on the 'business' part of the sale, thus outweighing any income tax advantage. This situation was altered in the 1978 and 1980 Budgets (see section below on Capital Gains Tax).

3. *Carriage, packing and delivery costs.*

4. *Wages and salaries.* Any sums paid to full-time or part-time employees. You cannot, however, count any salary you and your partners are taking from the business, but you can pay your wife a salary (provided she is actually doing a reasonably convincing amount of work for you). This is an advantage if her income from other sources is less than £1375 a year, because that first slice of earnings is free of tax – one of the reliefs we mentioned earlier.

5. *Entertaining.* Entertainment of overseas customers. The tax office may want to establish some correlation between the amount of export business you do and the sums you are claiming for entertainment in this connection. You are also allowed to claim for entertaining your own staff.

6. *Travel.* Hotel and travelling expenses on business trips and in connection with soliciting business. You are not, however, allowed the cost of travel between home and office, if you

have a regular place of work. In addition to these expenses you can claim for the running costs of your car (including petrol) in proportion to the extent to which you use it for business purposes.

7. *Interest.* Interest on loans and overdrafts incurred wholly in connection with your business. This does not include interest on any money you or your partners have lent to the business.

8. *Hire and hire purchase.* Hiring and leasing charges and hire element in hire-purchase agreement (not the actual cost, because this is a capital expense).

9. *Insurance.* Every kind of business insurance, including that taken out on behalf of employees, but excluding your own National Insurance contributions and premiums paid on your personal life insurance (though these premiums are subject to 17.5 per cent personal tax relief).

10. *The VAT element in allowable business expenses (unless you are a taxable trader for VAT purposes).* This would include, for instance, VAT on petrol for your car. The VAT on the purchase of a motor car is allowable in all cases, since this cannot be reclaimed in your VAT return.

11. *Certain legal and other professional fees.* You are allowed to claim for things like audit fees or court actions in connection with business, but not for penalties for breaking the law (eg parking fines!).

12. *Subscriptions to professional or trade bodies.*

13. *Bad debts.* These are bad debts actually incurred, though provision is generally allowed against tax in the case of specific customers whom you can show are unlikely to meet their obligations, for instance if their account is overdue and they are failing to respond to reminders. A general provision for a percentage of unspecified bad debts is not allowable against tax, however sensible it may be to make such provision in your accounts.

    Trade debts owing to you are counted as income even if they have not been paid at the end of the accounting period.

Likewise, debts owed by you are counted as costs, even if you are not going to pay them until the next accounting period.

14. *Gifts.* Business gifts costing up to £2 per recipient per year (but excluding food, drink and tobacco). All gifts to employees are allowable, but generous employers should remember that the employee may have to declare them on *his* tax return if their value is substantial.

Capital allowances

The business expenses listed above are all revenue expenditure items, incurred in the day-to-day running of your affairs. There are also capital expenditure outlays, such as the acquisition of motor cars, large items of machinery and permanent fixtures and fittings. Although these cannot be deducted from your profits as normal business expenses, there are concessions available on them under another heading. In Chapter 8 we dealt with the subject of depreciation as an element to be allowed for in considering the cost to the business of acquiring capital equipment.

1. The depreciation on a motor car can be deducted from your profits at the rate of 25 per cent a year as a 'writing down allowance'. However, in the case of cars costing more than £8000 this is limited to £2000 a year.

2. A writing down allowance is also given for other capital equipment (but not buildings). You can, in fact, take a 'first year allowance' which enables you to write off 100 per cent in the tax year of acquisition. It may, of course, not pay you to do it this way if you do not have profits to set it off against. In that case you can claim your allowance at the rate of 25 per cent a year. Each year, of course, the 25 per cent is claimed on the proportion that has not yet been written off. Thus, if you buy an offset machine for £500, in year one you claim 500 x (25/100) = £125; and in year two £375 x (25/100) = £94, and so on.

3. Equipment bought on hire purchase is eligible for the writing down allowance in respect of the capital element. The hire charges themselves can be claimed as business expenses, spread over the period of the agreement.

In calculating your writing down allowances you will have to take into account whether or not you are a taxable trader for VAT purposes, which depends on whether your annual turnover exceeds £15,000. If you are, you will already have reclaimed the VAT on your purchase in your quarterly or monthly VAT return. Thus capital allowances will be calculated on the net amount excluding VAT (except in the case of motor cars).

Stock valuation

If you are in a business which involves holding stock (which may be either finished goods for resale, work in progress or materials for-manufacture), it must be valued at each accounting date. The difference in value between opening stock and closing stock represents the cost of sales. Obviously, therefore, if you value your closing stock on a different basis from the opening stock, this will affect the profit you show. If you value the same kind of items more highly it will depress the cost of sales and increase the apparent profit. If you value them on a lower basis the cost of sales will be increased and the profit decreased.

Example A			Example B		
Sales		£150	Sales		£150
Opening Stock 100 Rose bushes @ £1.00:	£100		*Opening Stock* 100 Rose bushes @ £1.00:	£100	
Closing Stock 50 Rose bushes @ £1.50:	£75		*Closing Stock* 50 Rose bushes @ 60p:	£30	
Cost of Sales		£25	Cost of Sales		£70
Profit		£125	Profit		£80

Table 11.1 *An example of stock valuation*

Plainly, then, it does not make sense for you to upvalue your closing stock in order to show a paper profit. Equally, you are not allowed to depress it artificially in order to achieve the reverse effect. However, if you can make a genuine case that some stock will have to be sold at a lower margin than the one you normally work to in order to be able to sell it within a reasonable time, then a valuation in the light of this fact will generally be accepted by the taxman.

Stock relief

In times of high inflation it becomes almost inevitable that your stock appreciates in value, at least on paper. The snag is that when you come to replace it you will have to pay correspondingly more so that your profits, assuming you go on trading, are rapidly wiped out. It would be unjust as well as damaging to many businesses if these paper profits were taxed and in 1974 a provision was introduced to give tax relief in such cases. Initially, this was a temporary measure, but it has now achieved more permanent status. The 1981 Budget established that from November 1980 the relief given is based on a percentage of the opening stock (and work in progress) for the period of account. The first £2000 of stock do not qualify for relief. As far as the pre-November 1980 situation is concerned it could, of course, have happened that your stock actually decreased in value, for example, because you had decided to carry less inventory. In that case you would be liable to repay any corresponding relief previously granted, but there are quite generous provisions for deferring such repayments on which your accountant should be able to advise you.

Computing taxable profit

Normally your accountant will prepare a set of accounts for you for each year you are in business. Your accounting date need not coincide with the tax year (ending 5 April). The profits shown in these accounts will be the basis of your assessment.

As we stated earlier, certain costs which are genuine enough from the point of view of your profit and loss account are nevertheless not allowable for tax purposes, for example, entertaining customers other than foreign buyers or their agents. You are also not allowed to charge depreciation against your profit (though remember that you will receive a writing down allowance which, in the end, has a similar effect). These and other non-allowable expenses, therefore, must be added back to the profits.

Equally certain profits which you have made are to be deducted for the purposes of Schedule D assessment because they are taxed on a different basis and are subject to a return under another heading. Examples are gains from the disposal of capital assets, income from sub-letting part of your premises or interest paid by the bank on money being held in a deposit account.

In the 1980 Budget some new kinds of business spending came in for tax relief, notably incidental costs of raising loan finance and start-up costs incurred before you began trading.

Losses

If your business or professional occupation has made a loss on its accounting year (and remember that from the tax point of view non-allowable expenses are added back to profits and you will have to do the same in your return), you can have the loss set off against your other income for the tax year in which the loss was incurred and for the subsequent year. The set-off has to be made first of all against earned income and then, if you are still 'in credit', against unearned income. This is laid down because unearned income (income from investments) may be subject to a higher tax rate than the earned variety. However, you cannot set off business losses against liability for capital gains tax.

If your income for the year in which you made the loss and that of the subsequent year still does not exceed that loss, you can set off the balance against future profits; or you can carry the loss back and set it against earlier profits.

An important concession was made in the 1978 Budget to sole traders and partnerships. Since 1978 losses incurred in the first four years of a business can be carried back against income from other sources, including salary, in the three years before commencing business as a self-employed person or partner.

The basis of assessment

Schedule D tax is normally assessed on the profits for the preceding tax year. Thus your tax assessment for the tax year ending 5 April 1981, and which you have to pay in 1981, will relate to the accounting year which ended in the tax year finishing 5 April 1980. Your *accounting* year, as we have just said, need not coincide with the taxman's year: 5 April to 5 April. You can, if you like, run it to the anniversary of your commencing business, or on a calendar year. However, in the first year of operations, you will be assessed either on the proportion of profits for the accounting year represented by the time from your starting date to 5 April, or the actual profits during those months. You cannot, in respect of the first year, ask to be assessed on a preceding year basis.

Thus, if you commenced business on 1 October 1980 and your profit for the year ending 30 September 1981 is £1000, you will be taxed on the basis of six months' profit (1 October 1980 to 5 April 1981). This assessment will have to be met in 1981. It is not on a preceding year basis.

In the second tax year, in this instance, the one ending 5 April 1982, your Schedule D tax will be based on the actual profit for the first 12 months of business: here, £1000.

In the third tax year you will be assessed on your declaration for the preceding year which, as we have seen, is still the profit in your first 12 months of operations: in this case again £1000. Thereafter you will be paying tax on the normal basis of the preceding year's profits.

The object of these somewhat tortuous manoeuvres is to put you into phase for paying tax on the latter basis; but it has the disadvantage that if your profits are high in the first twelve months and thereafter shade off, you will be paying more tax than you should be in the second and third year. You can, therefore, elect to be taxed on your actual profits for those years. You should take your accountant's advice on the best course of action. He may also be able to demonstrate technical advantages, in terms of taxation, in starting business just after, rather than just before, 5 April in calculating the basis of assessment over the opening three-year period of a business.

Spare-time work

Even though you have a full-time job which is being taxed under Schedule E and thus being taken care of under your employer's PAYE scheme, you may also have earnings from part-time employment in the evenings and weekends which you have to declare. Your employer need not know about this second income because you can establish with your tax inspector that the tax code which fixes the amount of PAYE you pay (see below) only relates to the income you receive from your employer.

Your spare-time income is also eligible for the allowances on expenses 'wholly and exclusively incurred' for business purposes. This means that it is most important that you should keep a proper record of incomings and outgoings. If your spare-time activities are on a small scale, you will not need to keep the kind of detailed books of account described in Chapter 5; but you should certainly maintain a simple cash book, from which at the end of the year you or your accountant can prepare a statement to append to your income tax return.

Tax on spare-time work is payable in two half-yearly assessments: on 1 January within the year of assessment and on 1 July following the end of it.

Probably the largest item you will be able to set off against spare-time income is any sums you can pay your wife for her assistance up to the level of her tax-free allowance of £1375 and provided she is not earning as much as this from another source.

Partnerships

Partnership income is assessed between the partners in the same ratio as that in which they have agreed to split profits. However, the ratio will be the one that actually exists at the time the assessment is made which, since the tax is on a preceding year basis, may not necessarily be the same as that which obtained the year the profits were established.

Salaries, and interest on money put into the business by partners, are considered as profits for tax purposes and have to be added back as such in order to arrive at taxable profits.

For the purposes of assessment, the partnership is treated as a single entity, so the tax will be collected from the partnership as a whole, not from the individuals that constitute it.

Corporation tax

Corporation tax is payable by limited companies. Its provisions are somewhat complicated and it must be assumed, for the purposes of this brief chapter on taxation, that readers who are intending to set up businesses in this form will seek professional advice on tax aspects. However, the salient points are as follows:

1. Corporation tax is charged at a rate of 52 per cent on profits, though for companies with profits under £80,000 the rate is 40 per cent.
2. Dividends are paid to shareholders without deduction of tax, but 30/70ths of the dividends must be handed over to the Inland Revenue by the company within three months of the date of payment of the dividend. This is known as 'advance corporation tax' and is set off against corporation tax payable on profits.
3. Unlike Schedule D income tax, corporation tax is normally

payable nine months from the end of each accounting period.

4. Allowable expenses against profits for corporation tax purposes are roughly the same as those for other forms of revenue expenditure, with the important addition that salaries paid to employees (who include the owners of the company, if they are working in it) are deductible. However, in certain circumstances, the interest on loans made to the company by directors will not be treated as an allowable expense, but as a distribution of income on which advance corporation tax is payable.

If you are a director of a limited company, your income from this source will not be liable to the National Insurance levy of 5.75 per cent on income between £3150 and £10,000 a year. Your National Insurance contributions will be at the employed rate and you will be paying PAYE on your salary.

Capital transfer tax

Capital transfer tax was introduced in 1974 to replace estate duty and was potentially disastrous for many small businesses, which, having no liquid assets with which to pay the tax, would ultimately have been faced with no alternative but to sell out, when their proprietors would have come up against the further hurdle of capital gains tax.

The effect of CTT has been mitigated in the 1978 and 1980 Budgets. It has been recognised that small businesses are, in current jargon, a 'special case'. So, for the purposes of CTT, the value of a business is reduced by 50 per cent when it comes to assessing it for this tax. In the 1980 Budget the threshold above which CTT is payable was raised to £50,000. Thus on a business with assets of £100,000 no CTT is now payable. Furthermore, if its value exceeds that figure, payment can be spread over eight years, thus diminishing the possibility of forced sales of assets simply to pay CTT.

Capital gains tax

This tax is of longer standing than CTT and has therefore acquired the inevitable battery of judgements of what is and is not a capital gain. But, in essence, the situation is that if you sell or give away assets, which are usually cash, shares, property or other valuables, and your real or notional gain in any tax year from such transactions is more than £3000 (a figure set in the 1980 Budget) you are liable for capital gains tax at a flat rate of 30 per cent on the difference between the price at which you acquired the asset and its current net value.

Two loopholes have been created in this particular tax fortress which may benefit small businesses. First, if you sell a business and buy another one within three years you can defer payment of the tax until you finally dispose of the one you have bought and cease trading. Second, people who have been owners of a business for more than 10 years can, at the age of 60, obtain relief from CGT if they do sell their assets, at the rate of £10,000 a year and up to a maximum of £50,000.

This last benefit could be of particular value to people who have been using part of their private house as business premises and claiming tax relief on the charges incurred (heating, lighting, rates, etc) on a proportionate basis. Before 1978 they would have had to pay CGT on that proportion when they came to selling the house and this deterred quite a number of people from making such a claim, understandably when you consider the level of capital gain reached on house prices through the 1970s. Furthermore, in the 1980 Budget the first £10,000 capital gain achieved in these circumstances was in any case made exempt from CGT. Presumably the balance of any gain would be further exempt if it fell with the £50,000 limit.

Appeals

Every taxpayer, be he an individual or a corporation, has the right to appeal against his tax assessment, if he has grounds for believing he is being asked to pay too much. Such appeals have to be made in writing to the Inspector of Taxes within 30 days of receiving an assessment. They are usually settled by more or less amicable correspondence, but ultimately can be taken to a hearing by the General or, in more complex cases, Special Commissioners.

PAYE

If you employ staff you will be responsible for deducting PAYE from their wages. The same applies to your own salary from a partnership or a limited company. The sums have to be paid monthly to the Inland Revenue by the employer.

You will receive from the tax office a tax deduction card for each employee, with spaces for each week or month (depending on how they are paid) for the year ending 5 April. On these cards, weekly or monthly as the case may be, you will have to enter under a number of headings, details of tax, pay for each period and for the year to date. You will know how much tax to deduct by reading off the employee's tax code number, which has been allotted to him by the tax office, against a set of tables with which you will also be issued. Without going into technicalities, the way the tables work is to provide a mechanism, self-correcting for possible fluctuations of earnings, of assessing the amount of tax due on any particular wage or salary at any given point of the year.

At the end of the tax year you will have to make out two forms:

1. Form P 60 issued to each employee. This gives details of pay and tax deducted during the year.
2. Form P 35 for the Inland Revenue. This is a summary of tax and graduated National Insurance contributions for all employees during the year.

When an employee leaves, you should complete another form, P 45, for him. Part of this form, showing his code number, pay and tax deducted for the year to date, is sent to the tax office. The other parts are to be handed by the employee to his new employer so that he can pick up the PAYE system where you left off.

VAT

If the taxable outputs of your business, which for practical purposes means what you charge your customers for any goods or services that are not specifically 'exempt', exceed, or are likely to exceed £15,000 in a year (or £5000 in any quarter) you will have to register with the Customs and Excise (not the tax office, in this case) as a taxable trader for VAT purposes. This means that you will have to remit to Customs and Excise, either monthly or quarterly, 15 per cent of the price you charge on your 'outputs', this being the current standard rate of VAT. However, you will be able to deduct from these remittances any VAT which you yourself have been charged by your suppliers – your 'inputs'. This item covers not only materials used in producing the goods or services you supply to your customers, but everything which you have to buy to run your business, including such things as telephone charges.

Not all goods and services carry VAT. Some are 'zero rated' — basic foodstuffs, newspapers and exported goods being notable examples. Full details are contained in VAT Notices 700 and 701, issued by Customs and Excise, Kings Beam House, Mark Lane, London EC3, and you should obtain these from them, together with any other Notices about VAT which are relevant to your trade or profession. The significance of zero rating is that even though you do not charge VAT on goods of this nature that you supply, you can still claim back VAT on all your inputs, excluding the purchase of cars and business entertainment of domestic customers.

Zero rating is not, however, the same as 'exemption'. Zero rating carries a theoretical rate of VAT, which is 0 per cent. Exemption means that no rate of VAT applies at all and examples of exempt suppliers are bookmakers, persons selling or renting land and buildings, and various types of medical services. The exempt status is not particularly desirable, because if you are exempt you still have to pay VAT on all your inputs but have no outputs to set the tax off against.*

In this sense exempt traders are like private individuals and the question, therefore, arises as to whether you should, as you are entitled to do, ask to be registered as a taxable trader even though your outputs are less than the mandatory £15,000 a year level. Customs and Excise may, of course, refuse to register you on the grounds that your outputs are too low, though no hard-and-fast minimum figure for this has been fixed. Your accountant should be able to advise you on this point, but the main consideration would be the level of your taxable inputs. Thus if you are a part-time cabinetmaker you would be buying a lot of materials which carry VAT. But, if you were doing something like picture research, the VAT inputs might be quite low and the administrative work involved in being a taxable trader might not be justified by the amount of VAT you could claim back against your outputs.

The point to be realised is that if you register as a taxable trader, voluntarily or otherwise, you are going to be involved in a fair bit of extra administration. At the end of each VAT accounting period (quarterly or monthly, the latter being more

* The distribution between zero-rated goods and exempt goods is important in determining whether you should be registered for VAT. Exempt goods do not count towards total 'turnover' for this purpose, but zero-rated goods do. Thus, if your turnover is £15,000 *with* exempt goods but only £12,000 without them, you are not liable to pay VAT.

usual with traders in zero-rated goods), you will have to make a return of all your outputs, showing their total value and the amount of VAT charged. Against this you set the total of your inputs and the amount of VAT you have paid. The difference between the VAT on your outputs and that on your inputs is the sum payable to Customs and Excise. This obviously causes problems for retailers making a great many small sales and particularly for those supplying a mixture of zero-rated and standard-rated goods (eg a shop supplying sweets, which are taxable and other items of foods which are mostly zero rated). It also underlines the vital importance of keeping proper records and retaining copy invoices of all sales and purchases, because although your VAT return need only show totals, Customs and Excise inspectors are empowered to check the documents on which your return is based. There is obviously, therefore, a link between the records you have to maintain for ordinary accounting purposes and those that are needed to back up your VAT return.

There is also a close connection between VAT and the problem of cash flow. When you receive an invoice bearing VAT, the input element can be set off against the VAT output on your next return, irrespective of whether you yourself have paid the supplier. Therefore, if you are buying an expensive piece of capital equipment it will make sense for you to arrange to be invoiced just before your next return to Customs and Excise is due.

The boot is on the other foot, though, when you yourself are extending credit to a customer. The sale is reckoned to have taken place when the invoice has been rendered, not when you have received payment. Therefore you will be paying VAT on your output before you have actually received the cash covering it from your customer. This also means that except in some special cases no relief is given in respect of bad debts.

The black economy

One cannot these days write about taxation without some reference to the 'black economy'. There is a good deal of evidence to suggest that the response to the way inflated wages and salaries are pulling an increasing number of people into higher tax brackets has been tax evasion on a large scale by a variety of means such as straightforward non-declaration of earnings, making or receiving payments in cash, arranging remuneration in kind or, simply, barter deals. Some of these methods are easier for the tax inspectors to spot than others, but this is not the place to give advice on a highly contentious topic, except to say that all forms of tax evasion are illegal. In fact, there are enough loopholes and 'perks' available to self-employed people with a good tax consultant at their elbow to render law breaking an unacceptable and unnecessary risk.

If you're self-employed a Pension Plan offers you lifelong advantages.

From the moment you take out a Legal & General Pension Plan, your contributions qualify for tax relief at the highest rate you pay on earned income.

You can also vary your contributions each year which gives you the flexibility the self-employed need.

While you are still working your investment grows completely free of capital gains tax and income tax.

And when you retire you will receive a large tax-free lump sum and an income for the rest of your life.

Legal & General manage pensions for more people than anyone else in the country.

Ask your Broker about pensions for the self-employed from Legal & General.

Legal & General

We cover the things you care for.

Legal & General Assurance Society Ltd., Temple Court, 11 Queen Victoria Street, London EC4N 4TP. Tel: 01-248 9678.

12: Pensions

C B Cochran, *pensions consultant*

Although governments have made a number of concessions to the self-employed in recent budgets, one area where they have been more or less left out in the cold is that of state pensions. While the rest of the working population is entitled to two pensions, the basic state pension plus an earnings related scheme, the self-employed qualify only for the former. The problem is, of course, that it is very difficult to base an earnings related scheme on a figure which, as happens in the case of the self-employed, may fluctuate from year to year. This, however, is very little consolation to anyone who, not having made any other provision, faces retirement on a state pension which, for married couples, only amounts to £43.45 a week — considerably less than the national average wage.

The implication of all this would appear to be that the government has left the self-employed to care for themselves as far as pensions are concerned, though they made a number of tax concessions which were to have the effect of lightening the burden of making your own pension arrangements.

These have been somewhat eroded over the past couple of years. For instance, the National Insurance contribution has gone up to £3.40 per week, whereas benefits have only gone up from £17.50 to £22.50 per week.

A more significant step is that the band of profits on which Class 4 National Insurance contributions for the self-employed are payable has now been widened, with the lower limit standing at £3150 and the upper one at £10,000. On the other hand, the rate of contributions has been raised to 5.75 per cent.

More significant still are concessions introduced over a number of Finance Acts, relating to earnings earmarked for private pensions.

First, full tax relief may now be claimed on 17½ per cent of net earnings (earnings after allowable expenses) if these are applied to a private pensions plan. The 17½ per cent would, of course, be applied at the top rate of tax, making this a considerable benefit to high taxpayers. Moreover, the 1980 Budget abolished the £3000 upper level which previously restricted the amount that could be claimed in relief. Furthermore, if your contribution adds up to over 17½ per cent of net earnings, the excess can be carried forward to future years, when you hope your income will be high enough to enable tax relief to be claimed. This obviously makes sense in view of the fluctuation which is apt to occur in self-employed income and which itself, as has been pointed out above, makes it difficult to integrate you in an earnings-related state scheme.

Also, your contributions can be backdated for tax purposes within six months of your assessment for the year. Thus, if your accounts for the year to 31 December 1980 are not agreed by your accountant and the Inspector of Taxes until 30 September 1981, you will have until 30 March 1982 to pay and lodge with the Inland Revenue a claim to have your pension contribution allowed against your profits for the year to December 1980.

Apart from the personal tax relief element, there are three other reasons why making provision for a private pension plan provides some kind of haven against the tax blizzard.

First, all contributions are invested in a special pensions fund, which does not pay tax, hence the rate of growth is significantly greater than an ordinary savings fund. Second, a tax-free cash sum is payable when you begin your pension; and third, the pension itself is taxed as earned and not as investment income. So the advantages of personal pensions are considerable, even for those people who are only able to claim relief at a lower rate.

These advantages can be extended if you are paying your wife a salary as your employee. The Inland Revenue currently allows her to have a pension of two-thirds of her final earnings, increasing at 8½ per cent per annum. Thus for a woman of 35 it is possible to invest in a pension scheme to provide a pension at 60. This will count as a normal business expense by her husband in the same way as the salary itself, and would be allowed against his highest rate of tax on earned income. This would be more profitable than spending the same amount on the husband's pension, as that would probably increase his tax liability after retirement.

Leaving aside this option, however, we show in Table 12.1 four possible methods for someone aged 40 to save £500 per annum towards a retirement pension on his 65th birthday. This illustrates the benefit on the tax position of investing in a pension fund, as compared to other forms of savings.

While there are many types of plan available, basically they

Pensionplus
– for people who mind their own business.

When we designed Pensionplus we built in a great deal of flexibility – because that's what is needed in a personal pension plan.

Flexibility of contributions, of pension benefits and of retirement age – you'll find them all in Pensionplus ... **plus** flexible Family Security Benefits.

Pensionplus
– designed for people who mind their own business.

There are pensions experts at every Gresham Life Area Sales Office and at our Head Office. Call us, or write FREEPOST, no stamp required, to:

Gresham Life Assurance Society Limited
FREEPOST
Bournemouth BH4 9BR

Telephone: 0202 767655.

A member of the Life Offices' Association.

	Under the bed	Building Society savings accounts	Endowment with profits	Personal pension tax paid 30 per cent
Total contribution	£12,500	£12,500	£12,500	£12,500
* Interest on share account † Bonus on endowment ** Accumulation of pension fund	nil	£40,526*	£28,383†	£47,837**
Total investment	£12,500	£53,026	£40,883	£60,337
Annual pension	£1669	£9459	£7294	£7090
Tax-free cash sum				£21,271
Net cost	£12,500	£12,500	£10,312.50	£8750

Table 12.1 *The three types of pension plan*

THE M&G RANGE OF PENSION PLANS

M&G offer pension plans for self-employed people, plans for directors, senior executives, and employees of companies. Within the limits set down by the Inland Revenue all these plans can attract full tax relief on contributions. To obtain details of any of these plans, please tick the appropriate box.

FLEXIBLE PENSION PLAN ☐

A pension Plan for the self-employed offering the facility to switch between a range of tax-exempt funds including the highly successful Personal Pension Fund.

EXECUTIVE PENSION PLAN ☐

This Plan for selected directors and executives can be used to set up a separate pension scheme linked to eight tax-exempt funds.

SMALL SELF-ADMINISTERED ☐ SCHEME
Similar to the above but specifically designed for the requirements of a small company, with a facility for money in the pension fund to be reinvested in the company or elsewhere.

ADDITIONAL VOLUNTARY ☐ CONTRIBUTION
This Plan is only available to people already in a company pension scheme. It is specifically designed for individuals whose pension benefits are below the maximum allowed by the Inland Revenue.

ASSET MANAGEMENT ☐

This service enables the trustees of self-administered pension schemes to diversify their portfolios by investing direct into one of M&G's eight tax-exempt pension funds.

To: The M&G Group, Three Quays, Tower Hill, London EC3R 6BQ. Tel: 01-626 4588. | 01 | LN |

| 02 | Mr/Mrs/Miss | INITIALS |
| SURNAME |
| 04 | ADDRESS |
| | | 09 | POSTCODE |

| 27 | 74 | 30 |

PP 622211

Member of the
Life Offices Association

M&G

This offer is not available to residents of the Republic of Ireland

THE M&G GROUP

141

fall into three main categories: deferred annuity, cash-funded, and unit-linked.

Deferred annuities give a policyholder a basic guaranteed pension. In addition, each year a further bonus pension attachment based on a share of the pension fund profits may be added. These then become guaranteed in the same way as bonus attachments to with-profit endowment policies.

The cash-funded method is rather similar to saving in a building society account. Regular contributions are made and each year bonuses are added to the contributions to increase the size of the account. A large pool of money, therefore, accumulates and at retirement this pool is used to buy a pension at the then going rate. As this can and does fluctuate, companies offer a guaranteed basic pension, but this is usually 20 to 30 per cent below the likely current market rate.

Unit-linked contracts are probably best considered by those people who already have a secured and reasonably guaranteed income on retirement. Each year the contribution made is deemed to buy units at the current price. At retirement all these units are cashed in and the money is used to buy a pension at the current going rate. This is a very similar arrangement in method to the cash-funded plans, though, because of the fluctuation in the stock market, is a less secure way of saving for a pension. The amount of unit-linked pension depends very much on how the value of the units have grown over the period. Similarly, bonuses and interest make up a considerable part of the deferred annuity and the cash-funded pensions, so it follows that whatever contract is chosen it is best to chose a company which already has a good investment record.

A self-employed person is allowed to take his pension between the ages of 60 to 75, even lower for some special categories. However, many of the self-employed may wish to work part-time before they retire, and therefore to take a portion of their pension at the outset just to top up their earnings, and then to take the remainder when they finally retire. If this is the case it would be worthwhile looking to companies which offer flexible pension arrangements.

As with any other investment, you need to take advice and this comes best either from a pensions consultant with one of the larger firms of insurance brokers or alternatively direct from an insurance company.

In recent months there have been a number of developments in the self-employed pension field. Under current law one cannot touch one's pension until the age of 60 and prior to that date one cannot use a policy as collateral. The result is that many self-employed people have been investing money which they would like to use within their businesses (where it would be taxed) into pension plans (where it is not taxed).

A number of companies have now introduced a 'loan back facility' to overcome this. New and existing policy holders can now with certain companies arrange to borrow a sum of money which is related to the amount in their pension policy but which is not granted on the security of that policy.

Thus, if you have a policy worth say £7500 and need £5000 to build an extension to your business, your pension company might well now be able and willing to lend you that money secured by a first charge against your business property.

At the moment it is too early to say precisely how these new schemes will develop but they do mean that hundreds of millions of pounds of small business money which in the past has gone into stocks, big business and securities might now begin to flow back to the small sector.

144

13: Retirement and the Self-employed Person

Fred Kemp, *FCIS, FBIM, former director of the
Pre-Retirement Association*

Introduction: the dangers of self-employment

The desire to be one's own boss and join the self-employed is often very strong after a lifetime spent obeying orders and taking instructions in a large organisation. Ideally, for the person on the verge of retirement, the aims and objectives of running one's own business are to make it relatively trouble-free, to provide a secure additional income and to allow it to be sold easily after his death for the benefit of his or her spouse. Such businesses cannot be bought at a modest price and anyone with capital to invest who thinks otherwise is a likely target for the professional confidence trickster.

The person retiring from paid employment who is perhaps commuting part of his pension as a lump sum, or is cashing in an endowment policy, must exercise extreme caution in investing the fruits of perhaps a lifetime's work. Any offers of franchise arrangements or purchase of stocks for resale should be viewed with due suspicion, and the advice of both your bank manager and solicitor should be sought before any contract or agreement is signed. This seems plain common sense, but an article in the *Sunday Times* Business News on confidence tricksters states that 'Phineas Barnum's dictum that there is a fool born every minute was a gross underestimate!' Certainly the experience of the Pre-Retirement Association is that such warnings regarding investment cannot be repeated too often.

For the man or woman who has been an employee throughout life, the risks and stresses of running one's own small business full-time at the age of 60 plus can be hazardous. Take the typical local shopkeeper. He is working six or seven days a week. He has to meet ever rising costs: for rates, staff wages, electricity, heating and insurance. He must keep detailed accounts and VAT records. It is unlikely that he will be able to go on holiday with his family, and he dreads being ill. Should he die, his widow would have to cope with the business single-handed, and may decide to try to sell it at a time when prospective buyers will realise she wants to sell out quickly. If she has been living on the business premises she will have to buy a house and face the upheaval of moving at a time when she is still suffering from the shock of bereavement. This is no legacy for any person to force on to his spouse.

If you are on the verge of retirement you should be looking forward to a period of purposeful activity, and possibly the initial step for someone who still cherishes such ambitions is to take a part-time job in the type of business which interests him. He will then be able to sum up, on the basis of practical experience, the opportunities and problems of buying or starting an enterprise without risking precious capital.

The opportunities

It *is* possible for the employed person to choose a business opportunity to provide an income and interest in retirement provided he plans far enough ahead. There is, for example, a definite need in many places for boarding kennels where people can leave their animals when going on holiday or into hospital. There is also a steady demand for long-term quarantine homes for animals being brought to the UK by owners returning from work overseas (4100 dogs and 2000 cats a year). But do not underestimate the amount of work or capital involved. In the first place contact your local authority. Any kennel or cattery which wishes to keep animals in quarantine must be licensed by the Ministry of Agriculture, Fisheries and Food and the Animal Health Division of the Ministry handling this is at Government Buildings, Hook Rise South, Tolworth, Surbiton, Surrey KT6 7NF. If you write to this address, the Ministry will supply you with the relevant information and give details of the standards specified for the buildings including the types of materials. Also seek out the local veterinary surgeons. They might well know of a business for sale or suggest where one might be started.

One of the advantages with this type of business is not having to invest capital in holding a large stock! Such an enterprise could be started on a small scale by the wife whilst the husband continues his normal occupation until he reaches retirement age. The business could then be expanded when he is available full time to assist his wife. However, rather more capital is required for a quarantine home than for boarding premises.

Suburban houses and gardens are *not* suitable for kennels. A semi-rural area is essential as well as planning permission to run kennels.

146

The Scottish Life Awards for Industry

Everybody works for somebody–even the self employed.

The fact is, you work for the government. And the government, you'll agree, is a pretty hard taskmaster.

To prove it, just take a look at your income tax returns!

But we've got a few ways of helping people hang onto more of what they earn. A lot more. And we do so via an interesting selection of personal pension plans.

Each plan can be geared to the individual and his income, so you keep more of your hard-earned cash while you're working.

It's our award for acumen . . . and industry.

The Freepost coupon will bring you all the details.

NO STAMP Required

To: The Scottish Life Assurance Company Limited, 'Freepost', Edinburgh EH2 0DN.

I think it's time I had an award for industry. Please send full details of your personal pensions plans for the self employed.

Name ....

Address ....

....Date of Birth ....

Scottish Life
The Scottish Life Assurance Company

Despite the advantages of bulk buying, pet foods face ever increasing costs and these must be reflected in fees charged. Someone must be on duty seven days a week.

The retailing business

If you are approaching the age of 60 consider any retail business with a jaundiced eye. As a rough yardstick, we may say that today a business with a turnover of less than £50,000 a year is not economically viable because of the meagre profit margins and cost of overheads. Any retailer with a turnover of more than £15,000 a year must register for VAT. A supplier will rarely be able to deliver to a small retailer the goods he actually ordered. The haberdasher may request that 75 per cent of men's shirts he orders should be supplied in size 16½. In practice he is likely to receive only 10 per cent in that size. Often there is only part delivery of orders. Prices change frequently. The retailer must keep up to date with new fashion demands and tastes. He is at the mercy of TV advertisements. The public will expect him to have in stock next day any item they may have seen advertised the previous evening. A newsagent was swamped with orders for a particular book on football which was advertised one evening. Six months later he was still awaiting supplies. The small shopkeeper, despite recent efforts to merge with other small shopkeepers, will always have difficulty in competing with the huge multiple organisations, and the days of many small shops are numbered. Read the chapter on retailing in Part 2 and, above all, remember the three golden rules which dictate your choice: *location, location* and *location*.

Partnerships and consultancy

If you are considering entering a partnership, discuss any projected arrangement in detail with your solicitor and bank manager. If you have been employed in say the clothing industry and wish to set yourself up as a textile consultant, do not underestimate the cost of keeping yourself up to date. You will have to buy all the specialist trade journals (see Appendix 3) and not until you leave a large organisation will you fully appreciate the value of having all the secretarial and back-up facilities.

Pensions and National Insurance

In April 1975 a new state contribution scheme for the self-employed came into effect. If you are in doubt concerning your past contribution record in respect of your state pension the local office of the DHSS will obtain a computer print out of your details from Newcastle. Do not leave this until you are within a few months of the state retirement age. You can also seek advice concerning the desirability of continuing to pay a contribution after normal retiring age in return for enhanced benefits.

Any person within a few years of retirement will not benefit much from the new state pension scheme, and the wise man will plan to boost the state benefits with his own pension arrangements. Specialist companies will offer personal retirement plans which offer adequate pensions with options for lump sum benefits and widow's pensions. It is not widely known that men buying personal pensions, or self-employed annuities can also provide 'reversionary annuities' for their widows. In this case it is an annuity paid to the wife on the husband's death either before or after retirement. The Scottish Widow's Fund is one such company which has promoted a 'reversionary annuity'. Your insurance broker will give unbiased advice on pension schemes without charging a fee. If you send a stamped addressed envelope to the Pre-Retirement Association, they will send you a list of more than a dozen pension advisers from whom you can choose.

Other aspects of retirement

What are the essentials for a successful retirement? Let us give thought to the following, if we are to meet the problems and to explore fully the opportunities which retirement will offer:

1. Good physical and emotional health.
2. Adequate income, substantially beyond subsistence level.
3. Suitable accommodation.
4. Congenial associates and neighbours.
5. One or more absorbing interests.
6. An adequate personal philosophy of life.

Finance

The subject which concerns people most, before retirement, is money. Despite persistent inflation, the situation may not be too bad. Sit down (with a large sheet of paper) and write in column one your present budget, then in the next column show the pluses and minuses expected in retirement. Profits, salary, car and expenses from the business will be a minus: pluses will be private pensions plus the state pension, and income from investments. Present outgoings which will be reduced in retirement are obviously travel costs and lower income tax. At home you may have more meals, lighting and heating. Take into account mortgages and insurances which you may have planned to complete at retirement date. At the end of this exercise you will have a fair idea of how your finances will look, and you can decide if you will be able to retire completely or whether you need to look for a part-time job or set up a small business. If you need to supplement your income, remember to check the current amount of the 'Earnings rule' with the DHSS. If you are a man of 65 or a woman of 60, the State will reduce your State retirement pension if you earn more than the approved level. At the age of 70 (men) and 65 (women) restrictions on earnings are lifted.

If your income is such that you do not need a supplement, offer your services to an organisation that is looking for voluntary help. Be committed to some job or some person. A garden or a golf course will not get you out of bed, dressed and shaved at 10 am on a frosty January morning, but if you are responsible for driving a car with its boot full of food for a 'Meals on Wheels' service for the aged you will be there! You will enjoy it and you will get tremendous personal satisfaction from knowing you are being useful to others.

Leisure

Visit your local adult education centre. The centre may conduct a pre-retirement course covering in detail the aspects mentioned here. Such a course will give you an opportunity to discuss problems with the lecturers and other participants. Moreover, reduced rates for pensioners will mean you can take up such things as pottery, painting or old-time dancing for a nominal outlay, and you will meet people of all ages who live near you. Develop the hobby you have been thinking about for years and preferably also take up a completely new one — one that will challenge you and keep that trained mind active. At 60 you can

Too many people working for themselves are working for the taxman.

And the sooner they realise it, the better off they'll be.

If you're self-employed or in non-pensionable employment, it pays to invest in your future with a Standard Life pension scheme.

Because while providing for tomorrow, you benefit today. With considerable savings on tax and eligibility for loans to help you expand your business.

You can open a traditional With-Profits Personal Pension Policy and let the guaranteed benefits build up as bonuses. Or take out an investment linked Personal Pension Bond which provides a choice of six investment funds.

Your contributions are fully tax deductable within generous limits, and are invested by Standard Life free of UK Income and Capital Gains Tax.

Whichever scheme you choose, Standard Life offers a wide range of options plus a tax free cash sum. You can draw your pension at any age between 60 and 75 and the benefits may be taken in stages.

The advantages are numerous. And when your money's with the largest mutual life office in the EEC, you have the security of knowing that your retirement's being taken care of in the best possible way.

Contact your insurance adviser or your local Standard Life Branch today. They'll be pleased to give you details about how you can really start working for yourself.

Instead of for the taxman.

Standard Life

Head Office: 3 George Street, Edinburgh.

The largest mutual life assurance company in the European Community.

acquire a degree through the Open University while studying at home.

Living arrangements

Where to live in retirement? The cottage by the sea or the country may represent a lifetime's dream but do not be carried away by memories of 20 holidays spent in August at your favourite seaside resort. Go and visit the area in mid-January when half the shops are shut. Do not go to see the town's Director of Tourism. Seek out the Director of Social Services and ask if his area qualifies for the label 'Costa Geriatrica'. Ask him what are the social services and health services for the elderly. You must be practical and accept that eventually you might need such assistance as a home help, especially if by moving away from your home area you will be cutting yourself off from family and friends. Because many south coast areas have a high population imbalance caused by the retirement migration, the social services, working with limited funds, are unable to meet all the calls made upon them. Similar considerations apply to country areas. With the high cost of petrol an isolated cottage with one bus a day to town could become a virtual prison, and many rural areas now have no bus service at all.

Consider then staying in the area where your family and friends are and which is convenient (but not too convenient!) for grandchildren.

Do not necessarily stay in that large house where you reared the family. Choose a modern bungalow and move into it before you retire. While you are still earning money get all the essentials installed, including double glazing and roof insulation. If you cannot find or afford a modern bungalow (for you really should plan to avoid stairs in old age), look around for a suitable property to modernise, remembering that your local authority can dispense handsome grants towards modernisation and improvement. Make inquiries with the experts in your area: the local estate agents and the Citizens' Advice Bureau.

The essentials for the retirement home are economic central heating, privacy, good lighting, sensible electric wiring with plugs half way up the wall, and proper working levels. Make it a safe place to live — more people kill themselves in the home than on the roads! If you find such a home in an area where you are likely to have congenial neighbours and former business associates so much the better. The Retirement Homes Association runs specially designed retirement communities offering support services to residents.

Health

Everyone should remain as active and lively in retirement as possible. Take as much exercise as your body will permit. This does not mean a sudden conversion to a health and exercise 'kick'. It would be foolish at the age of 60 to start leaping about a squash court after an abstention of 20 years. It would be equally stupid to try to dig in a huge vegetable garden or allotment if you have not wielded a spade for ages.

There are facilities provided by the local authorities within reach of everyone's pocket. (Isn't it time you benefited from those rates you always complain about?) Local adult education centres provide yoga and keep-fit classes at low subsidised prices. Many courses are available at reduced fees for pensioners. Swimming is an excellent exercise for using muscles and is recommended for back pain sufferers. If your district boasts a heated swimming pool, why not use it?

Now, is all this advice you have had thrust at you worth it if you look at it in the terms of cost benefit analysis? It is surprising how many people are unaware of life expectancy figures. An average man of 60 can expect to live for another 18 years and the average woman can expect to live and draw the state pension for 22 years. So an investment in pre-retirement planning should give you a bonus in the years which lie ahead. Such preparation will enable you and your partner to enter this new phase of life with confidence. You will have planned your finances, have a safe suitable house, no bulging waistline, and you will be itching to have time at last to take up all the new activities you have arranged. *Choice* magazine, the only journal for retirement planning, can keep you up to date on matters relevant to the retired person. With the right attitude, retirement can be the most satisfying and fulfilling period of a person's life — the one period in life when the individual has complete freedom of choice to do what he wants to do, at the pace he decides. It is for you to decide in which direction you go.

Good luck!

Editor's Note: Fred Kemp was Chairman of the Council of Europe Working Party on Preparation for Retirement. Together with Bernard Buttle he is co-author of *Focus on Retirement* (1979) Kogan Page. The same authors have also written, in a lighter vein, *Looking Ahead: A Guide to Retirement* Macdonald & Evans. Both books can be obtained from the Pre-Retirement Association, 19 Undine Street, Tooting, London SW17 8PP.

Together with Bernard Buttle and Derek Kemp he has also written *Focus on Redundancy* (1980) which contains a chapter on self-employment. The book is available from Kogan Page, 120 Pentonville Road, London N1.

Part 2:
Running Shops and Other
Business Premises

We've formed more companies than any other company

We've been forming companies since 1864 – that's almost 100 years longer than anyone else in the business. Naturally in that time, we've formed a great many more companies than anyone else, and acquired a lot more experience. All of which is at your disposal when you come to Jordans to form a company.

At Jordans we specialise in Readymade, Standard and Custom-made Companies.

So whatever kind of company you need, simply contact:

David Hodgson in London 01-253 3030
Or Michael Counsell in Bristol 0272 32861

Jordans
the best of companies

14: Starting Your Business

Introduction

To buy and stock a shop, or start and run a hotel or restaurant, is a sizeable investment — in your time, energy and, above all, money. True, if you buy premises for any type of business and the venture fails, you can cut your losses by selling the premises. You may avoid significant losses, provided you have bought at a *realistic* price, but losses there will be: on stock, on any refurbishing you carried out, and on the opportunity cost of your time and capital. So, do not rush into anything: consider the size of the investment and the possibility of failure and, conversely, recognise the personal sacrifices you must make to achieve success.

Buying a business

All investments in business ventures are a risk, but they should not be too much of a risk. Do not over-commit yourself, and aim to finance your business as far as possible from your own resources. Of course, self-financing is often not feasible and you will probably depend on finance from a clearing bank, merchant bank, insurance company or building society. In practice, clearing banks are by far the most usual service of finance for small businesses. Merchant banks and finance houses lend larger amounts, often as a short-term basis, at relatively high rates of interest. Insurance companies are important sources of *personal* finance, but are less willing to lend money to commercial ventures, as assurance policies rarely cover the size of the loan required by the aspiring businessman. And building societies are rarely prepared to give mortgages to commercial ventures.

Thus, it is usually to the high street bank that a small businessman will turn (though, with expert financial advice, good use can be made of the other sources of finance). Banks (and individual bank managers) vary considerably in their willingness to lend to new enterprises and expanding businesses.

Ask friends, people in other businesses and an accountant for advice on which bank(s) to approach. Then, build up a working relationship with the bank manager, and convince him of your commitment and ability to make the project work. The proposal you make to him should be clear, accurate and realistic. You must be clear about how much you need, for what purposes, for how long, etc. The onus is on you to prove your case. The following suggests a possible framework for your argument: make notes on each point and be ready and *able* to cover each point objectively and fluently.

- ☐ What type of venture is it? Where will it be located?
- ☐ What is your experience of the trade, and how did you become involved in this particular project?
- ☐ What is the structure of your organisation, and who owns it? Is it a limited company or a partnership, or are you a sole trader?
- ☐ What business objectives have you set yourself: profitability or expansion, diversification or specialisation, etc?
- ☐ How will you market your work: advertising, representation, etc?
- ☐ What are your overheads: property, capital equipment, staff, running costs, etc?
- ☐ How will you price your work?
- ☐ What is the value of your assets?
- ☐ Can you estimate the amount of money you need, and the length of the period before you achieve profitability? Be realistic and thorough on this, as on all points.

You must be able to sell yourself and the project. This is a good test of whether *you* believe in the workability of the scheme.

A good relationship with your bank is invaluable. As well as a bank loan or overdraft agreement, your bank will offer a range of other loans for short-term purposes, such as the acquisition of property and the funding of expansion.

Chapter 3 gives a more detailed treatment of the subject of raising capital, but some points have been reiterated here because this section is aimed at people who will be making a large investment in property and capital equipment. Subsequent chapters deal with major business areas in which property held by lease or on freehold is central. Certain principles apply to all these areas:

☐ Pay a realistic price for whatever you purchase.
☐ Make all agreements you sign legally binding and use a solicitor to protect your investment.
☐ Do not underestimate the size of the investment.
☐ Do not over-commit yourself financially, and retain something as security.
☐ Consult an accountant before borrowing money from any source and make certain you know the provisions of all financial agreements.
☐ Have a watertight proposal to make to any potential lender.
☐ Use *bona fide* sources of finance.
☐ Your relationship with a lender must be based on mutual *trust* as well as mutual *interest*.
☐ Be realistic about your credit needs: buying the business is only the prelude to refurbishing and stocking it, insuring and perhaps fireproofing the premises, purchasing capital equipment and paying current expenses at a time when you are struggling to build a reputation and establish a business structure and clientele.
☐ Know when (and how) to pull out if things go badly: where to sell stock, how to sell the premises, how to terminate long-term loans, etc.
☐ If things go well, know when (and how) to expand and diversify: do not over-extend your resources; ensure that you have a capable staff, able to cope with greater pressures.

15: Farming and Market Gardening

The 'back to the land' movement has been quite fashionable in recent years, with all kinds of people giving up their jobs and homes in cities to live on smallholdings (communal or otherwise) where they try to be completely self-sufficient. Others, more commercially minded, may take up market gardening, which gives them a pleasant life in the country while they sell the fruits of their labours to others. Some more conventional souls may simply decide to buy a farm and rear cattle, grow corn or keep pigs or poultry.

In all cases, the romantic glow soon disappears. There are two essentials for any of these occupations, neither of them romantic: capital and the capacity for hard work. Take advice from professional bodies such as the Ministry of Agriculture's Advisory Service or the local county office of the National Farmers' Union. The local authority is responsible for agricultural education and you should make inquiries about courses that might be available in your area. The soaring costs of fuel and animal feedstuffs have already put many market gardeners and farmers out of business, so it is obviously essential to go into the finances of the operation very thoroughly before making a decision.

It is also essential to have the complete support of your family. This can be a very hard life, getting up early in all weathers to feed animals, breaking your back hoeing and weeding, and you have to be extremely keen and enthusiastic to take it on. If your nearest and dearest is not equally enthusiastic, forget it, for you are going to need their active help, since labour is both expensive and hard to come by.

Farming

The old joke that there are only three ways to get into farming — matrimony, patrimony and parsimony — applies even more strongly today. Unless you stand to inherit a farm, you are going to need an awful lot of money: agricultural land at the moment averages over £1700 an acre and good quality land regularly sells at £2200 plus an acre. The acreage you require will depend on the type of farming and the quality of the land. It could vary from 100 acres for dairy farming to, say, 300 acres for arable farming. And it does not stop there. You are then going to need working capital to buy cows, sheep, tractors, combines, etc. Even to start in a modest way could need £40,000 to £50,000, not including running costs.

You may be lucky enough to possess that kind of money, or at least have access to it; if not, you are going to need a bank loan, and here you are going to discover the other essential qualification for a farmer nowadays — technical know-how. Farming has become a technological occupation, requiring all kinds of special skills and knowledge. Unless you can convince a bank that you have this know-how (and some business experience) you are unlikely to get your money. Long-term loans for the purchase of land are available from the Agricultural Mortgage Corporation Ltd, but here again, properly prepared budgets and a realistic and comprehensive proposal will be required if the application is to be successful.

Farming is now a highly risky occupation giving only a 3 to 4 per cent return on the land. The failure rate is very high, particularly among the kind of people who take it up, with absolutely no experience, because it seems to offer a pleasant way of life. Unless you know about fertilisers, pesticides, animal husbandry and farm machinery, you are likely to make some expensive mistakes, and remember that two bad years could wipe you out financially. The farmers who are most successful are those who start young, probably in a family owned business. By the time they take over, they have acquired the necessary experience, usually backed up these days with a course at one of the agricultural colleges. You should not contemplate farming without some practical experience, or a degree or diploma from an agricultural college, or preferably both.

A cheaper way in is to try to become a tenant farmer. You do not have the enormous expense of buying the land, but once in you are protected for life and can run things to suit yourself (except for mismanagement of course). The snag is that tenancies are in tremendous demand, and there are often as many as 100 applicants for one farm. You can also try intensive farming, where you again save on the cost of land, though remember that here your working capital requirements are going to be higher. Battery hens or other animals require a lot of outlay in the form of equipment and feedstuffs, while market gardeners will find themselves spending a fortune on heating greenhouses. Soaring costs in fact have meant that intensive farming is not as profitable as it was, and many people have gone out of business. The trend in farming at the moment is in fact towards bigger, not smaller, units, because it is the only way to make a decent living.

Another idea which is very popular at the moment with the 'get-away-from-it-all-brigade' is to buy a smallholding and try to be entirely self-sufficient, perhaps even setting up a commune. It is an attractive idea, and the initial cost need not be great, but be warned: this is subsistence farming and you will find yourself working as hard as the American pioneers did. Also, even on a commune you may need a tractor and, for that, you are going to need money. You really need to be dedicated or rich (preferably both).

If the foregoing has not deterred you, get some professional advice, either from ADAS (the Agricultural Development Advisory Service of the Ministry of Agriculture) or from your local agricultural college or institute. There are also various farm management consultants and land agency firms who will (for a fee) give advice on what to do.

Even running a smallholding will demand considerable capital and expertise, as well as determination and immense hard work. Pat Burke, who runs one such smallholding, says: 'You must start with sufficient capital to carry you through the first year since you will almost certainly make nothing at all until your second year. All the self employed work long hours but running a smallholding involves particularly long hours — weekends don't exist.'

Market gardening

Unless you take over an established business, the main problems for the would-be market gardener are acquiring the necessary land and a greenhouse. You may be lucky enough to own a suitable piece of land already, or a garden big enough (two to three acres)' to be worked commercially, otherwise you may have to pay anything up to £2800 an acre. A greenhouse is the other big expense. It is a vital piece of equipment, enabling you to grow tomatoes, bedding plants, pot plants for the winter months and seedlings for early vegetables. You can do without one, but you must then make enough money in the spring and summer to make up for the lean winter months when you have virtually nothing to offer except a few winter vegetables. You also have to make provision for the cost of heating a greenhouse: recent price increases in fuel have sent the cost sky-high, so you must make sure that every inch of space is working for you, if your profits are not going literally to disappear in smoke. Even the cheapest second-hand greenhouse is likely to cost at least £1400, while a new one costs five to six times as much.

If you are not a trained horticulturalist, it is a good idea to employ someone who is, or who has at least had practical experience of running a big garden and greenhouse. One full-time helper is probably all you will be able to afford in the early years. Seasonal help picking tomatoes, strawberries, beans, etc, costs about £1.80 an hour, and is often difficult to find. You (and your family) must be prepared to work long hours and turn your hand to anything.

For general information, particularly on the economics of growing produce, contact the National Farmers' Union which has a very good horticultural section. Another excellent source of information on what crops to grow, soil tests, etc, is the Agricultural Development Advisory Service of the Ministry of Agriculture.

One basic decision to be made, once you have decided on your crops, is how you are going to market your produce. If you are on a busy main road you may decide to rely heavily on local advertising and passing trade from tourists, etc, sending the surplus to the local market, or even taking a stall in the local market yourself. You can also send your produce to one of the big central markets, but you then have to pay a fee to the auctioneer, as well as transport costs.

Selling produce

Anyone who has a big enough garden or allotment can make money selling produce: flowers, fruit, vegetables, herbs, honey, home-made jams and chutneys and eggs.* If you live on or near a main road the easiest way to sell things is simply to put up a stall or barrow at your gate, or else a notice directing people to your house. If you live right off the beaten track you might find it easier to sell to your village store or to one of the 'farm shops'

---

* Before you start apply for planning permission and ask a lawyer or the local Citizens' Advice Bureau whether your action would contravene sales legislation or EEC regulations on the sale of farm produce.

that are to be found now in many villages. In the summer you can make a lot of money from passing trade — tourists and city dwellers on the lookout for country produce.

Two worthwhile investments, when you have made enough money, are a deep freeze and a greenhouse. With a deep freeze, you can freeze surplus fruit and vegetables to sell in the winter, or for people to transfer to their own freezers. This enables you to make a bit more money in the lean winter months. With a greenhouse, you can grow some of the more exotic vegetables such as green peppers and aubergines, potted plants, especially for the Christmas trade, and offer bedding plants such as tomatoes for sale to other gardeners.

How much should you charge? A quick scout round the local shops will tell you what the going rate is for the more usual fruit and vegetables. You should of course charge more than shop prices for home-made jams, jellies and chutneys.

16: Retailing

Buying a shop

No book can answer all the questions or anticipate all the problems that buying a shop or starting a retail business entails, but it can warn you of the main reasons for failure:

☐ Paying an unrealistic price for the business.
☐ Lack of experience in the trade you enter.
☐ Cash flow problems caused by underestimating current costs.
☐ Failure to recognise the level of competition to the type of goods you sell or the service you offer (are you setting up a general food store next to a round-the-clock supermarket?).

The character of areas and shopping precincts changes rapidly. The 'centre' of your town is perhaps moving, through lack of space, to an open-plan area with a multi-storey car park and a wide range of shopping units. Long-established shops in the 'older' part of town are often unable to survive, so be wary of being offered this type of business. There are wide variations in the desirability and potential profitability of even apparently similar retail businesses.

Ask where the business you have seen advertised is. Is it well-positioned or far from the centre of trading activity? What is its reputation? Be sceptical of the seller's claims to a fund of 'goodwill' from long-standing customers. There is no guarantee that they exist and, if they do, that they will be as loyal to you. How much stock have you been offered as part of the purchase price? Does the shop need redecoration? What terms are you being offered: freehold or leasehold? What is the nature of the competition to your enterprise?

Such questions do not allow simple answers. These vary according to the type of business you intend to conduct. For example, a more specialised shop (selling, say, good quality hi-fi or photographic equipment at competitive prices) does not need to be as central as a grocer's, butcher's or general goods store.

Customers will hear about it and seek it out and, having been satisfied once, will return for accessories, improved equipment and advice.

Think, too, about general location and the composition of the local population: is it predominantly young or old, middle class or working class, close to sports facilities or not, and so on. Is there a seasonal trade that you might capture? Are there shops nearby that may attract certain types of people, whose custom you might aim to tap? Would you have to work special hours to fit in with the habits of your potential customers (by for example, staying open until 7 or 7.30 pm in suburban residential areas)? Would those habits affect your trade adversely at certain times (low 'traffic' at weekends in business areas, for instance)?

In short, you must consider a whole range of locational factors before choosing to buy an established business or deciding *where* to start a new shop. Four rules:

☐ Talk to people who know the trade and the locality.
☐ Take the advice of an accountant and solicitor who will, respectively, assess the financial worth of the purchase and the legal commitments you will enter into.
☐ Do not buy the first shop offered to you unless *everyone* thinks it is an unmissable opportunity (and, even then, think again!).
☐ Always assume the seller is asking too much.

This is not sophisticated business thinking; it is plain commonsense. George Thorpe, a food retailer, stresses the need for forward planning. He says: 'Even if you have to borrow money, do not be under capitalised. Keep your shelves full and well stocked since this will attract customers . . . Apart from fruit and veg you will have to have five to seven times your weekly takings tied up in stock.'

You and your business

On a more personal level, can you and your family bear the strain of managing a shop: the hours of work, the tedium of filling in tax forms and keeping books; the problems of receiving early morning deliveries; the pressure of having always to be polite to your customers? (You might not wish to follow the dictum that the customer is always right, but would you survive? Small businesses depend on customers returning and on word-of-mouth promotion.)

Working hours are long, but made tolerable by a commitment to *your* business. You will grow to dislike VAT returns and difficult customers, and you will encounter a host of petty day-to-day administrative difficulties, but if you are serious about the move in the first place, you should survive these. But ask yourself: is my immediate family as dedicated to the project as I am? What is a challenge to you may be a burden to them. So, be as sensitive to their needs as you are to your own.

Buying an established business

Shops for sale are sometimes advertised in the local and national press and in some trade journals,* or you can consult a firm of business valuers and transfer agents. It is a good idea to write down the specific requirements that you are looking for: this will not only help you to brief your agent and any other advisers such as your accountant and bank manager, but will also help you clarify your ideas.

Shops are generally rented on a leasehold basis, and you have to pay for fixtures and fittings, existing stock, and 'goodwill'. (If the shop is bought freehold, this obviously gives much greater security of tenure but also involves a much higher capital investment.) How this price is arrived at depends on a number of factors, which you must analyse carefully before you commit yourself. *Stock* is generally valued for business sale purposes at current market cost price, and an independent valuation of the stock is desirable. *Fixtures and fittings* should also be independently valued, and an inventory of these should be made and attached to the contract of sale. 'Goodwill' is a nebulous concept to which an exact value cannot be attached. Obviously, the more the shop relies on regular, established customers, the higher the value of the goodwill; conversely, the more it relies on casual, passing trade, the lower the goodwill value. The price of a shop will also to a large extent depend on the potential of the local area. You will need to make a careful assessment of factors such as:

1. Competition. Do not make the mistake of thinking that the absence of a nearby competitor *necessarily* guarantees

* It is advisable to read trade journals (some of which are listed in Appendix 3) not only for lists of specific businesses for sale, but also to get a grasp of average prices of shops, etc and of the general concerns and problems of the trade in which you are interested.

success. A shop that has done reasonably well in the face of nearby competition is a safer bet than a shop with a similar record which has had a virtual monopoly of local trade. There is always a danger that if there is no competition, someone else may move in after you. Another common mistake is to see only shops of the same trade as competition. Indirectly, all other traders in the area are competition, since all are competing for a share of the consumers' spending power.

2. Nearness to railway stations, bus stops, etc: this may substantially increase the flow of passing trade. A map may help to clarify the exact potential of the location.

3. Any future local development plans – check with the local authority.

It is important that you and your accountant study the books thoroughly. In particular, examine the trend of the profit and loss account over the past few years to determine whether the business is improving. Another important point to note is whether the previous trader has been paying himself a salary, or whether this has to be deducted from the net profit figure.

We spoke to the owner of a general goods shop who makes these points strongly: 'Location, potential competition and overheads are the three key points to watch. If you're buying an existing store scrutinise the accounts minutely. Is it possible to run it with one less member of staff for example? Are home deliveries being made – these can be very, very expensive? Don't try to compete on prices with the big boys – you'll lose! Stock lots of lines and if needs be sell say sugar at a loss knowing you've got a good margin on shampoo. There's no guarantee that goodwill will pass over to you on completion of the sale – your face might not fit and there's little allegiance nowadays from customers.'

Starting from scratch

You may want to take over premises which have previously been used for other purposes, in which case you should look closely at the previous owner's reasons for closing down and determine to what extent the same factors will affect you, even though you are engaged in a different trade. If you are going to use them for another type of business, you must get planning permission first. Or you may want to rent newly built premises, in which case you will probably have to pay a premium. The premium is based on the potential of the area, but try to get some *exact* idea of what that potential is: the number of new flats being built nearby, for example. In general, the premium should be lower than the goodwill price you would pay for a going concern, since it only indicates potential, not a record of success.

Legal obligations

The most important Acts* affecting shops are:

- ☐ Contracts of Employment Act
- ☐ Offices, Shops and Railway Premises Act
- ☐ Shops Act
- ☐ Trade Descriptions Act
- ☐ Weights and Measures Act
- ☐ Sale of Goods Acts
- ☐ Local Authority By-laws
- ☐ Consumer Credit Act
- ☐ Redundancy Payment Act
- ☐ Payment of Wages Act
- ☐ Employment Protection Act
- ☐ Sex Discrimination Act
- ☐ Health and Safety at Work Act.

These fall into three categories. First, employment legislation (see Chapter 10). Check the ages of your employees; ensure that they are taxed and that you pay your share of their National Insurance contribution; cover them regarding pensions and superannuation; know where they stand in relation to the Employment Protection Act (if they work more than 16 hours a week and more than 52 weeks (or, in a small firm, 104 weeks) a year, they will be covered by its provisions and eligible to claim against wrongful dismissal, etc).

Second, safety, security and planning. You should insure your premises and stock, and cover yourself against liability (potential liability will vary widely depending on the goods you sell and the services you offer). In the case of a food shop, you must satisfy a health inspector, and other types of premises will have to be passed fit by a fire officer. Check these and local planning laws before you start trading. The quickest way to find

---

* Other Acts, such as the Pet Animals Act, affect specific types of shops.

out which of these laws apply to you is to contact your local Shops Act inspector. He will also provide details of by-laws on opening hours, Sunday trading, pavement displays, etc.

Third, fair trading. Know and follow the provisions of the Consumer Credit Act and the Trade Descriptions Act. There are strict rules on how you display prices, on recommended prices and 'special' offers, on the giving of guarantees, on the rates of hire purchase you can offer and the other types of credit you make available, and so on. Again, cover yourself against expensive litigation by going through existing legislation with a solicitor, looking at standard practice in businesses similar to your own, and taking advice from the local Weights and Measures Inspector.

Keeping accounts

A great deal of bookwork will be inevitable: keeping count of stock levels and daily sales (for personal use and for VAT purposes); an elementary statistical breakdown of what is selling; keeping tabs on credit customers, orders, returned goods, etc. Your accountant and bank manager will wish to see comprehensive and up-to-date accounts to check your progress. See Chapter 5 for an introduction to simple accounting, but be warned: for anything more than day-to-day bookkeeping it is worth using a qualified accountant.

Value Added Tax (VAT)

VAT is an indirect tax of 15 per cent levied on all goods and services except a few zero-rated basic commodities and exempt goods and services. If your business has a taxable turnover greater than £15,000 or you *anticipate* that your annual turnover will be greater than this figure, you must register at a Customs and Excise VAT office. You should include VAT in the prices you charge customers, and log the VAT portion of all sales. This amount is payable to the Customs and Excise at the end of the accounting period designated for that business. Payments are usually quarterly.

All self-employed people are classed as businesses for the purposes of VAT and those with gross receipts greater than £15,000 per annum are liable to VAT.

Detailed VAT records should be kept. If the Customs and Excise office consider your assessment to be incorrect, they may make their own assessment. If you feel you have been improperly assessed or unfairly treated, in most cases you have recourse to the VAT Tribunal.

Security

Never leave cash lying about. If there is a lot of money in the till, take out a round sum in notes and leave a chit in the till to remind yourself where it is. Watch out for shoplifters, and ensure against them as far as possible by not leaving small, valuable items in easily accessible positions. Do not leave customers or visitors unattended. Remember that you must be insured right from the start, even before you have opened up for business. The Home Office produces a pamphlet on theft by staff, which is a danger which must not be overlooked. Consult your local crime protection officer who will advise you on ways to combat both dangers.

Stock

It is sensible to buy your stock from a wholesaler, or cash and carry or from a manufacturer's agent, since you will generally need frequent deliveries of small quantities of goods. Have as few sources of supply as possible, to cut down your workload. There are a few exceptions to this. In the case of cigarettes, for example, it is better to deal directly with the manufacturer.

Make sure you know at all times what your stock levels are, and devise a system whereby you know when to re-order, before stocks run too low. The stock should be cleaned and dusted regularly and any stock that remains unsold over a long period should be discarded. Stock-taking should be carried out at least once a year.

Layout and display

Try to keep the layout of the shop flexible, and use space as efficiently as possible. Make the interior of the shop as attractive as you can: displays, however small, should have a focal point, and should be changed frequently. You may want to hire a freelance window dresser occasionally.

Case studies

It would be impossible to cover the whole range of shops: general and specialist, selling goods and offering services, urban and rural, central and suburban, business and consumer orientated, and so on. A few case studies are included here only for illustration, and a note added on sub post offices which are a rather special case. But no one *type* of shop or method of operation will necessarily work. Find something that suits you, and let what you do and the style you adopt reflect your personality.

Antique shops

This is a prime example of an area where you must be experienced: you must have a thorough knowledge of antiques, of the business and of other dealers. Whether you are starting off from scratch or buying an established business, you will need funds to buy stock. If you buy a going concern, you may find that the stock consists of all the duds and non-sellers of the previous owners, and you will have to get rid of it all and start again.

You will learn the technique of buying things at auctions: always go to the preview first and mark on your catalogue the items you are interested in and the price you are prepared to pay. Beware of being 'trotted' — other dealers running up the bidding and then dropping out at the end leaving you to pay an unrealistic price. Country auctions are usually widely advertised in local papers and you will soon get to know local dealers and their specialities. You must then build up a body of reliable clients, who will form the backbone of your business. These may include other dealers and foreign buyers.

You are most likely to make a success if you specialise, and learn as much as you can about your speciality, whether it is pictures, brass and copper, china or furniture. Use *The Lyle Official Antiques Review* if at all in doubt about the auction value of any item.

One main drawback is the hours you will be expected to keep — this is *not* a 9 to 5 job! Evenings will probably be spent entering up sales, pricing new acquisitions, etc, and then foreign dealers have a nasty habit of travelling overnight and arriving on the doorstep at 8 am ready to do business.

Robert O'Connor, an antique dealer, gives would-be dealers four pieces of advice: 'Buying is the key to success — you can't ring up a wholesaler and order twelve dozen. Selling is not so difficult as long as it's the right piece and the right price. You have to know and love your subject and not be motivated by profit. Work hard at developing lines of supply and specialise in an area that particularly interests you. Go to sale rooms, visit other dealers, study, read and handle the items and your instincts will develop.'

Bookshops

The location of a bookshop is all-important when deciding what sort of books to stock: children's books, textbooks, hobbies, gardening, etc. If you live on the tourist route it might be worthwhile stocking a lot of local history, while in another area it would be a good idea to find out what the local evening classes are.

You need to be devoted to your work, since you are going to work long hours, dealing with all sorts of queries from the public and some days you may be lucky to sell one cheap paperback, despite having had an infinitely varied range of browsers in your shop. What often makes a big difference is cultivating a connection with your local public library: if you can become their main supplier it will make a tremendous difference to your sales. School books are mainly bought centrally nowadays, but if there is a college in your area it is well worth finding out what textbooks are required and stocking a selection. You could even put a small ad in your window to that effect and perhaps develop a secondhand and exchange system with students.

The antiquarian book trade is extremely specialised and you really need to be an expert in the subject before you can hope to make any money in this area. People do make a lot of money, but they have to be prepared to invest thousands. They also need the patience to acquire the specialised knowledge needed.

Newsagents and tobacconists

Extremely hard work and long hours are involved in running this type of shop, and it is not a particularly profitable area. You will probably need to organise a daily delivery service for newspapers, which will involve getting up very early, marking newspapers, paying delivery agents, keeping books of customers' credit, etc. You will have to deal with a large number of suppliers, whose representatives will call regularly. You will have all the headaches of VAT and the constant small price rises which particularly affect cigarettes and confectionery. Moreover, you will have to keep the shop open for as many hours as possible — most newsagents close only on Good Friday, Christmas Day and Boxing Day, the only days when newspapers are not printed. If a member of your family is available to work in the shop, the extra help will be invaluable, and you can avoid the problems which taking on staff might entail.

Ironmonger's/do it yourself shop

The principles for this type of retail outlet differ from those which apply to a newsagent's in several important respects: trade will often be more specialised, so location is likely to be less important; stock will often be expensive and heavy initial capitalisation may be necessary, and, because some items will be bulky and a wide range of stock must be held, relatively large premises will be required.

Russ Morgan, who runs a DIY shop, also emphasises the degree of expertise you need to have: 'You must know the tools you stock and the jobs they're capable of doing so that you can advise your customers correctly. You are not merely selling products you are also a key source of advice and if your advice is good and your products are right then people will return again and again.' He is also aware of the high cost and the importance of stock control. 'Get your stock level right. Too little and word gets around that you can never get anything there. Too much and the cost of keeping your stock on your shelves eats into profits. If you are taking £500 a week then your stock should be about £4000. But do remember if someone buys a very expensive plane to reorder immediately — if you don't someone is bound to come in next week asking for it and you won't be able to help him.'

Travel agency

Anyone can buy a shop and set up a business as a travel agent — you do not need any special licence or authorisation. On the other hand, if you want to become an authorised agent for British Rail, or any of the major airline companies, or for any of the big shipping companies, there is rather more involved. Before you can earn commission on the sale of tickets from these various bodies, you have to satisfy them that you are a reputable company; and their requirements can be fairly stringent.

Two essential requirements if you are setting up on your own are contacts inside the business and sufficient capital. Most people will acquire the necessary experience *and* the contacts by working in an agency for a year or two until they have learned the ropes. At the same time they will probably work part-time for the examination of the Association of British Travel Agents.

Most reputable agents belong to the Association of British Travel Agents, who also have to be satisfied that you are a reputable firm. If you are a limited company, they require you to have an issued share capital of £5000 and also to put up another £5000 as a bond for your bank or insurance company. To gain approval of IATA (International Air Transport Association) and British Rail (who do all their own, very thorough, investigations) you have to prove that you are a reputable firm with sufficient financial backing, that you are generating sufficient business to warrant selling their tickets (the financial requirements vary according to the locality), that your staff are sufficiently trained and knowledgeable, that your premises are of a sufficiently high standard and promote the right image. Then, and only then, will you be able to advertise that you are an authorised agent.

It will take at least one or two years to work up the necessary volume of business. In the meantime, most people concentrate on hotel bookings and package tours. You can deal in air and rail tickets, but only through another friendly agency, and of course *you* do not then earn the commission (it is illegal).

Choosing the right area is obviously important — centre of town, busy suburb, prosperous market town, for example. There is a great deal of competition and you will survive and prosper only if you provide a friendly and *reliable* service which is also competitively priced. Remember, too, that the most lucrative business is done with firms: you should cultivate every contact you can find in the hope of becoming *the* company agency for nearby business firms.

Sub post offices

As a sub post master you are effectively a 'franchisee' of the Post Office. You offer its services and sell its products at prices

175

which it dictates and for which you receive payment. The postal services you provide will often be only part of the overall service, and the Post Office will not usually restrict other sales. But it will be an important part of the business, attracting a steady stream of customers who, once inside the shop, may be tempted to buy other things.

A sub post mastership is not *automatically* transferred from seller to buyer and the change has to be ratified by the Post Office. You should realise this when purchasing any business that includes postal services.

Owing to the decline in the number of rural and sub post offices and the demand for such businesses, competition is fierce and it is becoming increasingly difficult to obtain a sub post-mastership.

Bored with success?

Franchise
your business

Business good? Maybe it's time for you to step up to another level. If your business is franchiseable, you could have a whole new career ahead of you.

Our team of experienced franchise specialists can provide a total franchise development package for your business — franchise agreement — prospectus — marketing materials & publicity scheme — even a franchise sales programme (the sales development of your franchise is our particular skill) — your applications for NPA approval and BFA membership.

In fact, total co-ordination of your franchise.

Make the Irish franchise connection through FCL. Our Irish office will represent selected established franchisors of substance in Northern Ireland and Eire.

Franchise Concepts Limited

118 High Street
Sevenoaks
Kent
Tel. 01-228 4743

178

17: Franchising

Martin Mendelsohn, *author of* The Guide to Franchising
Pergamon Press

What the franchisor offers

One method by which it is possible to start in business and reduce the risks inherent in such a venture is to take up a business format franchise.

The business format franchise is a stage in the development of agency, distributorship, licences, and know-how type of manufacturing and marketing transactions. Instead of being limited to one aspect of business activity there has developed the concept of licensing an entire package comprising all the elements necessary to establish a previously untrained person in a business to be run on a predetermined basis. These elements comprise:

☐ The entire business concept
☐ A process of initiation and training in all aspects of the running of the business according to that concept
☐ A continuing process of assistance and guidance.

The entire business concept

This involves the development by the franchisor of a successful way of carrying on a business in all its aspects. The franchisor will develop what may be described as a 'blueprint' for conducting the business. The blueprint should:

1. Eliminate so far as possible the risks inherent in opening a new business, for example, the product range should be thoroughly market tested in pilot operations run by the franchisor.
2. Enable a person who has never before owned or operated a business to open up in business on his own account, not only with a pre-established format but with the backing of an organisation (ie the franchisor) that would not otherwise be available to him.
3. Set out in detail exactly how the business should be run.

Process of initiation and training

The franchisee must be trained in the business methods that are necessary to operate the business according to the blueprint. This may involve training in the use of specialised equipment, marketing methods, preparation of produce and application of processes. The franchisee should be trained so that he is relatively expert in those spheres that are necessary for the operation of that particular business.

Continuing process of assistance and guidance

The franchisor will in many cases provide the following range of services on a continuing basis depending of course upon the particular type of business:

☐ Regular visits from and access to a 'trouble-shooter' to assist in correcting or preventing deviations from the blueprint which may cause trading difficulties for the franchisee.

☐ Liaison between the franchisor, the franchisee and all other franchisees for exchanges of ideas and experiences.

☐ Product or concept innovation including investigation of marketability and compatibility with the existing business.

☐ Retraining facilities and training facilities, for the franchisee's staff.

☐ Market research.

☐ National and local advertising and promotion.

☐ Bulk purchasing opportunities.

☐ Management and accounting advice and services.

☐ Publication of a journal.

☐ Research into methods.

It will be seen that the business format franchise is a comprehensive and continuing relationship in which the initial concept is always being developed. The resources available for such development are those contributed to by the franchisor and all franchisees and are therefore much more considerable than any one individual could reasonably afford.

It will be noted that reference has been made to the *business format franchise*. The expression *franchise* is now popularly used to describe all those transactions in which one person licenses another rights to do something. For example, petrol filling stations, car dealerships, the use of a sportsman's or entertainer's name are commonly called franchises. It is important that you recognise what sort of franchise you are dealing with so that it is clear what can really be expected.

The word franchising can be used as a vehicle for abuse and indeed it already has been. It is the sort of transaction that readily lends itself to fraudulent practices. Invariably the transaction falls into two stages, the first is the provision of pre-opening services, the second the continuing relationship thereafter. If therefore the franchisor charges too much at stage one and is not there to provide stage two the fraud is obvious. A fraud could be committed by franchising an untried and undeveloped concept resulting in a franchisee being charged fees for a right to conduct a business which in reality does not exist.

Pyramid selling

The most serious frauds which have been perpetrated upon the unsuspecting were described as pyramid selling or multi-level marketing schemes. These schemes are presented as foolproof and very tempting methods of making easy money and are

181

often marketed by presenting successful 'franchisees' who speak of their great financial success. These schemes involve the sale of distributorships to purchasers who may divide and subdivide them and sell them on to those whom they recruit as sub-distributors. Expansion of these enterprises takes place on the chain letter principle.

The ostensible object is to build up a sales force which will sell the company's products or services from door to door. In fact, selling the goods or services is difficult; they are usually expensive and areas are often saturated with other distributors. Selling distributorships is much more lucrative and becomes effectively the company's business.

These schemes were quickly recognised by the government as containing elements which are dishonest and, accordingly, the Fair Trading Act 1973 contains provisions which prohibit pyramid-type schemes. The Act also contains provisions which permit the making of regulations:

☐ To control or prohibit the issue, circulation or distribution of documents which contain invitations to persons to participate in a scheme.

☐ Prohibiting the promoter of a scheme from performing functions which are vital to the operation of such a scheme, such as supplying goods or receiving payment for goods.

It is important to be able to recognise involvement with a pyramid-type scheme. And, obviously, before signing any contract or parting with money you should take proper professional advice. Be suspicious if you are offered or told that there will be a reward (ie payment, supply of cheaper products or any other disguised benefit) for doing something totally unrelated to the sale of the basic product or service with which the scheme is involved. For example, you may be offered a percentage payment of any sum paid to the promoter of the scheme for recruiting another participant, or for persuading such participant to purchase a higher position in the scheme. Other rewards could include a profit or commission on sales, or the provision of services or training to other participants in the scheme, or a commission on sales effected by other participants in the scheme.

Advantages and disadvantages of franchising

Advantages to the franchisee

1. The franchisee's lack of basic or specialised knowledge is

overcome by the training programme of the franchisor.

2. The franchisee has the incentive of owning his own business despite the background of assistance from the franchisor. He is an independent businessman within the framework of the franchise agreement and can by his own hard work and effort maximise the value of his investment.

3. The franchisee's business opens with the benefit of a name already well established in the mind and eye of the public.

4. The franchisee invariably requires less capital than is required in setting up independently by reason of the assistance given by the franchisor. However, many franchised businesses are organised in a highly sophisticated way and a franchisee may well have a larger investment to make than he would if he were to open for business without the franchise umbrella. On the other hand, a more modest investment may jeopardise the success of the business.

5. The franchisee should (where appropriate) receive assistance in:
   □ site selection
   □ preparation of plans for remodelling the premises, including the obtaining of any necessary town planning or by-law

consents
- [ ] obtaining finance for the acquisition of the franchised business
- [ ] the training of his staff
- [ ] purchase of equipment
- [ ] selection and purchase of stock
- [ ] getting the business open and running smoothly.

6. The franchisee receives the benefit on a national scale (if appropriate) of the franchisor's advertising and promotional activities.

7. The franchisee receives the benefit of the bulk purchasing and negotiating capacity of the franchisor on behalf of all the franchisees.

8. The franchisee has at his fingertips the specialised and highly skilled knowledge and experience of the franchisor's Head Office organisation in all aspects of his business while continuing in a self-employed capacity.

9. The franchisee's business risk is reduced. However, no franchisee should consider that because he is coming under the umbrella of the franchisor he is not going to be exposed to any risk at all. Any business undertaking involves risk and a franchised business is no exception. To be succussful, the franchisee will have to work hard, perhaps harder than ever before. The franchisor will never be able to promise great rewards for little effort. The blueprint for carrying on business successfully and profitably can rarely be the blueprint for carrying on business successfully without working.

10. The franchisee has the services of 'trouble-shooters' provided by the franchisor to assist him with the many problems that may arise from time to time in the course of business.

11. The franchisee has the benefit of the use of the franchisor's patents, trade marks, trade secrets and any secret process or formulae.

12. The franchisee has the benefit of the franchisor's continuous research and development programmes designed to improve the business and keep it up to date.

13. The franchisor obtains the maximum amount of market information and experience which is circularised for the benefit of all the franchisees. This should give him access to information which would not otherwise be available to him.

14. There are also usually some territorial guarantees to ensure that no competitive franchisee is set up in a competing

business within a defined area around the franchisee's business address. This can give rise to some legal difficulties under the Restrictive Trade Practices Act and must therefore be handled with care.

Disadvantages to the franchisee

1. Inevitably the relationship between the franchisor and franchisee will involve the imposition of controls. These controls will regulate the quality of the service or goods to be provided or sold by the franchisee. It has been mentioned previously that the franchisee will own his own business. He will, but he must accept that for the advantages enjoyed by him, by virtue of his association with the franchisor and all the other franchisees, control of quality and standards is essential. Each bad franchisee has an adverse effect not only on his own business, but indirectly on the whole franchised chain of business and all other franchisees. The franchisor will therefore demand that standards are maintained so that the maximum benefit is derived by the franchisee and indirectly by the whole franchised chain from the operation of the franchisee's business. This is not to say that the

franchisee will not be able to make any contribution or to impose his own personality on his business. Most franchisors do encourage their franchisees to make their contribution to the development of the business of the franchise chain and hold seminars and get-togethers to assist in the process.

2. The franchisee will have to pay the franchisor for the services provided and for the use of the blueprint, ie franchise fees.
3. The difficulty of assessing the quality of the franchisor. This factor must be weighed very carefully by the franchisee for it can affect the franchisee in two ways. First, the franchisor's offer of a package may well not amount to what it appears to be on the surface. Second, the franchisor may be unable to maintain the continuing services which the franchisee may need in order to sustain his efforts.
4. The franchise contract will contain some restrictions against the assignment of the franchised business. This is a clear inhibition on the franchisee's ability to deal with his own business but, as with most of the restrictions, there is a reason for it. The reason is that the franchisor will have already been most meticulous in his choice of the franchisee as his original franchisee for the particular outlet. Why then should he be any less meticulous in his approval of a replacement? Naturally he will wish to be satisfied that any successor of the franchisee is equally suitable for that purpose. In practice there is normally very little difficulty in the achievement of successful assignments of franchised businesses.
5. The franchisee may find himself becoming too dependent upon the franchisor. This can affect him in a number of ways; for example, he may not achieve the motivation that is necessary for him to work and build his business to take full advantage of the foundations that the blueprint provides.
6. The franchisor's policies may affect the franchisee's profitability.
7. The franchisor may make mistakes of policy; he may make decisions relating to innovations in the business which are unsuccessful and operate to the detriment of the franchisee.
8. The good name of the franchised business or its brand image may become less reputable for reasons beyond the franchisee's control.

How to decide

In order to judge these advantages and disadvantages and the way in which they are likely to concern a prospective franchisee there should be a detailed examination of the franchisor and his scheme. However, one must not lose sight of the fact that in deciding whether or not to go into a franchise one is also deciding to go into business on one's own account, albeit a particular type of business structured in a particular type of way. It is necessary, regardless of the fact that it is a franchised business which is contemplated, to indulge in the same sort of self-assessment in which one should indulge when deciding to embark on any business venture. If one has a particular franchise in mind the self-assessment exercise is less academic but one should be asking some, if not all, of the following questions:

- ☐ Am I qualified physically and temperamentally for self-employment?
- ☐ Do I possess sufficient financial resources to enable me to start a business and survive while it is struggling to become established?
- ☐ What are my natural aptitudes and skills? Do I do my best with mental or physical tasks? Do I mix well with people?
- ☐ Do I have the ability to work hard?
- ☐ How will my family be affected by my decision? Do they

187

wholeheartedly support my proposed venture?

Having submitted oneself to this exercise in introspection, one then has to consider three other specific areas in relation to a franchise scheme.

1. The product or service which is given.
2. The franchisor: who is he and how does he rate?
3. The operational details.

We shall examine each in turn.

The product or service which is being offered

A number of questions arise for consideration.

1. Is the product or service new? Has it been thoroughly proved in practice to be successful? Does it have staying power?
2. Is the product or service in a business area which is in decline?
3. How highly competitive is the market for the particular product or service?
4. How competitive is the price for the product or service? Can this competitiveness be maintained?
5. What is the source of supply of any products? How certain is it that the source will be available for the future? Are alternatives available?
6. Are the products or services based upon any trade mark or patented equipment and the protection thereby afforded?
7. Is there an adequate back-up in terms of guarantees and service facilities if relevant?
8. Could the supplier easily bypass the franchisor and you, and set up his own competitive franchise?
9. What is the reputation of the product and supplier?

The franchisor

The following questions should be put to a franchisor to enable one to assess him, his financial involvement and the quality of his personnel.

1. How long have you been franchising?
2. Did you run your own pilot schemes before franchising?
3. If not, why not?

4. Whether you did or not, what is the extent of your own cash investment in the business?
5. How many franchised businesses are you running at the moment?
6. What are the addresses of these businesses?
7. May I please interview any number of these franchisees? May I choose whom I interview?
8. How many outlets do you yourselves run as at the present time?
9. What does your head office organisation consist of?
10. Can you demonstrate your capacity to provide the necessary follow-up services?
11. May I take up your bank references?
12. Are there any other referees whom I may approach?
13. How many business failures have been experienced by your franchisees?
14. On what basis do you choose your franchisees – how selective are you?
15. What is the business background of the directors and executives of the franchisor company?
16. Have you or any of your directors or executives ever experienced any business failures? If so, please provide details.
17. Has any of your directors or executives ever: been bankrupt; entered into an arrangement with his creditors; been convicted of any criminal offence; been involved as a shareholder or executive in any company which while he was a director or executive or shortly after he ceased to be a director or executive went into liquidation? If so, please provide details.
18. Have you or any of your directors or executives been involved in any material litigation with franchisees? If so, please provide details.

The operational details

1. What is the initial cost of your franchise? What does this price include? What capital costs will be incurred in addition to this price, and what for?
2. How much working capital do I need?
3. What are the costs incurred in the business likely to be, broken down into *gross* profit and *net* profit?
4. May I see actual accounts which confirm or fail to confirm

your projections?

5. What financing arrangements can you make and what terms for repayment will there be? What rate of interest will be required and will the finance company want security?
6. Is the business seasonal?
7. When is the best time to open up?
8. What fees do you charge?
9. Do you take any commission on supplies of goods or materials to a franchisee?
10. Will I be obliged to maintain a minimum fee or a minimum purchase of goods? What happens if I fail to meet this commitment?
11. What advertising and promotional support do you provide?
12. Do I have to contribute to it, if so, how much?
13. What initial services do you offer?
14. Do you train me? Who pays for my training? Where do I go for training?
15. What continuing services do you provide after the business has commenced?

CONTRACTS

1. May I have a copy of your franchise contracts?
2. Does this contract permit me to sell my business? What restrictions are there affecting my rights to sell the business?
3. For how long is the franchise granted?
4. What do I get at the end of that period? Do I get automatic renewal?
5. What will happen if I do not like the business? Upon what basis can I terminate the contract?

OTHER ASPECTS

1. Who will be my link with you after I have opened for business? Can I meet some of your staff?
2. What point of sale and promotional literature do you supply and what do I have to pay for it?
3. What will the opening hours of business be?
4. Will I own the equipment necessary to operate the business when I have cleared the finance company?
5. How soon will I have to spend money on replacing equipment?

6. Will you find me a site or do I have to find it?
7. What systems do you have for keeping franchisees in touch with you and each other? Do you publish a newsletter? Do you hold seminars?
8. What help will I receive in local advertising and promotion?
9. What exclusive rights do I get?
10. How will I cope with my bookkeeping?
11. What can I sell and what can I not sell?
12. Do you provide instruction and operational manuals?
13. What would happen if you misjudged the site and it did not produce the anticipated figures but resulted in a loss?
14. What would happen if I ran into operational problems I was not able to solve? What help would I get?
15. How can I be sure you will do what you promise?

The British Franchise Association (BFA)

The formation of the British Franchise Association in 1977 introduced a new element. Membership is open only to those whose franchise scheme has been operating successfully for a period of time. The franchisor is investigated before admission to membership and must accept and observe a strict code of ethical behaviour. The BFA has a disciplinary procedure which can be invoked against a member who acts contrary to the code of ethics or otherwise engages in questionable practices. New franchisors do not qualify for membership until they have been in operation for a time, though this is not to say that non-members automatically run unethical operations or should necessarily be avoided. Current members of the Association are listed in Appendix 4.

Conclusion

The advantages and disadvantages listed above, as well as the replies to the questions, must be weighed up and considered before making the decision on whether or not to enter into a franchised business venture. One must decide whether the advantages with the training and support they provide are worth having in return for the surrender of some independence to the degree of outside control which is inherent in the franchise transaction. The prospective franchisee must decide whether the particular franchisor is the right person with whom to do business; he must also decide whether he is personally and temperamentally suitable for this type of relationship.

Having weighed up all the factors and taken proper professional advice, he may also consider the advice of his bank manager or businessman whose judgement he respects; he should certainly discuss the matter with his immediate family, though he has to make his final decision. If he is not able to take this decision with confidence, after having heard all that his advisers have to say, he should consider whether he is indeed capable of running his own business.

There is not much guidance available for those considering a franchise. There is one book available, *The Guide to Franchising*, published by Pergamon Press, and a free pamphlet *Obtaining a Franchise: A Guide for Small Firms*, published by the Small Firms Centre, but this is in limited supply. There is a magazine, *Franchise World*, published quarterly, obtainable from Franchise World, 37 Nottingham Road, London SW17. This magazine contains articles about franchising in general and about specific franchise opportunities as well as a mass of franchise news. *Franchise World* has also published two booklets: *How to Evaluate a Franchise* and *How to Franchise Your Business*.

There are those who describe themselves as franchise consultants but many of these represent franchisors and are selling franchises. They may be more interested in selling a franchise than in offering objective and unbiased advice.

The British Franchise Association of 15 The Poynings, Iver, Buckinghamshire may be approached, and is always willing to give advice and provide information sources. The Association also has a very active programme of seminars on the subject of franchising which may provide the answer to the questions which are in one's mind.

Checklist

Musts

1. Weigh advantages and disadvantages.
2. Assess oneself.
3. Assess the business.
4. Assess the franchisor.
5. Assess the franchise package.
6. Speak to existing franchisees.
7. Consider advice of others who are qualified to give it.
8. Make up your own mind.

Beware

1. Heavy initial franchise fees.
2. Pyramid-type schemes.
3. Franchisors whose ongoing fee income is too low to support services.
4. Contracts which do not match promises.
5. The hard sell.
6. A franchise consultant who is offering a franchise for sale and purporting to offer objective advice.
7. Get rich quick offers.
8. Franchisors who have not invested in pilot operations.

18: Hotels, Catering*
and Entertainments

Hotels, pubs, clubs and the range of independently owned eating places from simple corner shop cafes to long-established, expensive restaurants constitute a vast business. There are over 30,000 hotels and large guest houses and a vast number of pubs and clubs. And catering is, in employment terms, one of the biggest industries in the UK. The range of opportunities and business options is so wide that we can barely scratch the surface, but an outline of each area will be given and some general conclusions drawn.

The business

What is true of running a shop, that you need unstinting energy and commitment, is even truer in this field. Your hours will be long and irregular. You are likely to have to work 365 days a year. You may have to deal with dissatisfied and difficult customers. There is a mountain of paperwork to monitor and national and local regulations to understand and abide by. Your family, which is in any case likely to be directly involved in the running of your hotel, restaurant or cafe, should be as committed to succeeding as you are.

Offsetting these disadvantages, these areas, particularly owning a restaurant or hotel on which you can stamp your personality and deal very closely with your customers, have many attractions. Indeed, perhaps too many: new restaurants open with great frequency but often quickly collapse because of poor planning, bad management, lack of finance, or a simple lack of realism about the scope for *that* type of restaurant in *that* locality.

---

* Catering is also considered in Part 3, the distinction being the use of business premises. All caterers dealt with here are assumed to have business units open to the public. The self-employed caterers dealt with later tend to produce cakes, rolls, etc to order for business functions, parties, wedding receptions, and so on.

Location

As in retailing, location is crucial. Decide what sort of operation you wish to conduct and then look for the premises. If you want to start a hotel or guest house, look for an expanding inland tourist spot or popular seaside resort. In the latter think about the problems of surviving the winter, with only limited and erratic custom. Ask yourself what type of visitor the place attracts and who might be attracted by price reductions out of season (pensioners or the disabled perhaps). Understand the character of the area in which your business will be sited, and have some idea *whose* needs you will cater for. This applies as much to services as to manufacturing firms, and is crucial when you decide how to market that service.

Restaurants

New restaurants open every week, particularly in the London area. But almost as many close, and only the gifted and the adaptable survive.

There are basically two kinds of people who open a restaurant — the gifted amateur or professional cook, and the 'ideas man' who knows how to fulfil a taste and buys premises and finds the staff to meet that need (many of the 'in places' in London are now more rated for decor, music and clientele than for their cuisine). The main problem for the amateur or professional is likely to be how to maintain standards without wasting an enormous amount of food and losing money. One answer is to have a *small* choice of dishes which are changed regularly. He will have to spend quite a lot of time finding the best sources locally for fresh meat, fish and vegetables since his reputation depends on it. The restaurateur who has a speciality (such as steaks) and sticks to it will find life a lot simpler.

Where your restaurant is located is obviously essential. If it is in the centre of town, well and good. If not, you must set about advertising, make sure your friends spread the word around, find an eye-catching decor and try to get yourself written up in the local paper. If you are sufficiently confident, you could try writing to the restaurant critics on some of the big magazines (such as *Harpers & Queen*) or newspapers.

If your restaurant is quite small, you will probably find it more economical in the long run to be as mechanised as possible with chip machines, dishwashers, freezers, etc, rather than hiring a lot of expensive, possibly unreliable, staff. Costing can be quite difficult, with the rising price of food, but beware of undercharging. There is a temptation to court trade with low prices, but you will soon find it impossible to keep up standards. It is a good idea, too, to realise your limitations and not try to be grander than you are — if you are basically steak and chips there is no point in trying to produce cordon bleu menus: you will soon be found out!

We spoke to a restauranteur who points to seven problem areas:

1. Wastage.
2. Overheads — heating and lighting cost £50 per week for a 30-seat restaurant!
3. Payment of VAT.
4. Establishing good and appropriate decor.
5. The need to change the menu — don't let you or your customers get bored with it.
6. Maintaining your profit margins.
7. Coping with fluctuations in demand — no customers one night, 50 the next!

Cafes, snack bars, etc

The large restaurant has very different problems to the small, unpretentious cafe. The former provides particular foods with (one hopes) a distinctive touch, and will seek to build up a clientele. It may encounter problems in employing staff, dealing with alcohol licensing, regulations on opening hours, fire precautions, and so on. Moreover, it may be vulnerable to economic downturns and changing consumer tastes. By contrast, the cafe offers a simple service to the local workforce and others at a reasonable price. Fads of taste and the vagaries of economics count for little.

Owning a cafe is more closely allied to general retailing than to being a restaurateur. True, you must be able to prepare a reasonably wide range of good food cheaply, quickly, efficiently and hygienically. But this should not be beyond the capabilities of the average person.

Re-read the retailing section: location will be important and your business must be located in heavy 'traffic' areas. Recognise that each day will have peaks and troughs — a rush at 12 to 2 pm perhaps? Can you cope and, if you can, will you then be overstaffed for the rest of the day?

197

Your business must be covered by health and safety regulations and must be passed by a food inspector and a fire officer. Regulations on bookkeeping and VAT returns apply to you with equal force as to any other retail business.

The hotel business

You must choose your hotel or guest house with great care. It is a big investment to make, so be sure to examine the following points:

The area

What is the competition like? Are there any plans for redevelopment locally which might involve one of the big hotel groups? Is it on a main road or tourist route, or is it hidden in the back streets or down a country lane? Does the area as a whole seem to be coming up in the world, or going down?

The customers

Ideally, you want to attract a variety of clientele, so that you are fairly busy all year round. Seaside hotels are full up for most of the summer, but virtually deserted in the winter: are you going to make enough profit to cover those lean winter months? Other hotels in industrial or commercial areas will find that they are full of businessmen during the week, but that the weekends are very quiet. The most successful hotels are those which have a good mix of commercial, holiday, conference and banqueting business. Study the accounts if you can and see what the pattern of business is.

The fabric

What state is your hotel in? You must find out how much renovating or decorating needs to be done and how much this is going to cost. What are the maintenance costs likely to be?

The law

There are a number of laws that the hotelier is subject to, particularly health and safety legislation. Insure your property and protect yourself against liability; make sure you meet the necessary safety levels for fireproofing and hygiene or your insurance may be worthless. Another important set of regulations, if you are opening a new hotel, covers licensing. There are various guides to the licensing laws, but if you have to apply for a new licence, it is wise to do it through a solicitor.

Also very important is the Fire Precautions Act. Every hotel, if it sleeps more than six people, must have a fire certificate from the local fire authority. When buying a going concern, find out if it has a fire certificate, or if an application for one has been made (if not, the hotel is being run illegally). If the fire authority has already inspected the building, check on the cost of any alterations required to bring the premises into line with the Fire Precautions Act of 1971.

Staff

Good staff are obviously essential for the smooth and efficient running of a hotel, but they are very difficult to come by. This is an industry with a very high staff turnover, especially among unskilled staff, and you must expect to spend a lot of time interviewing, supervising and training. Everyone in the business agrees that it pays to take your time (however inconvenient) and select staff very carefully, rather than always employing the first person you see because you are busy.

Goodwill

Does the hotel you are considering buying have a good reputation? Will regular visitors return even though the hotel has changed owner?

Past performance and potential

How has it operated in the past: could you improve upon it? What is the sleeping capacity? Could it be increased without reducing standards? Can seasonal fluctuations be reduced by good marketing? How great are staff expenses and other overheads as a proportion of turnover? What is the hotel's net profit as a percentage of turnover?

Pubs

The following section refers to brewery tenants, not to pub

199

managers (who are not self-employed) or to the owners of free houses, which are now so few and far between as to make the possibility of finding a vacant one very unlikely.

Tenants rent their pubs from the brewery company, paying an agreed sum to the outgoing tenant for fittings, equipment and stock. They agree to buy their beer from the brewery, and generally cannot buy stock (even of items other than liquor) from any other source without the brewery's permission. They keep their own profits and are responsible for their own losses, the brewery receiving only the rent on the premises and the guaranteed outlet for its product.

There are more applications from prospective tenants than there are tenancies available, so the breweries are able to 'pick and choose' to some extent. The qualities they look for in a prospective tenant are:

1. Sufficient capital resources to purchase fittings, equipment, and stock in hand, to cover immediate running expenses, and to provide a sufficient reserve to cover the tenant in the event of a temporary reduction in trade.
2. Married tenants are preferred. Running a pub is very much a family affair, and your spouse's experience and attitude can be a decisive factor.
3. Good health, since running a pub involves hard physical work and long hours.
4. Some managerial experience, in any trade, would count in the applicant's favour, though it is not strictly necessary. Similarly, experience or training in the liquor trade would be useful, though again it is not a mandatory requirement.

We spoke to one publican who offered this advice: 'Watch the optics, the fiddles and the free drinks to friends. Watch that the brewers don't send you lines you don't want. Don't commit yourself to loans and brewers' discounts — there'll be conditions in the fine print you won't like. The Weights and Measures boys will be calling often to check your measures and make sure you have price notices and age warnings up.'

Tenancy agreements

Most breweries have a standard form of agreement to be signed by the tenant. The procedure for taking over the fittings, furniture and equipment is the only area in which there may be a substantial difference between breweries: some require that the new tenant buys these items from the outgoing tenant, whilst in other cases they remain the property of the brewery, and the tenant lodges a deposit, returnable when he gives up the tenancy. Other items covered in the tenancy agreement include rent (usually paid quarterly), the term of the tenancy, responsibility for repairs, a requirement that the tenant take out employer's and public liability insurance, the terms on which the stock is purchased, the brewery company's right of access to the premises, requirements connected with transfer of the licence, and terms on which the tenancy can be terminated.

Licences

The tenant usually takes over premises that are already licensed, so he has to negotiate the transfer of the licence from the outgoing tenant to himself. It is advisable to be represented by a solicitor in your application for transfer of the licence.

Training

If you are accepted by a brewery for a tenancy, and neither you nor your wife have any experience of the trade, it is likely that both of you will be asked to attend a short residential course, run by the brewery company and lasting from one to two weeks. While you are waiting for a suitable tenancy, or applying to different breweries, it is advisable, if you have no experience, to work part-time in a pub. This will give you some experience, and will help you to decide whether you are really suited to what is in fact a very arduous job.

Other opportunities

It is possible to run clubs, cinemas, theatres and so on independently. Indeed, the attractions for the music lover or cinema buff are considerable as it seems to be possible to mix business with pleasure. But base any decision on *business* sense, not on a romantic notion of making your leisure interests pay. Can the town support another cinema, particularly if you intend to show nothing but *avant garde* and experimental films? (Whether you want to show more obscure films or not, if the major companies have tied up the distribution of the money-spinning movies you may have no option!)

You will face the same problems as the hotelier and restauranteur in choosing the right location, employing staff, perhaps getting restrictions on opening hours lifted, obtaining a licence to serve alcohol, meeting fire regulations.* (Some of these problems can be circumvented if you make your institution a private club, admitting members only at some sort of fee, though future legislation may close this loophole.) And do not forget the less well-known legislation on health, hygiene, noise abatement, etc, which may involve you in short-term inconvenience or, worse, long-term and expensive rounds of litigation.

Which business?

Whatever type of service you provide will need sound financial backing, commercial acumen, the ability to offer something distinctive and market it accordingly, and patience in choosing the right opening. Fix on a 'target' population: advertise in newspapers and periodicals which they are likely to read, and be prepared for an initial struggle while you attempt to build up the business. The business field you choose to enter should be one in which you have some expertise, something distinctive to offer and a practical marketing strategy. But, even then, you will need resilience and the ability to work hard for long periods.

---

* This could be extremely expensive if alterations to a club or cinema have to be made to comply with regulations. Consider this when you buy a property which you hope to convert, and check that an established business has a fire certificate.

Part 3:
Directory of Opportunities
for the Self-employed

19: How to Market Your Skills

There are hundreds of examples of self-employment: from window-cleaners to tax consultants, from the home typist to the famous author living in his tax haven abroad. In this section of the book we cover some of the more popular and more accessible areas of self-employment. If the area you are particularly interested in is not covered here, the best advice we can give is to talk to someone who has tried it (and preferably someone who has been successful).

Freelance work

Freelance work is especially attractive to young people with few commitments, and to married women, less so to those with families to support, because of the element of risk involved. It can include either part-time work, done for a short time to raise extra cash or it can be a full-time job.

Freelance work has several major advantages as opposed to full-time employment. First, it offers a certain degree of flexibility and freedom. The freelance is free from the necessity of *having* to work from nine to five, from rush-hour travel, from having to 'create' work if he does not really get anything to do, from being directly under his employer's supervision.

The second advantage is the possibility, though not the certainty, of high earnings. Taken on an hourly or weekly basis, freelance work is more highly paid than ordinary employment, though your pay does not include sick pay, pension contributions, holiday pay, the employer's National Insurance contributions, or payment for the almost inevitable slack periods which occur in most full-time jobs. From the employer's point of view, it is sometimes cheaper to use reliable freelances, as he does not have any commitments towards them. From the freelance's point of view, the main problem is ensuring that he or she has a continuing supply of work. Remember when calculating charges that you must allow for slack periods, and if you expect to earn over £15,000 a year you will be liable to pay VAT as well as income tax.

The other major advantage of freelance work is that for tax purposes you are on Schedule D (self-employed) which means that you can claim all business expenses against tax, and that your tax is paid at the end of the year, rather than on the PAYE system. (For detailed information on taxation, see Chapter 11.)

There are a number of drawbacks to freelance work, however. As already mentioned, there are slack periods. Moreover, you don't get holiday pay or sick pay, you have to buy your own National Insurance stamps and pay the Class 4 levy (5.75 per cent of earnings), and you may have to pay VAT.

For some people, though, the main drawback is the need for self-discipline. If you are at all inclined to put things off until tomorrow, you will probably find it hard to work as a freelance. Some people need the stability of a nine-to-five environment to get any work done at all; others (and these are the ones who turn out to be successful freelances) are quite happy to stay up all night working, if necessary, and will put in a tremendous effort to keep to deadlines. Remember that you need to put more effort into freelance work than into an ordinary job: if you are not reliable, you will not get any more work.

Efficiency and reliability are thus the ways to being a successful freelance in any field. You will tend to develop contacts and clients, who, if they trust your work, will use you repeatedly and pay promptly for your services.

How to start out

It is difficult to give general guidelines about how to start out as a freelance: there are so many different types of freelance work that it is very difficult to generalise. People often start by working on a part-time basis and then graduate to full freelance status. This provides them with some security while they establish themselves.

The following chapters include suggestions for the kinds of work which can be done on a freelance basis. We have tried to give some indication of the ways in which you can find work. In some areas, advertising may pay off; for others it will be worse than useless. Much freelance work is obtained through personal contacts, and this is usually the most fruitful source. There are a few employment agencies and other bodies which operate in this area, and details have been given where appropriate.

Charges

One of the hardest problems facing you will be the all-important question of calculating your charges. Will you charge per hour, or per job? How much are other people charging for similar work? How much will people be prepared to pay you? Much freelance work is paid on an hourly basis, and you will probably want to start off by being paid by the hour, until you have some experience of calculating how long it will take you to complete a job. Otherwise, you may find yourself out of pocket, having initially quoted a low price and then finding that the work has taken you longer than you expected. However, if you intend to make a real career as a freelance, on a long-term basis, you should eventually aim to charge per job rather than per hour, as you will in the long run make more money in this way.

Where possible we have tried to give some idea of the hourly rates of pay for different kinds of freelance work, but pay varies between localitites and the types of possible jobs are almost infinite, so check up with other freelances if possible. Do not underprice yourself too much: you will get plenty of work, but will exhaust yourself trying to complete it. Better to do less for more money: but do not price yourself out of the market either. There is an important balance to be struck: initially, you may need to be very competitive to establish yourself, but do not set your prices too low as your customers may not accept higher charges later.

Travelling time and expenses

There seems to be some dispute among freelances about whether to charge for the time spent travelling to collect and deliver work. If you are doing something like typing letters, or small design jobs, you could spend up to 30 per cent of your time travelling around between different jobs, and obviously this is a complete waste of time, from your point of view, unless you are being paid for it. It is difficult to establish any general rule which applies to travelling time, but the following guidelines may help:

1. If you are being paid £4.00 per hour or less, it is

reasonable to expect to charge for at least *some* of your travelling time and fares, particularly if a lot of your time is spent travelling.

2. If you are being paid more than this, or are doing jobs that take more than a week or so to complete, it is not really fair to charge for travelling time.

3. If you choose to live a long way from your various employers (if you live in the country, for example and travel to town once a week to collect and deliver work) then it is not reasonable to charge for the time it takes you to travel into town. Similar rules apply to expenses. If you have to buy a piece of equipment solely for a particular job, the expense can be passed on to the employer, but you cannot really charge for something that you use all the time, such as hiring a typewriter or buying paper.

Keeping records

For tax purposes, you need to keep a record of your invoices (a small duplicate book will do) and a record of your expenses. It may be worth employing an accountant to help you with your tax return: he will probably save you more money than you have to pay him in fees (see also Chapters 4, 5 and 11).

You may find it helpful to keep a record of the number of hours worked in each week and tick them off when they have been invoiced. Examples of a typical freelance's invoice and weekly record of hours are shown opposite.

It may be worth adding to the invoice the terms of payment which you expect to be met: 15 days net, 30 days net, etc. Conversely, if you have a very good relationship with a client, you may consider this to be unnecessary and likely to damage the relationship. But remember: most of your business will be for firms to which you will be one creditor (and probably one of the smallest) among many. You may have to chase up payment and, if this happens too frequently and for too many jobs, time which should be spent on new work will be wasted. This is another argument for dealing with people you know on the basis of mutual trust. But, look forward to the day when your business is large enough to employ a general administrator or secretary to do the chasing.

Weekly record of hours

Invoice sent

For London Advertising ☑
Monday: 5 hours & £2 expenses (stamps)
Charge: £4.00 per hour

For Thames Press Ltd ☐
Tuesday: 10 hours
Friday: 7 hours
Expenses: £1.00 fares
Charge: £4.00 per hour

For Rev L Green ☑
Wednesday: 8 hours
Charge: £3.00 per hour

Invoice

4/9/78

To: London Advertising Ltd
From: Jane Smith, 20 Norton Road, London NW10

For 5 hours typing at £4.00 per hour	£20.00
Expenses (purchase of postage stamps)	£2.00
	£22.00

Part-time or full-time?

This question can only be resolved by you. Are you prepared to
risk all or would you prefer to combine a steady income from a
salaried job with freelance work. This is often a good way of
building up contacts, measuring how much you can do, how to
present your work, and so on. It is also a better time to make
mistakes than later, when you support yourself exclusively from
freelance work.

Taxation and National Insurance

You are responsible for your own National Insurance
contributions and tax assessment (see Chapter 11). If you have a
regular job, assessed on a PAYE basis, you will be covered for
National Insurance, but additional earnings up to the specified
ceiling will be subject to a further payment. And you must, of
course, declare earnings additional to your salary on your
annual tax declaration.

The law

It is unlikely that the law will interfere with the service which
you intend to provide (there are exceptions but these are not
covered in this publication!). However, you should be careful
where you conduct your business from. If you set up your
business in what was previously a residence, you may need
planning permission, which you should obtain *before* con-
structing your design studio or building your workshop. Moreover, restrictions on operating businesses from privately rented
and council accommodation are very strict. If you cannot
obtain the necessary permission, remember that you can often
rent a small studio for upwards of £30 per week. This is not an
extravagant amount if you are confident of a reasonably
high and constant workload.

Selling is governed by a plethora of laws. You will need a
licence from the borough council for street vending and door-
to-door selling (the latter is now so strictly monitored as to be
almost prohibited). Similarly, if you try to turn your front
room into a showcase for your home-made jams, pots, clothes
and carved statues, you may fall foul of the law. There are
exceptions to this, and often the law is not enforced, but it is
as well to be informed on the legality of your activity and to

apply for planning permission and a licence to sell.

Self-employment overseas*

Many people do work overseas, often only for a few years, to earn high salaries as teachers, engineers, designers, technicians, managers and consultants of various types. Another group includes semi-permanent 'exiles', such as executives of major companies with bases overseas.

If you work and live overseas, you are exempt from UK tax unless you reside in the UK for more than 90 days in a single tax year (6 April to 5 April of the following year). However, gains on UK investments will be taxed as normal. You will, of course, have to pay tax in the country in which you are resident (unless your salary is tax-free). If you reside in the UK for more than 90 days you may have to pay tax on your income in both countries. Consult the Inland Revenue before you leave on the level at which you will be taxed, as rates on overseas earnings differ from standard UK rates.

A number of other points should be considered by the person who will be self-employed overseas:

1. You will not be as advantageously placed as someone sent overseas by his company. He will be protected and insured, will receive relocation allowances, and will be supported by his company in periods of difficulty, whereas you will have to fend for yourself in all these matters.†
2. Take out health insurance.
3. Have a contract with a *bona fide* employer *before* you leave if possible. Check his references, and be sure his company is not going to collapse as soon as you reach your (perhaps remote) destination.
4. Be aware of the cost of living in your chosen workplace: it is, for example, very high in parts of the EEC.
5. Make sure your documentation is correct: passport, visa, work permit, etc.
6. Check the currency regulations in the country where you will work: in particular, how much money can you bring out of the country?

---

* See Godfrey Golzen and Margaret Stewart (1980) *Working Abroad: A Guide to Living and Working Overseas.*

† This is less true in the other EEC countries, which have reciprocal arrangements with the UK to protect their respective citizens.

211

7. What are the working and living conditions there?
8. Is there an accessible UK or European community which will ease the transition to a new environment?
9. Will your UK interests be protected in your absence?
10. What will be the effect of the move on your immediate family? And, if they are travelling with you, how will they cope with your new surroundings?

20: Arts and Entertainment

The following are performance-based activities, about which little can be said except that you must offer something distinctive, be self-confident in performance, and not underestimate the competition and the problems such a career inevitably holds.

Acting

A career in acting is attractive to many people but demands talent, dedication, perseverance and luck. You will probably require training at a good drama college, and a place there will be attained only if you have a wide range of acting experience, proven ability and obvious enthusiasm. You may or may not make it from there: many would-be actors never graduate from walk-on parts or part-time and school entertainments. It is advisable to have a 'second string to your bow' if possible, such as a marketable degree or some other qualification. But this is almost an admission of defeat: if you are serious about acting, go ahead and do it and, if you fail, at least you have the consolation of knowing the attempt was not half-hearted. For information and advice contact Equity, the actors' union, and join the organisation as soon as possible. You will amost certainly have to be a paid-up member before you can undertake professional stage, TV and other work.

Peter Penry-Jones, a successful actor, emphasises the need for sound financial management: 'Get a good accountant and good professional/financial advice at an early stage. Everybody in the arts tends to get so immersed in their work that, with irregular cash flow and no interest in money, they end up in a financial mess. You can have an excellent quarter and go over the VAT threshold but then have hardly any other work for the remaining nine months of the year. Don't get so deep in your work that you ignore situations like this since they can eventually cause you tremendous headaches.

Cabaret artists

These vary considerably in quality and type. If you are not unduly worried about a career, just go ahead and enjoy it and, if you make some money too, fine. If you think you have talent (and others agree with you!) find a reputable agent, who will fix up dates at clubs, and wait to be discovered. Do not be bashful about putting yourself forward: take as many engagements as you can — the experience will be useful in developing a style to cope with difficult audiences and encourage 'thin' houses, etc.

Disc jockeying

Most people start doing DJ work because they enjoy entertaining people and listening to music. Essential requirements for the DJ are a lively, outgoing personality, a good knowledge of pop music (some DJs specialise in one particular type of music) and as large a selection of records as possible. Disc jockeys are engaged by clubs, pubs, etc, either on a regular basis or for one-off sessions. They are generally expected to bring their own records, but equipment may be provided.

The minimum equipment needed to run a mobile disco is a pair of turntables, an amplifier of about 50 watts, more if you think you will play at outdoor gigs or bigger venues, at least two 20-watt speakers, and some form of transport, preferably a van rather than a car. Shop around and find out what discounts are available through the Disc Jockey Federation. Above all, sound quality must be high and no amount of 'extras' will compensate for poor sound.

For the more ambitious, and those with more money to invest, a magnetic cartridge, which improves the quality of the sound, is recommended, and this involves the use of a pre-amplifier and a mixer. You will probably want to use more than two speakers, and a more high-powered amplifier. You may want to invest in stereo equipment, although you will find that this can create problems caused by the many different kinds of rooms in which you will want to use the equipment. Beyond basic equipment, you will decide to provide 'extras' such as a light show, a microphone for the DJ, a strobe, all of which can push your costs up considerably.

If you are going to operate a mobile discotheque as part of a public performance, which is defined as one which takes place 'outside the domestic or home life of the participants', it is necessary to obtain a licence from Phonographic Performance Ltd, 14-22 Ganton Street, London W1. A licence is needed for *any* kind of public performance: even a performance at a firm's dinner dance, for example, would need to be covered. The fees for a licence are on a sliding scale, depending on the amount of time and size of audience for which it is granted.

Playing a record involves two copyrights: that of the record company, which is covered by the licence from Phonographic Performance, and that of the music publisher and composer, which is covered by the Performing Right Society Ltd, 29 Berners Street, London W1. Most public halls are covered by a licence from the Performing Right Society, but you should check up on this before operating in a public place.

There are a large number of mobile discotheques operating, particularly in London and the Home Counties, so you will find that competition is keen. Demand tends to fluctuate seasonally, with November and December being the best months for bookings.

Advertising in local papers and magazines and the distribution of printed leaflets or business cards are recommended ways of getting bookings.

Pay is variable, according to the type of function and equipment used. Mobile discotheques charge between £40 and £60 a night for private parties, more for weddings and public functions. You must 'cost' your time to a certain extent: if you are playing at a private party, for example, it is likely that you will have to carry on well after midnight, and you should allow for this.

Music

The range of options is enormous: classical, jazz, folk, pop, rock; vocal or instrumental; in a band or solo, etc. The only rule is that you need ability and tenacity. Rock and pop venues will book you if you are good. Appearing gives you the chance of being seen, getting a recording contract, making discs, etc. Without record company backing, your position is difficult. Studio time to make demonstration tapes is extremely expensive. Even finding a good place to practise may be difficult, but persevere, practise, play as many gigs as possible, carve out a musical identity for yourself and you may succeed.

The position of the classical musician or singer is rather

different. He will probably have had a long period of formal, performance-based training and will aim to obtain a salaried position in an orchestra, ensemble, quartet etc, or recognition as a soloist. Competition is fierce: you have to be highly accomplished to play in any full-time orchestra, let alone one of the great British or international orchestras, and only the few, very finest talents work as soloists. Training is rigorous and, at the end of the course, those destined for a career as a professional musician will probably already be marked out.

Painting and sculpture

There are few ground rules in fine art and related areas. You will need a distinctive style, the capacity to carry through commissions, a good dealer to market your work, and great dedication. Competition is considerable, but the rewards of success are high. If you enjoy neither instant success nor financial patronage, be prepared to support your art with a second occupation, perhaps as a freelance designer or art teacher.

21: Media and Communications

This is an area in which much work is carried out on a freelance basis: design, research, writing, editing, etc. It is a good idea to work in a selected area and get to know it well before starting on your own, and talk to your peers, many of whom will probably work on a freelance basis.

Art and design

There are numerous opportunities for freelances in this area if you have talent, creativity, the ability to meet deadlines and a range of contacts in the business. You may be a book designer, illustrator, clothes designer, cartoonist or three-dimensional designer. The message is the same: if you are good and people who have used you have liked your work, you will be given a steady stream of work, for which you will be well paid.

You will probably have a design qualification, and you should specialise, but your chosen specialism does not have to be the area in which you qualified.

If you are successful as a freelance designer, you should invest in a good, well-lit, well-ventilated studio in which to work. And if demand for your services is very great, think about expansion: is there someone whose work is good who could be taken on as a business partner, perhaps, and could you delegate administrative chores to someone?

Editorial work

For proof-reading and copy editing, experience in a publishing house is a prerequisite. People tend to feel that proof-reading, in particular, only requires a good command of spelling and an eye for detail, but in fact it really requires some knowledge of the way a book is actually put together, and an eye for the kinds of mistakes that an inexperienced person would not necessarily pick up. No inexperienced person would be able to obtain freelance editorial work from any publishing firm.

However, if you have worked in publishing, you may be able to obtain freelance work through personal contacts. Forget the idea of advertising your services: it will almost certainly not work.

Editorial work is particularly suited to freelancing: most of it can be done more quickly and thoroughly in the quiet of one's own home than in the distracting hubbub of an office atmosphere. It also has the advantage of being time-consuming; once you have obtained a particular piece of work, you will usually find that it guarantees you one to two weeks' employment, and so you do not get into the situation in which some freelances find themselves, of having to spend up to half your time collecting and delivering work.

Freelance journalism

In theory, it is very simple to become a journalist: pick up a pen, buy a typewriter and offer your services to newspapers and magazines. In practice, it is very difficult: will anyone want your services? Join the freelance branch of the NUJ or the Institute of Journalists and try anything to get work, however mundane, on your local newspaper. With a range of varied writing and research jobs behind you, specialise — in art, music, business, book reviews, etc — and submit your work to national newspapers. Be prepared to write articles of any length, perhaps even a book on a topic in an area in which you can claim some expertise. In short, take whatever commissions come along until you have established a reputation and developed a relationship with a particular newspaper or magazine and its editor. Then, and only then, can you afford to pick and choose.

Indexing

Publishers have a constant need for indexers who they can trust to work quickly, efficiently and thoroughly. Indexing requires the ability to understand the arguments and principal themes a book and organise the material by keywords, often to a brief given by the author or publisher.

Various professional qualifications are obtainable in indexing, and the Society of Indexers operates a scheme of registered indexers for those with experience. Indexing is a skilled task and hourly rates for a qualified indexer are £3 to £4. As in many other areas, freelance indexers will tend to develop relationships with particular publishers, perhaps even with individual editors, especially if the indexer concentrates on a specific subject area.

Literary agency

The main 'qualifications' for establishing a literary agent's are long experience in and a thorough knowledge of publishing. You must know how and where to place books: how to put together a proposal to ensure a high percentage of acceptances; whether a book is a marketable commodity; and how the manuscript in front of you might be changed to make it more marketable. You will usually receive a commission on your client's (the author's) royalty. This may be easily earned – sending a manuscript to a publisher who knows instantly that he wants it, or very hard earned – reading the script, doctoring it, adding a contents, synopsis, proposal, etc.

Becoming a literary agent seems very attractive but it is very difficult to succeed: reputations take many years to be established, and a good list of authors is similarly difficult to develop. You will only succeed if you have a touch of creativity, strong business sense, a capacity for organization, patience and an entrée into the rather closed media and publishing worlds.

Market research interviewing

Market research interviewing mainly involves either visiting people in their own homes to ask them their views about commercial products (or possibly about social issues) or stopping people in the street to ask them a series of questions about a particular subject.

Basic requirements for the job are patience, perseverance, and the ability to relate to a wide variety of different types of people. You must be available to work some evenings and weekends, and possibly to spend the occasional night away from home. A car is not absolutely necessary, although it does help; and you must be on the telephone.

A short training course is provided by the large, reputable market research companies. It is fairly easy to be accepted for a training course, as interviewers are generally in short supply, but is is important to show that you are going to be available for work on a long-term basis, as the company sees your training as an investment.

Most interviewers put their names down with several market research companies. They can expect a steady flow of work, particularly in London, though probably less in the rest of the country.

Opportunities exist for promotion from interviewing to supervisory and managerial posts, but after promotion one would no longer be working on a freelance basis. Other types of freelance work, besides interviewing, are sometimes available from market research firms: clerical work, for example, or the coding of questionnaires.

If you are interested in working as a market research interviewer, write to the Market Research Society who will supply on request a list of research companies employing interviewers. Or you can contact one of the bigger, more reputable market research agencies such as the British Market Research Bureau Ltd or Research Bureau Ltd.

Pay rates are about £14 to £20 for a six-hour day, plus expenses. Pay can be higher for experienced interviewers.

Film-making

This is a notoriously competitive area; for every success, there are 99 (perhaps 999) failures. You will need experience of a range of techniques, including video and slide presentation, and you should work quickly and creatively, fulfilling commissions on time and to the specified budget. Only the fortunate few will *choose* which films to make; the rest will have to be satisfied with industrial, training and promotional films. But, remember, these often require great skill and imagination, will provide good experience and may lead to more ambitious and more personally fulfilling projects later.

Photography

As in other fields, in freelance photography you are more likely to succeed by organisation, reliability and perseverance than by sheer talent alone. If you are submitting samples of your work to magazines, journals and newspapers you must expect to have a large proportion of your work rejected; but on the small proportion that *is* accepted you can gradually build up your reputation with your clients.

Don't be misled by camera fanatics — it is important, of course, to have good, reliable equipment, but you don't necessarily need the most expensive, up-to-date gadgets and accessories to be a successful professional photographer. Far better to have sound, reliable equipment which you are happy with and you *know* that you can take good pictures with, and to take great care with the presentation of your work.

How to get work

Freelance photography covers such a wide area that it is difficult to cover all the possible avenues of entry to the profession. One fact stands out: there are a great many competent photographers, and so to be successful your pictures will have to have some special quality that makes them stand out, not necessarily in terms of technical proficiency but in terms of ideas. If you are trying to break into the women's magazine field, for example, it is no good taking along a portfolio of photographs which are almost exactly the same as the ones the magazine uses already; they know photographers who can produce these, and you must give them a very good reason for using you, as opposed to people they already know and trust.

Most of the larger magazines commission work, for which the photographer is paid on a fee basis. Standard practice for obtaining commissioned work is the submission of a portfolio, backed up by one or more personal visits, and it is likely that your personality and ideas will carry more weight with the art editor than your technical expertise, though of course you must be technically competent.

Submitting work 'on spec'

It is possible to make a living by submitting selections of prints to magazines 'on spec', particularly if you concentrate on small, specialised publications and local magazines and newspapers.

Presentation of your work is very important. Prints should be of the highest quality possible, and should be carefully packed to avoid damage by the Post Office. Your work should be clearly labelled, and it is a good idea to have a referencing number to each photograph, to avoid confusion.

You should offer 'single reproduction rights': this means that the print can be resold at a later date, and you retain the copyright.

Wedding photographs, passports, portraits

This area is one of the most attractive to people who want to make extra money from photography on a part-time basis, possibly graduating to full-time freelance work when they have established themselves. Work can be obtained through local advertising and personal contacts, and your local camera club should be able to give help and suggestions.

Payment

Rates of pay vary tremendously, since the work itself is so varied. Fees for commissioned work for the high-circulation magazines can be substantial, but most of this work goes to established photographers.

It is important to remember when dealing with magazines that payment may be delayed by as much as six months, and if you try to push for early payment you may make yourself very unpopular. It is unlikely, in any event, that you will be paid before publication. If you are going to be a full-time freelance photographer therefore, you shouldn't under-capitalise yourself, as it may be a year or so before you really begin to make enough money to live on.

PR and advertising consultancy

This is an expanding area with good opportunities for the self-employed person who has worked in promotion and marketing and now wants to work independently. But there are problems: how do you compete with large agencies with massive resources? The answer is that, for the most part, you do not: you offer consultancy (often to the agency rather than to the firm) on specific projects, in areas in which you have expertise. You can then allow your enterprise to develop, perhaps employing staff, developing and diversifying your services and challenging the larger organisations. In the short term, cultivate contacts, specialise in a single area, show very personal attention to clients and be satisfied with a steady flow of small projects.

We spoke to a public relations consultant who gave this advice to people thinking of going it alone: 'You have to do two things simultaneously — first the work in hand and second the constant search for new clients. Doing the former will obviously help with the latter, but don't get so tied up in your current work that you neglect to look ahead. If you start getting fairly regular work from a client then suggest you move from billing on a job by job basis to an annual contract; this will help your cash flow enormously and such a contract is also of very high value when talking to your bank manager or building society.'

Research

The term 'research' covers a broad area. Many researchers for television and radio, for various companies, for advertising agencies and marketing organisations — are not freelance. Some people do part-time market research (for which a telephone and car and an outgoing personality are necessary). Others work in individual research projects, for which particular academic and professional qualifications may be necessary. In general, a researcher should have had varied experience, have the capacity to work independently and quickly and to understand a library cataloguing system, be able to write reasonably well and to type. Opportunities to work may be erratic, and a range of very different projects may be taken on. There will probably be less opportunity to build relationships with particular clients, and assignments will often be one-off jobs. Rates of pay will also vary considerably.

Teaching and tutoring

If you have a degree, teacher's diploma or some other qualification, it is worth thinking about private coaching, especially if you have children of your own and perhaps find it difficult to work normal school hours. Try advertising in your local paper or, better still, in the personal columns of *The Times, Daily Telegraph* or *Times Educational Supplement*. State the subjects and the level to which you are prepared to teach. Demand will depend a lot on the area in which you live: you might do better in the 'smarter' areas where parents tend to worry more about their children's chances of winning scholarships, achieving university entrance, etc. There is a particular demand for tutors in mathematics and science subjects. As well as normal school subjects, there is also a demand for people who can teach the piano and other musical instruments or give extra coaching in various languages. The average rate for private tuition is £5 to £8 an hour, depending on the level.

You can register with a local or national educational agency such as Truman & Knightley or Gabbitas-Thring. It is also worth contacting your local education authority, which may have received an inquiry from parents or students. They might also put you on their books as someone who can do supply teaching in an emergency, which is also paid by the hour.

Teaching English as a foreign language (TEFL)

This has become a major area of employment, particularly for young people and recent graduates trying to earn some money in the UK or eager to go overseas. There are numerous language schools, particularly in south-east England, offering a variety of language courses to foreign students, businessmen etc. But be warned: some of these are rather fly-by-night operations and you should work for and be trained by a large and reputable company such as International House.

Whether you are working in the UK or overseas, you will probably need an EFL qualification, some teaching experience and/or a degree. If none of these is required, you can assume that the credentials of the organisation are doubtful. Be careful, if you plan to teach abroad, to check the status of the organisation for which you will work. Make certain that you have (and have checked) a contract of employment, that you know where you will stay and how high living costs there are. Too often, EFL teachers turn up to find they are being poorly paid for unreasonably long hours, or that the accommodation which comes with the job is poor but expensive, or that classes are large and difficult to handle.

Translating/interpreting

The growing emphasis on exports and on our links with the continent means that this is an expanding field. It is also a highly competitive one, though, and you need to have quite a lot to offer to make a successful living. Most translators work in French and German, for example, so it helps if you are an expert in one of the more unusual languages: there is a great demand at the moment for specialists in Chinese, Japanese and Arabic.

As well as having a language qualification, either a degree or college diploma (such as the Institute of Linguists qualification), you should also have some other skill or professional qualification to offer. Few firms employ translators for their knowledge of the language alone. They want people who can deal with business correspondence, translate engineering and computer manuals, medical textbooks, technical leaflets, advertising brochures for all kinds of products etc. It always pays to cultivate a special subject and become known as the expert in that field.

To get started try writing to all the translating agencies in the Yellow Pages. Business firms tend to put their work through these agencies, so unless you already have good contacts with a few firms, it is a good idea to get on to the books of an agency. If you fancy literary translating, the best idea again is simply to write round to all the publishing firms -- one of them might just happen to have some work going.

Rates of pay vary considerably, depending on the quality of your work, the degree of difficulty and the quality sought by the employer. Chinese and Japanese translators are the best paid, and European language translators the worst, with Arabic and Russian specialists somewhere in the middle. If you work for a company direct, without going through an agency, you can charge more. You *can* take on work for private individuals — letters, etc, but it is unlikely to be worthwhile financially, since you can't charge so much.

Being an interpreter requires very special qualities. Apart from having perfect knowledge of two foreign languages, you also need tremendous mental and physical stamina, very quick reactions, above-average intelligence and a good, wide education. These qualities are especially needed for conference work -- very few people are good enough, and there are only about 50 conference interpreters in the country, but you can also find work at exhibitions, business meetings, as couriers for travel agencies and guides for the London Tourist Board or the British Tourist Authority.

Writing

Freelance writing is a profession to which many are called but comparatively few are published and from the outset it should be said that, unless one is working or has worked on the staff of a newspaper or magazine of some standing, by which a network of professional contacts has been built up, it is a very difficult field for the total newcomer to break into. The best policy then is initially to consider freelance writing as a means of earning extra money over and above that earned from a regular job which will provide the safety net of a dependable income. If the job is in a related field, such as public relations, advertising or book publishing, so much the better from the point of view of giving the potential writer constant practice at the basics of word craft as well as the opportunity to make new and helpful personal contacts. For the purpose of this section it is assumed that the would-be freelance writer is considering producing articles and short fiction for newspapers or magazines, since first novels, always a favourite with new writers, are notoriously hard to place and, as the recent pressure for Public Lending Right shows, even well-established novelists find the financial returns on their work almost impossible to live on.

Unfortunately, many new freelance writers make the mistake of believing that they have only to write fluently and consistently, with perhaps a welcome seasoning of wit, to be successful in regularly placing their articles. In fact, ease and agility of verbal expression are merely the basic requirements of the journalist's draft and the key to success in placing articles lies firmly in:

1. The choice of a subject to write about.
2. Ensuring that the subject is presented in such a way that it can be readily assimilated into the publication to which you submit it.

The choice of a subject to write about is a more subtle and demanding undertaking than simply avoiding the submission of cookery articles to political weeklies. Such publications as *The Writers' and Artists' Year Book* list the basic spheres of interest of hundreds of periodicals and newspapers, but after such listings have been scanned for initial guidance, the freelance writer should then study with care several issues of the publication to which he would like to submit material. He should then aim to research and write up a subject which will fall within the sphere of interest of the publication, but which is unlikely to be covered by the full-time or regular part-time contributors to the publication. Similarly, it is best to avoid initially articles which involve a political or serious economic stance, since these are subjects for which even well-established staff are chosen carefully.

The aim, then, is to select a subject which is original and about which one may even have special knowledge in the hope that it will land on an editor's desk as a delightful addition to his page rather than a dubious repetition. Sometimes this oblique approach to freelance subject selection can turn into a more permanent proposition if one happens to stumble across a subject which a magazine or newspaper feels it is worth ultimately retaining a correspondent for. A classic example of this is beer, a subject for which at least one national newspaper now retains a correspondent in the manner of the already well-established wine or food correspondent.

In the case of writing short fiction a major market is the supply of romantic short stories to women's magazines. Here, although the choice of subject is in principle already determined the detailed development of the subject needs to be very accurately tailored to a specific magazine.

Many fiction editors on women's magazines receive a steady supply of short stories from literary agents, but it is virtually useless for the new freelance writer to attempt to place work by these means. The vast majority of literary agents will not agree to place short fiction, or indeed any short pieces, for writers who are not already on their books either as novelists or full-length non-fiction writers.

Presentation

Having thought out a suitable subject, equal care should be expended on the literary style of the potential piece. Here again, range of vocabulary, approach and length, not only of the piece but of paragraphs, can only be judged by a careful study of the publication to which the piece will be submitted. Major points to observe in the presentation of work may be summarised as follows:

1. Work should be typed, using one and a half or double spacing on one side of a sheet of paper only. Always retain a carbon copy.
2. Always read your typescript carefully before submitting it and make any corrections, which should be very minor, as clearly as possible.
3. Never submit a manuscript without a covering letter, but keep the letter brief. A covering letter should give the gist of your piece in no more than a sentence or two and draw to the editor's attention any recent or particularly

prestigious published work which will help him to get a fuller picture of you.

4. Before writing a covering letter, telephone the publication to obtain the name of the person to whom you should submit the work. This is particularly useful when submitting material to newspapers which tend to be very departmentalised.

5. If your article has any particularly topical connections which give it a limited 'shelf-life' say so in your covering letter and then telephone after several days for a decision. Many articles, rejected by one publication, can quite often be quickly but sensitively revamped and successfully placed with a rival magazine.

6. When submitting articles to illustrated magazines it is often useful to team up with a freelance photographer, if, and only if, your article directly benefits from illustrations.

7. Never submit uncaptioned photographs and present captions typed on a separate sheet. Remember that two apposite and technically excellent photographs are better than half a dozen fuzzy snap-shots.

8. If your article is rejected accept the editor's decision cheerfully and courteously and never attempt to get him to change his mind by arguing. Rejecting scores of unsolicited articles by telephone is one of the least pleasant editorial jobs and whether you agree with them or not, editors know what they want. Nor should you expect editors to constructively criticise your work, after all they are running publications, not a school of journalism.

Finally, two rules:

1. Never turn a job down, however small and anonymous that job may be and always get commissioned work in on time.

2. Spare no effort when checking that your facts are right. The beginner who acquires a reputation for inaccurate reporting or slip-shod research may as well give up. If a paper or magazine accepts your article, but holds it over for several months, remember to keep abreast of any new developments in the interim: accuracy applies not only to the time or writing, but more important, to the time of publication.

One full-time writer we approached gave this advice: 'Discipline, discipline, discipline! These are the three key words for any budding writer to remember. Get up early and keep at it. If you're stuck for words get something down regardless — you can always change it later. Work hard at your contacts, the people who will buy or recommend buyers for your work. It's no good writing the finest short story or the best technical description of a new widget if you can't then sell your piece.'

22: Crafts

All types of crafts can be conducted from the home or a studio and many talented individuals can earn a living as a potter, dressmaker, etc, or simply earn a little extra money knitting, mending clothes, etc.

Dressmaking

There are various types of dressmaking that can be done at home: outwork for the garment trade; running up made-to-measure clothes; repairs and alterations; and specialised work such as leather work, embroidery or crochet, which can be sold to boutiques or through mail order. 'Outwork' is repetitive and the pay is low: it is not recommended. Making clothes for friends and for customers brought in by advertisements and recommendations is much more interesting, though even here the rewards may not be high. The easiest type of work is when the customer presents you with a commercially produced pattern and fabric for it, so all you have to do is cut it out and sew it together. Making your own patterns, on the other hand, requires a fair amount of skill as translating a flat piece of paper into a three-dimensional garment is quite a complicated business. If you *do* know how to make your own patterns, then the customer can present you with a rough sketch, or even just a description, and you work from there.

If the customer does not present you with the fabric for the garment she may give you vague instructions and then be unhappy with your interpretation of them. A compromise could be for you to go shopping with her, to ensure that the chosen fabric is suitable and that sufficient quantities are bought. Thread, zips and trimmings can be bought at the same time. Alternatively, you could build up your own stock. by buying remnants and reduced lines, and offer the customer a choice from these.

It is important to have a fitting as soon as the garment is in one piece, and a second fitting may be needed to check on details such as the hang of a sleeve or to make sure that the collar lies flat.

Alterations (zips, hems, etc) form quite a high proportion of the work of many home dressmakers. These jobs can be fiddly and time-consuming, but it is not possible to charge much for this type of work, so if you advertise your services you may find it worth your while to emphasise the fact that you do not do alterations.

Embroidered, leather or crochet garments can be sold to boutiques or by mail order (most women's magazines carry small ads for clothes). You must make sure that you have sufficient stock to cover any bulk orders you may receive. You also need a talent for sensing fashion trends almost before they happen, as it will take several months before your garments appear in the shops.

You really need an electric sewing machine: a swing-needle one will enable you to do zigzag stitches, useful for buttonholes, neatening off raw edges and simple embroidery. A zip foot for the machine is also desirable. Other pieces of equipment you will need are pins, shears, needles, thread (keep two or three reels of black and white in stock, and buy other colours when you need them), french chalk, a buttonhole cutter, a tape measure and a steam iron.

Jewellery

The designing and making of jewellery is a highly competitive business. Before investing in expensive materials and equipment, you must prove to yourself that you have some flair for design and are suitably skilful with your hands. Starting off with lapidary work is a good way of finding out if you have the necessary artistic ability, and, most important, if anyone wants to buy your designs. From there, the best plan is to take an art college or City and Guilds course in jewellery, and sell the results while you develop some expertise. The great advantage of doing this is that you can use college equipment while you gradually build up your own collection of tools.

The most successful students find that they have no difficulty in selling their work while they are still at college. Start by showing off your handiwork to friends, if your work is good enough your reputation will spread by word of mouth and you will soon find the orders coming in. From there you can progress to taking samples of your work round the various jewellers and department stores in the hope of getting orders. You can also hire a stall in a street market on Saturdays and see how successful you are.

The initial outlay on tools can be quite small, especially if you are able to use college equipment as well. Eventually, of course, you will need your own equipment and this can be expensive so you would be wise to save some of your initial profits towards buying equipment. Materials are also expensive, and it is important to get the pricing right, if you are going to make a reasonable profit. Here your best plan is simply to show samples to a well-established jeweller. He will soon tell you how much he would charge, since he obviously does not want to be undercut by a newcomer.

Knitting and crochet

If you are a quick skilful worker, good at spotting fashion trends, you will probably be able to make a living making hats, scarves, sweaters, children's clothes, etc. Buy the wool wholesale from one of the Yorkshire mills (they advertise in the women's magazines) and be prepared to spend all your free time slogging away. The quicker you are the better, of course. Take samples round the local craft and gift shops and suitable stall-holders in local street markets. If your work is really eye-catching and original, try some of the big department stores.

If you want to take on big orders, the best plan would be to find a few housebound housewives with the necessary skill who would be glad of some pocket money. You might even think of going into partnership with another knitter.

Knitwear firms are often on the lookout for people who can knit or crochet specialised merchandise, but be careful: they pay very low rates.

Knitting with a machine is much faster, and you might consider investing in a second-hand machine. ILEA runs courses for the use of knitting machines; consult your local public library for courses in other areas.

How much should you charge? You can price similar goods in the shops, but remember that the shop wants its cut too, so you will have to be content with less than the shop price. On the other hand people are usually willing to pay more for hand-made goods; if you charge too little, you will have to slave away for hours and hours to make any money at all.

Lapidary work

Lapidary is the art of working in gemstones or pebbles and it forms an excellent introduction to the art of making jewellery, since the basic materials are not so expensive as in jewellery proper.

Learning the techniques of lapidary work is quite simple: there are many books on the subject, as well as clubs and societies. *Gems* is a monthly magazine which lists suppliers, as well as clubs and organisations. Most books will also give you a list of the tools and equipment required. The main item of equipment for lapidary work at home is a tumbler, which is used for grinding and polishing the stones (obtained from craft shops) which are then set in silver, copper, steel etc to make rings, pendants or brooches.

You will have to be patient; it can take up to 12 weeks to polish a consignment of stones. But you should then have no trouble selling your pieces via local shops, stalls in the local market, department stores, even coffee mornings. Do not undersell your work, look round the shops and see what comparable pieces fetch before offering your work to a shop.

Making loose covers and curtains

To make a living sewing, you must be an experienced and fast worker. Loose covers in particular involve far more work than the inexperienced would ever imagine, so do not gaily undertake to re-cover someone's sofa over the weekend. There are plenty of good handicraft books that give step-by-step directions, and provided you follow them accurately you should not have any problems, even as a beginner. The most important point with loose covers is to know how to measure up accurately, and this is essential when dealing with expensive fabrics.

You will need a sewing machine with a piping foot, enough room to lay the material out properly for cutting and measuring, a really good pair of dressmaking scissors, and a good deal of patience.

You will soon find work by advertising in the local papers, and by word of mouth, once you have done a few jobs. To find out what to charge, ring up one of the big department stores that offer this service and ask them for a quote: make sure your quoted price is then a few pounds cheaper and you will have no trouble finding more work.

Beware of taking on too much and so failing to deliver the goods in time. Take on one job at a time, until you know exactly how long it takes you to do a pair of curtains, or a chair cover, etc. Otherwise, you will end up with a lot of irate clients and a bad reputation for being unreliable.

Picture framing

Some local authorities run evening courses in picture framing. It is also possible to learn the craft by working in a gallery, though usually galleries are rather a 'closed shop'. Basically, as with all crafts, it is best to experiment as much as possible before you undertake commercial work. You need a good work table and some large shelves on which to store your work. Basic tools are a mitre saw for the corners; clamps, to hold the corners together while they are being glued; accurate rulers and a set square; hammer and nails, and a vice and mount cutter are useful, though not strictly necessary.

You will also need mouldings, a backing board, which can be either card or hardboard, and glass. Your local glass merchant will cut glass to the right size for you: this is easier than doing it yourself.

Suppliers are often unwilling to supply materials in small quantities, but if you look around, you should be able to find some small firms who are willing to do so. If you are keen on jumble sales, you will find that you can often pick up old picture frames for next to nothing, and these can be revamped.

For making the actual frames, great care and accuracy is needed in order to get the mitred edges to fit exactly. Step-by-step instructions for making different types of frames are given in *Framing* by Eamon Toscano. Compare prices by asking galleries and picture-framing shops for quotations.

Pottery

It is possible to 'teach yourself' by reading and experimentation, but if you want to take a course many local authorities run evening classes in pottery (they are popular so book as early as you can).

Unless you are going in for pottery in a small way, you will need plenty of space for working and storage. It is a good idea to convert your garage, or an outside shed, into a work room since it then won't matter if you make a mess. Your work room should ideally be equipped with a decent-sized sink, a solid work-surface, preferably with a plain wooden top, plenty of shelves, a damp cupboard (which can be a wooden cupboard lined with plastic sheeting or with slabs of plaster which are periodically soaked in water), and a waterproof container for storing clay. Other basic requirements are the kiln (if you are eventually planning on a high turnover of work, you will need to buy the largest kiln you can afford); the potter's wheel (though this is not absolutely necessary for a beginner, since you can do mould, slab and coil pottery without one); an assortment of bowls, buckets, basins, sieves, etc; and a set of small tools — cutting wire, a knife, scrapers, 'bats' (squares of hardboard used for carrying and drying pottery), sponges, brushes and modelling tools.

You may prefer to use your own local clay, in which case you will have to devote time to its preparation; or you can buy it ready-prepared from a potter's merchant or pottery supply house. Local brickworks will often supply clay cheaply, though it may need some extra preparation. It is usually supplied by the hundredweight, and smaller amounts are proportionately more expensive. It is important that it should be kept in a cool, damp place.

You can buy ready-made glazes, though it is possible to mix your own. You will also need sand, slow-setting potter's plaster grog, oxides, slips (englobes) and wax. A detailed list of suppliers is given in *Simple Pottery* by Kenneth Drake, an excellent book which is recommended for the beginner.

If you visit craft shops with samples of your work, you will find that some will take pots on a sale or return basis, whilst others will buy a small quantity of your work outright and order more if it sells. Alternatively, you may want to sell your work direct to the customer, in which case you could start off by hiring a market stall, with the eventual aim of owning your own shop.

Upholstery

This is an area where it really pays not to price yourself out of the market. The real dyed-in-the-wool professional is so expensive that many people cannot afford the prices. If you have served a long apprenticeship you are of course entitled to charge the top rate; but if you are planning to work as you learn, set your sights a bit lower financially and you will find far more work. You can either buy junk furniture to do up yourself, or advertise to do up other people's furniture. Until you have had some experience, it is probably best not to invest too much money in buying furniture, unless you have lots of storage room and no immediate need for the cash.

You can start out via evening classes, or inquire at your local public library. There are plenty of good books on the subject, and you should soon be able to tackle bedroom or dining room chairs, footstools, etc, without any trouble, but do not attempt buttoning, springs, chaise longues, etc until you have had a bit more experience.

There is a tremendous demand for reasonably priced upholsterers, so you should not have much trouble finding work. Advertise in your local paper or even in the national press, once your work is good enough to tackle big pieces. It is also worth visiting a few antique shops, since they often have upholstery jobs to be done.

The right tools are very important and not too expensive. You will need a webbing stretcher, tack hammer, set of upholstery needles and a regulator. You can buy the tools and materials from specialist suppliers, which are listed in the Yellow Pages.

Trevor Constable, a furniture restorer, mentioned some of the pitfalls to beware: 'You can't go for work like a bull at a gate. Antique dealers will promise you lots but little will materialise. If you've got the skill word will get around and work will come in. Don't put all your eggs in one basket. Get a range of customers and don't rely on one source for more than say a third of your total work. If you are totally committed to one source and it dries up . . . you're out of business.'

23: Construction, Building and Maintenance Services

Builders, carpenters, plumbers and electricians are in constant demand. Established firms charge high labour rates, and people qualified in these trades can obtain a steady income by taking on extra work at reasonable rates. Alternatively, if you are more ambitious, you may start a building or redecoration company. You will need some capital, the necessary equipment, some means of transport, and a rudimentary administrative system - - to take commissions for work, send invoices, check payments, keep tabs on costs, etc.

You may also need a tax exemption certificate, which customers (such as the local authorities) will require to ensure that you are a Schedule D taxpayer. If you work solely for private householders, small shops, etc, you will not need this certificate. But, if you work for a main contractor, local authority or government department, you will have 30 per cent of all bills (except the cost of materials and VAT) automatically deducted by them, unless you have this certificate.

The Inland Revenue publishes a guide on how to apply for and use these certificates. If you are refused a certificate, and without one you will find work difficult to get, you can appeal within 28 days to the local general commissioners.

Training

The orthodox training for these trades is by entering into apprenticeship after leaving school, but it is now also possible for older people to learn these skills at government training centres (details from your local employment office). Courses for manual trades last six months, after which there is a year's probationary period with an employer. Trainees are paid an allowance whilst taking the six-month course.

Much of the work available in private households consists either of very small jobs, such as putting up shelves or wall-papering, or conversion work, for which you must take into account building regulations and you or the house owner should get planning permission if applicable. You will find that the wider the range of skills you can offer, the more you will be in demand, since one job might involve both carpentry and decorating for example.

It is advisable to work with a partner, since you will often need help with lifting, measurement, etc. You also will find that it is invaluable to have contacts who specialise in other, related trades, since you will often find that you cannot complete a job without the help of, say, an electrician. Contacts will also help you to find work since they will get in touch with you to finish jobs that they themselves cannot complete.

The building regulations

Major structural changes must conform with national and local building regulations. If in doubt, consult your local authority (ask for the District Surveyor or Building Inspector).

Planning permission needs to be granted for external extensions exceeding 1300 cubic feet. If the building you are working on is listed as being of historic interest there may be regulations against changing its external appearance — again check with the local authority. These problems concern the person who commissioned the work more than you, but it is as well to guard yourself against liability.

How to get work

As explained above, contacts in related trades are invaluable. You might also obtain subcontracted work from small building firms. Landlords and property agents are useful people to cultivate, as they often provide a great deal of maintenance and conversion work. You may also wish to advertise in the local press. But beware of making claims which you cannot support: do not, for example, say that you are a master builder if you hold no such certificate.

Sources of information

1. The Department of the Environment publishes a leaflet called *How To Find Out: Getting the Best from Building Information Services,* listing 80 important information

sources for the construction industry. They also publish a large number of advisory leaflets on subjects such as *Emulsion Paints, Frost Precautions in Household Water Supply, Sands for Plasters, Mortars and Renderings,* etc. These are available from HMSO bookshops or from *Building Centres* and other booksellers.

2. There are 13 *Building Centres* in different regional locations. The address of the London branch is 26, Store Street, London WC1. The other branches are at Belfast, Birmingham, Bristol, Cambridge, Coventry, Dublin, Glasgow, Liverpool, Manchester, Nottingham, Southampton, and Stoke on Trent.

3. The Building Research Establishment is the largest and most comprehensive source of technical advice available to the construction industry. It operates from three centres --Watford, Birmingham and Glasgow.

Industrial/window cleaning

Cleaning, traditionally low-paid, unskilled work, can be a useful 'filler-in' for people in unreliable, chancy professions such as acting or modelling. Its great advantage is that work can often be obtained at very short notice and then dropped once something more lucrative comes up.

Alternatively, you may wish to do it on a much more organised and long-term basis. Companies and shops are increasingly using outside cleaning agencies rather than their own staff to clean their premises. This means regular and reasonably well paid work for those able to offer a thorough and dependable cleaning service, often at unseasonable times and perhaps in bad conditions.

Local advertising, once again, is one of the traditional methods of finding domestic cleaning work. Personal contacts and local women's organisations are another source. Domestic cleaners are usually in great demand, so you should not have any problems.

You may prefer to do office cleaning, in which case you should telephone small offices and ask for work, advertise in the local paper, or start an office or industrial cleaning company.

Setting up your own cleaning agency is a relatively straightforward affair, since you can initially do the cleaning yourself and then graduate to a purely administrative and coordinating role, taking on casual workers as and when the need arises.

Pay for domestic cleaners in London is usually about £2.00 an hour, and a little less outside London. Fares are often paid as well. Rates paid to industrial and window cleaners vary considerably, depending on the size and nature of the job, the number of cleaners involved, the frequency of the service, etc.

Painting, decorating, plumbing and electrical work

These are areas which attract numerous 'cowboys', offering little or no expertise and a generally poor service. Fortunately, because continued custom depends so much on word of mouth, the rogues tend to fall by the wayside and only those offering a professional service survive. If you are experienced in one of these areas, try it for a while on a part-time basis and, if you have a steady stream of jobs and apparently satisfied customers, enter the profession full time.

You will probably have been employed with a firm in this capacity and may at first worry about days (or weeks) without work and a long-term shortage of orders. But you must learn to live with the downturns, and price your work for jobs accordingly. These services are always in demand, and if you do a competent job at a competitive price you will survive. Word of mouth will win you most orders but, if you can cope with additional work, go out and look for it: put ads in the windows of local shops, in local newspapers and in the Yellow Pages.

We spoke to a painter and decorator who offered this advice: 'It's silly to start with no work in hand so make sure you have sufficient work before you take the plunge. By "sufficient" I don't mean bits and pieces but solid full time jobs. Recommendation is better than advertising and do a good job for a fair price.'

24: Selling

Selling anything calls for a lot of self-confidence, determination and perseverance. You have to be prepared to go out on the road and meet perfect strangers, chase up every contact, however vague, ring up firms that might conceivably be interested, and always be prepared for rebuffs, rudeness or just plain indifference. It helps if you have previously had a job that involves meeting lots of people, such as market research.

Selling insurance

To get started, write to several of the big insurance companies. If you are accepted by one of them, you will be sent on a short training course. After that, you are on your own, though of course most firms give a lot of guidance at first and may even send someone out with you on a few calls to give you a bit of confidence. You will be expected to work from home, though some companies do provide a desk and a telephone (otherwise you have to pay your own telephone bills). How much time you spend in the office with colleagues, picking up tips and discussing plans of campaign, is entirely up to you.

The various companies do operate slightly different systems of payment: some pay a salary, of varying size, in conjunction with commission, while with others you will be on a straight commission basis. It helps to have some money behind you while you are getting established, as it may take a while for the first cheque to come in.

There are also opportunities for those experienced in insurance to establish themselves as brokers, and Chips Carpenter, one such broker, gives this advice: 'When you start up make sure you have enough capital to carry you through the first one to two years. That way you cannot be influenced to give the wrong advice to a client in a commission war, ie you will not be open to inducements.

Familiarise yourself thoroughly on the taxation and accountancy front for three reasons:

1. For your own bookkeeping purposes.
2. So you know where you stand all the time and are not reliant on your accountant/taxman to tell you your profit and tax liability.
3. In order that you can give the best possible advice to your clients.

Represent say a dozen good companies so that you can assist all types of clients with all types of needs.'

Freelance representation

Most firms have representatives who liaise with clients. The majority are attached to, and paid a salary by, the company, but some are freelance. Freelance terms differ widely: some reps receive expenses plus fee plus commission on orders taken; others are paid expenses plus commission; still others are on a straight commission (percentage of orders personally obtained or area sales). Before you sign an agreement to act as a company's representative, make certain that you understand the terms of the contract and, in particular, the method of remuneration.

'Repping' for any company and selling any product demands self-confidence, a degree of brashness, the ability to communicate and conjure up enthusiasm where perhaps none exists, a 'track record' in salesmanship, good references and, probably, a clean driving licence. Peter Ayres, a manufacturer's agent, offers some sound advice on how to keep up your flagging spirits: 'Do not get despondent if you do not do much business one week. It's your results over a period of a year say that count. Keep pressing on and remember that the last call of the day could be the best. Also do not carry too many different lines (ie too many agencies); do a good job for a few companies and build up gradually.'

On the credit side, you are to some extent free to choose an area in which to work and largely unrestricted in choosing a 'style' or approach. However, these advantages are to some extent illusory, for to be successful it may be necessary to concentrate on, obtain a knowledge of and build up contacts in, one trade and one location. Very few salesmen can sell freezers in Alaska (and those who do will have an intimate knowledge of freezers *and* of Alaskans).

Door-to-door selling

Restrictions on what can be sold 'door-to-door' and on methods of selling and a very rigorous code of practice have severely curtailed this practice. In any case, it is hopelessly inefficient, given the prospective customer's innate hostility to unsolicited offers. If you have a product which you think you can sell, there must be a better way of doing it!

Street vending

There are important regulations on street selling which must be observed. A vendor will almost invariably require a licence from the local authority to sell a particular product at a particular place. It may also stipulate days and times when the vendor may operate. This licence may be renewable, and the vendor's stall may be inspected to ensure that the conditions of the licence are being observed.

It is usually worth setting up a stall at an established street market, particularly if you select a market where you think the audience is suitable for your product. Though you may have to pay a fee to pitch your stall at an established market, it will prove financially worthwhile as you are guaranteed a large audience. The only problem is that some markets have long waiting lists, so apply early.

Mail order selling

Many people, particularly women, earn money acting as agents for mail order companies. Anyone over 18 can apply to become an agent, based at home and offering the company's goods as advertised in catalogues which are produced once or twice a year. They receive a commission of 10 or 12½ per cent on sales they make, in return for which they collect and record payments from customers and send regular payments to the mail order company. There may be additional problems of receiving and distributing goods, returning faulty products, dealing with bad debts, etc. These may be considerable if the agent tries to build up a large number of clients, drawn from a wide circle. Many do not do so, preferring to use the catalogues as a source of goods, purchased on credit terms, for friends and family. Few people earn a decent income as an agent, and some who do experience administrative and other difficulties.

25: Transport

Light removals

If you can afford to invest in a reasonable, fairly large second-hand van, you can do light removals. This service is in great demand, particularly in the larger cities. All that you need is a van, a telephone, a few advertisements in local shop windows, recommendations from friends, and you are in business! This sort of work can easily be done on a part-time basis, as people moving flats are likely to want to move at weekends or in the evenings. If you want to work full-time, though, it might be worth setting up a partnership with two or three other van owners, with a central office and a full-time receptionist to answer the telephone and arrange bookings. People wanting to hire a van for a couple of hours are likely to ring another firm if you are not in or cannot come at a particular time, but if you have a receptionist to allocate the work, three of you are each likely to get more work than any one of you could handle independently. A small van can also be used to handle small deliveries for private firms, distributing magazines, for example.

You should charge from the time you leave home until the time you arrive back (ie you include the time it takes you to get to and return from a particular job).

Cab driving

Apart from orthodox taxi firms, which employ full-time drivers 'plying for hire' (ie to a large extent picking up fares on a casual basis in the street), there are also cab hire firms who supply cars with drivers on demand, in response to a telephone call or some other kind of prior arrangement. These firms do not maintain a vehicle fleet of their own but employ outside people, generally part-timers, who drive their own cars, picking up the cab hire firm's clients. The cab hire firm thus acts in somewhat the same way as an employment agency; they supply the leads for drivers on their books.

To get this type of work you should have a clean driving

licence and you must take out a special 'hire and reward' insurance. Remuneration varies from place to place and from firm to firm, but like ordinary taxi fares it is based on the mileage, the time the job takes and the hour at which it is carried out. The cab hire firm lays down the rates and a percentage of the fare has to be paid to them on each job, though there are some firms that make a flat weekly charge to drivers on their books.

Work is obtained initially by phoning in to base, which is obviously chancy. However, once you have established your status as a regular, many cab hire firms will offer to lease to you or otherwise supply you with a two-way radio and this is a much more reliable way of keeping up the flow of jobs.

Cab driving involves working long hours in order to make an adequate income, and remember that you must allow for petrol, depreciation and insurance. However, the casual nature of cab driving makes this a suitable occupation for those who are filling in time between salaried work.

Cab hire firms are to be found in Yellow Pages. Alternatively, your local garage may be able to advise you of good firms who are looking for drivers with their own cars.

Heavy goods transport

This is a very different proposition to light removals. You will require a heavy goods vehicle (HGV) licence, which is obtained only by passing a rigorous driving test, and an operators' ('O') licence, which is only issued if you can prove that you can finance a successful haulage operation.* Moreover, even if you do obtain a licence, the outlay needed to establish a haulage firm is considerable: buying or hiring vehicles, servicing them, buying parts, employing drivers. It is difficult just to operate locally: you need to be able to transport goods throughout the country, at reasonable rates, in competition with long-established and heavily-capitalised haulage operators. Do not be deterred by these problems, but be aware of them, particularly if you have to prove how workable your scheme is to a bank manager or some other financer.

---

* The criteria for acceptance by the licensing authority include proven professional competence, sound financial backing, and satisfactory premises from which to operate.

Repairs and services

Every car owner believes himself to be a mechanic, but to be able to work on a wide range of cars and deal with many different types of problem requires considerable expertise. So, do not set up a car workshop if you do not have the necessary training and experience. Moreover, you will require a good deal of capital – to acquire large premises, and the range of materials and fittings needed to undertake the work. Competition is also severe – there are many large, established garages with a team of mechanics. Can you provide services at competitive prices and with comparable efficiency and speed? Garage mechanics get a bad press, but this does not necessarily make the area an easy one in which to establish a new operation.

Dennis Edmonson, who specialises in car repairs and servicing, emphasises the need for expertise: 'Don't be tempted to take on work you are not sure you can complete to a high standard. Familiarise yourself with all the rules and regulations which surround the transport industry today, and don't get flustered by the bureaucrats who will constantly be on at you. Be wary of the travellers and agents who will call every week trying to con you into purchasing materials/machinery you don't really need.'

26: Miscellaneous Services

Catering

A freelance cook can find plenty of work catering for small social functions such as church gatherings or club meetings, as well as private functions such as dinner parties. Simple buffet catering for small gatherings of up to 50 people or dinner parties for up to 20 guests can be managed singlehanded: a team of several caterers, of course, could handle larger functions.

The key to successful catering on a small scale is careful organising and planning. Costing is an important element in planning, and costs can be kept to a minimum by buying in bulk and eliminating waste. It is recommended that you work out your overall costs, taking into account overheads such as petrol, equipment, etc, and then add on a percentage for your own labour. Twenty-five per cent is reasonable. Careful timing and coordination, so that you do not find that the coffee is slowly getting cold while the last speech is still in progress, is also important.

Equipment can be bought from cash and carry centres. You will also need some form of transport, preferably a van rather than a car. Food can be bought wholesale from cash and carry centres. Keep everything simple. Do not take on elaborate menus or complicated dishes until you have mastered the organisational problems involved in catering for groups.

Contacts can be made through church organisations, local social clubs, etc and direct mail or the local paper is a good way of advertising your services.

We spoke to a self-employed caterer who described some of the problems you may face in this area: 'You've got to have stamina and be prepared to work long hours . . . You have to be on the ball, leaving nothing to chance. You are wide open to fiddling and pilfering — anything from teabags to sides of meat goes — so you have to have good controls. Make yourself different or special in some way and offer impeccable service. It might be just one more wedding to you but it's the day of a lifetime to your client's daughter. You have to be able to step in and do any job that's needed, from waitressing to cooking to cleaning out the loos.'

Home typing and secretarial work

This kind of work is well suited to those who wish to work from home. Little capital investment is needed; obviously one's own typewriter is necessary, but a second-hand electric typewriter can be hired for around £50 per month, or bought for about £250 upwards (depending on the model). No one is going to make a fortune doing typing at home, but the skilled typist may be able to make more money at home than in the average secretarial job, provided she can find sufficient work to do. There are certain pitfalls to be avoided, such as envolope typing, which is notoriously underpaid, but on the whole this is an area in which it is possible to make a reasonable amount of money, and which has the advantage of being flexible enough to fit in with domestic commitments.

We talked to a secretary working at home who gave three pieces of advice to other competent typists/secretaries thinking of working independently: 'Aim your services at the person who does not have sufficient work to employ a secretary (eg local small businesses) or the person with the one off major job (eg the PhD student with a 500-page thesis). Price your regular work by the hour and for one-off jobs quote an overall fee. Be wary of offering to let your clients quote your phone number as a place that messages can be left. You'll be woken up during the night and if you pop out to the shops a desperately urgent call will go unanswered.'

How to find work

Classified advertisements are one source: authors sometimes advertise for people to type their manuscripts, for example. However, you will probably do better to insert your own classified advertisements in selected newspapers or put a note on the local university notice board, offering to type manuscripts. theses, etc. Another good place to advertise is the trade press, particularly if you have experience of doing secretarial work in a specialised area. Local advertising in shop windows, local newspapers and magazines might also be effective, as people requiring your services would have the advantage of knowing that you were close at hand.

248

It is perhaps better, though, to contact potential employers directly. People such as clergymen, MPs, doctors and architects, and various clubs, associations, and even some businessmen often require part-time secretarial serivces, which can easily be provided from home. For this kind of work, it helps if you can do audio-typing, as you can then collect tapes and take them home, rather than having to take shorthand dictation.

Rates of pay

Pay for home typing is around £3.00 to £5.00 per hour, or more if you are particularly skilled, if you are typing mathematical formulae or if you are working to a tight brief. Thesis and manuscript typing is sometimes paid according to the number of words typed, with a fixed charge per 1000 words. If you are doing this kind or work, and your typing is fast, it is probably more profitable to charge a fixed fee per thousand words. For letter typing, however, an hourly charge is probably preferable. Remember to keep an accurate record of the number of hours worked, and include the time that you have to spend collecting and delivering work.

Running your own typing agency

The employment agency field no longer offers the kind of opportunities it once did, as many large firms have moved into the area. However, there is one type of agency, admittedly limited in scope, which is a reasonable proposition for the independent operator. This is the small envelope typing and direct mail agency. You contact firms which do a lot of their business by sending circulars out to people, offering to handle their whole distribution, typing envelopes or labels, inserting circulars into envelopes and postage. The administrative work for this kind of business can easily be handled by one person (from their own home if convenient) and the actual mechanical work of envelope typing and stuffing can be farmed out to outworkers.

Typesetting

If you are a *very* good typist, one of the most interesting and worthwhile possibilities for freelance work would be typesetting. A high degree of skill is needed, and a fairly large investment (particularly for a compugraphic machine) but this area offers far greater potential for high earnings and job involvement than straightforward typing.

The job involves preparation of typed matter which will eventually be printed photographically. Many small magazines, advertisements and books are now produced in this way rather than by traditional letterpress printing.

The matter to be printed is typed out on an IBM or word-processing typesetting machine, which produces copy similar in every respect to that produced by normal printing.

The best way to get involved in this area would be to gain some initial experience by working for a small typesetting firm, before setting up on your own. It may also be important to be unionised, since many printers will not accept work from non-union typesetters. Check this out thoroughly before setting up your own typesetting operation.

Rates for jobs vary considerably — according to the type of job, the deadline to be met, the quality of your machine, your accuracy, etc. It is best to quote per page rates, though you will need experience to be able to assess and 'price' manuscripts! Work can be obtained from publishing firms, design consultants, advertising agents, etc.

Modelling

All kinds of people are needed as photographic and still-life models for advertisements, posters, etc. The main requirements are self-confidence, poise, and a reasonably well stocked wardrobe; but most important of all, your face and figure must be just what the photographer or artist wants at the time.

The work can be very varied, involving short bookings lasting an hour or so, or location sessions lasting several days. You must be prepared, sometimes, for long delays whilst equipment and props are arranged, so you must have a reasonable degree of patience; it is also important that you should be absolutely punctual and reliable.

A lot of the opportunities for photographic models are in London, but it is possible to obtain modelling work elsewhere, particularly fashion modelling.

How to get work

The first step is to find an agent: look in Yellow Pages under 'model agencies'. You can also make direct approaches to photographers and art colleges: look in Yellow Pages under 'commercial and industrial photographers'.

If you are registered with an agent, get him to recommend a photographer, and have some sample pictures taken These will form the basis of a composite, or montage, of the model's best pictures, printed on two sides of a single sheet or on four sides of a small folder. Fees are usually paid through the agent, who deducts commission, normally 15 per cent of any modelling fee. Avoid agents who ask for a registration fee before taking you on to their books.

Playgroup leaders

Playgroups cater for pre-school age children, and are usually run on a fairly informal basis, either by one woman in her own home (possibly with the help of a friend or neighbour) or, for larger groups, by several people using a public hall or similar premises.

No formal training is needed. The criteria for playgroup leaders are laid down by each local social services department. Many local authorities now organise courses for playgroup supervisors, and the National Extension College (32 Trumpington Street, Cambridge CB2 1SQ) runs a correspondence course.

If you are planning to run a playgroup in your own home, you must be prepared to invest a certain amount of money in sturdy, sound equipment (climbing frame, sandpit, painting equipment, constructional toys, etc). You will need insurance, and you will have to make sure that your home meets the required safety standards, so the Fire Officer will have to inspect your premises. You will also need planning permission, and you are legally obliged to register your playgroup with the local Department of Social Services. It is able to reject planning permission and prohibit that group being organised if it feels that the applicant is not suitable to hold the position.

Most of these requirements also apply to larger, hall-based groups, though you will probably not need to apply for planning permission, since most halls have permission for a variety of community activities which would include playgroups. Larger groups are often run by a committee consisting of the supervisor, at least one parent, the local health visitor, a secretary and chairman. Staff requirements for a large

251

group (of, say, 25 children) would include a supervisor, one or two paid assistants, and helpers working on a rota basis.

Fees can be calculated by adding together total costs (wages, rent, insurance, a fund for equipment, day-to-day expenses such as postage, repaires, etc) and dividing the total by the number of children that will be attending. If you find that the resulting fees are too high for local mothers to afford, the playgroup can be subsidised by fund-raising activities such as fetes and bazaars. It will help you to cover your costs if you charge fees in advance, and it is also a good idea to charge an 'absentee' fee of half the normal rate for children who are unable to attend for short periods. For further information, contact the Pre-School Playgroups Association (PPA).

Appendices

BE YOUR OWN BOSS!

How many people do you know who are making more money than you, often with much less knowledge and effort? Chances are they are in business for themselves, enjoying the freedom and opportunity that comes with being your own boss. But what sort of business should you start?

How do you go about it? Who can you turn to for sound, impartial advice? The answer is BUSINESS IDEAS LETTER, the monthly newsletter of THE INSTITUTE OF SMALL BUSINESS. Over the past 12 years BIL has covered thousands of business ideas and helped hundreds of people like yourself to get started on their own. Whether you simply want to make a few extra pounds each week in your spare time, or lay the foundation of your own business empire, BIL and THE INSTITUTE OF SMALL BUSINESS can help and advise you. And what is more, you can try our service FREE for one month, with no obligation whatsoever.

Complete the coupon or telephone us today for details.

The Institute of Small Business
Business Ideas Letter, FREEPOST, 13 London Road
Bromley, Kent BR1 1BR (No stamp)

Name _____

Address _____

_____

_____

Please send me without obligation details of your one month FREE trial offer, services and publications

Telephone 01-464 8686 — Now! Please quote WFY

Further Information

Before taking the plunge, it is absolutely essential to get all the help and advice you can, especially if you are planning to invest a lot of money in a business. Ring one of the specialist bodies listed below, go to the public library, do as much background reading as you have time for, consult your bank manager, solicitor and accountant, and talk to any friends who have succeeded in the area in which you are interested.

Small Firms Division Department of Industry
Abell House
John Islip Street
London SW1
Tel: 01-211 3000/6018
The Department of Industry has also established a number of regionally-based small firms centres.

London and South Eastern Region
Bulstrode Street
London W1
Tel: 01-487 4342
Freefone: 2444

South Western Region
Colston Centre
Colston Avenue
Bristol BS1 4UB
Tel: 0272-294546
Freefone: 2444

Northern Region
22 Newgate Shopping Centre
Newcastle upon Tyne NE1 5RH
Tel: 0632-25353
Freefone: 2444

North West Region
320-5 Royal Exchange
Manchester M2 7AH
Tel: 061-832 5282
Freefone: 2444
and

Working for Yourself

1 Old Hall Street
Liverpool L3 9HJ
Tel: 051-236 5756
Freefone: 2444

Yorkshire and Humberside Region
1 Park Row
City Square
Leeds LS1 5NR
Tel: 0532-445151
Freefone: 2444

East Midlands Region
48-50 Maid Marian Way
Nottingham NG1 6GF
Tel: 0602-49791
Freefone: 2444

West Midlands Region
Ladywood House
Stephenson Street
Birmingham B2 4DT
Tel: 021-643 3344
Freefone: 2444

Eastern Region
24 Brooklands Avenue
Cambridge CB2 2BU
Tel: 0223-63312
Freefone: 2444

Scotland
57 Bothwell Street
Glasgow G2 6TU
Tel: 041-248 6014
Freefone: 2444

Wales
16 St David's House
Wood Street
Cardiff CF1 1ER
Tel 0222-396116
Freefone: 2444

Northern Ireland
Department of Commerce
Chichester House
64 Chichester Street
Belfast BT1 4JX

Agricultural Cooperation and Marketing Services Ltd *(advice for farmers)*
Agricultural House
25 Knightsbridge
London SW1
Tel: 01-235 7853

Agricultural Development Advisory Service *(advice for farmers)*
Ministry of Agriculture, Fisheries and Food
Great Westminster House
Horseferry Road
London SW1
Tel: 01-216 6311

Agricultural Mortgage Corporation Ltd
Bucklersbury House
3 Queen Victoria Street
London EC4N 8DU
Tel: 01-236 5252

Association of British Travel Agents
55-7 Newman Street
London W1
Tel: 01-637 2444

Alliance of Small Firms
279 Church Road
London SE19 2QQ
Tel: 01-653 4798

Back Pain Association
Grundy House
Somerset Road
Teddington TW11 8TD *(send SAE)*

BBC External Services *(translation/interpreting work)*
Bush House
Strand
London WC2

Booksellers Association
154 Buckingham Palace Road
London SW1
Tel: 01-730 8214

British Franchise Association Ltd
15 The Poynings
Iver
Bucks SL0 9DS
Tel: 0753-653546

The British Hotels, Restaurants and Caterers Association
13 Cork Street
London W1
Tel: 01-499 6641

British Institute of Management
Management House
Parker Street
London WC2
Tel: 01-405 3456

British Tourist Authority *(interpreting work)*
64 St James's Street
London SW1
Tel: 01-629 9191

The Building Centre *(building trades work)*
26 Store Street
London WC1
Tel: 01-637 9001

Building Research Establishment *(building trades work)*
Bucknalls Lane
Watford WD2 7JR
or
Scottish Laboratory
Kelvin Road
Glasgow
or
Birmingham Engineering and Building Centre
Broad Street
Birmingham B1 2DB

Choice Magazine *(retirement planning)*
Bedford Chambers
Covent Garden
London WC2

Confederation of British Industry (CBI)
Centre Point
New Oxford Street
London WC1
Tel: 01-379 7400

Council for Small Industries in Rural Areas (COSIRA)
141 Castle Street
Salisbury
Wiltshire
Tel: 0722-6255

Disc Jockeys Federation
c/o 196 Stapleton Hall Road
London N4 4QL
Tel: 01-341 2785

Equipment Leasing Association
18 Upper Grosvenor Street
London W1
Tel: 01-491 2783

Federation of Master Builders
33 John Street
London WC1
Tel: 01-242 7583

Finance Houses Association
18 Upper Grosvenor Street
London W1
Tel: 01-491 2783

Hairdressing Council
17 Spring Street
London W2
Tel: 01-402 6367

Highlands and Islands Development Board
6 Castle Wynd
Inverness
Scotland IV2 3ED

Hotel Catering and Institutional Management Association
191 Trinity Road
London SW17
Tel: 01-767 1431

Hotel and Catering Industry Training Board
PO Box 18
Central Square
Wembley
Middlesex
Tel: 01-902 8865

Industrial and Commercial Finance Corporation (ICFC)
91 Waterloo Road
London SE1 8XP
Tel: 01-928 7822

Institute of Linguists
24a Highbury Grove
London N5 2EA
Tel: 01-359 7445

Institute of Directors
116 Pall Mall
London SW1
Tel: 01-839 1233

Institute of Personnel Management
Central House
Upper Woburn Place
London WC1
Tel: 01-387 2844

Institute of Small Businesses (Association)
1 Whitehall Place
London SW1A 2HD
Tel: 01-839 7645

International Air Transport Association *(licensing for travel agents)*
West London Air Terminal
London SW7 4ED
Tel: 01-370 4255

Lapidary Publications
84 High Street
Broadstairs
Kent

London Chamber of Commerce
69 Cannon Street
London EC4
Tel: 01-248 4444

London Tourist Board
26 Grosvenor Gardens
London SW1
Tel: 01-730 0791

Market Research Society
15 Belgrave Square
London SW1X 8PF
Tel: 01-235 4709

National Farmers' Union
Agriculture House
Knightsbridge
London SW1
Tel: 01-235 5077

National Federation of Retail Newsagents
2 Bridewell Place
London EC4
Tel: 01-353 6816

National Federation of Self-employed and Small Businesses Ltd
32 St Anne's Road West
Lytham St Annes
Lancashire
Tel: 0253-720911
and
45 Russell Square
London WC1
Tel: 01-636 2828

National Research Development Corporation
Kingsgate House
66 Victoria Street
London SW1
Tel: 01-828 3400

**The National Union of Small Shopkeepers of Great Britain
and Northern Ireland**
Westminster Buildings
Theatre Square
Nottingham NGL 6LH
Tel: 0602-45046

Northern Ireland Development Agency
Maryfield
100 Belfast Road
Hollywood
County Down

Pre-Retirement Association
17 Undine Street
Tooting
London SW17 8PP

Pre-School Playgroups Association
Alford House
Aveline Street
London SE11
Tel: 01-582 8871
or
7 Royal Terrace
Glasgow
Tel: 041-331 1340

Research Bureau Ltd *(market research)*
PO Box 203, Green Bank
Wapping
London E1 9PA
Tel: 01-488 1366

Retirement Homes Association
Southdowns
South Darenth
Dartford
Kent DA14 9LG

Scottish Development Agency
Small Business Division
102 Telford Road
Edinburgh

Society of Indexers
28 Johns Avenue
London NW4 4EN
Tel: 01-203 0929

Translators' Association
Society of Authors
84 Drayton Gardens
London SW10
Tel: 01-373 6642

Welsh Development Agency
Treforest Industrial Estate
Pontypridd
Mid-Glamorgan

Select Bibliography*

Part 1

Be Your Own Boss: How to became Self-employed, by John Blundell
(National Federation of the Self-employed)
Business of Your Own Today, by B Fraser Harrison (World's Work)
Buying and Running Your Own Business, by Ian Ford (Business Books)
Company Law, 5th edition, by M C Oliver (Macdonald & Evans)
The Complete Guide to Managing Your Business, ed Maggi McCormick
(Eagleman Publications)
Croner's Reference Book for the Self-employed, ed Daphne McAra
(Croner Publication Ltd)
Daily Telegraph Guide to Income Tax, by B Budibent (Collins)
Everyday Credit Checking, S Barzman (Thomas Y Crowell, New York)
Financing of Small Business, by J Bates (Sweet & Maxwell)
Focus on Redundancy, by Fred Kemp, Bernard Buttle and Derek Kemp
(Kogan Page)
Focus on Retirement, by Fred Kemp and Bernard Buttle (Kogan Page)
Going Solo, by William Perry and Derek Jones (BBC Publications)
A Guide to Franchising, by Martin Mendelsohn (Pergamon Press)
The Hambro Tax Guide, by A S Silke and W I Sinclair (Macdonald &
Janes, published annually)
How to Read a Balance Sheet, 5th revised edition (ILO)
How To Start Your Own Craft Business, by H Genfan and L Taetzsch
(Watson Guptill, New York)
Looking Ahead: A Guide to Retirement, by Fred Kemp and Bernard
Buttle (Macdonald & Evans)
Management of Trade Credit, by T G Hutson and J Butterworth (Gower
Press)
Managing for Results, by Peter F Drucker (Pan Books)
The Money Book, by Eamonn Fingleton and Tom Tickell *(Penguin)*
More Profit from Your Stock, by E A Jensen, 2nd edition (available from
the author, 39 Withdean Crescent, Brighton)
Occupation: Self-employed, by Rosemary Pettit (Wildwood House)
Rapid Company Growth, John Hazel and Alan Reid (Business Books)
Run Your Own Business, by Peter Douglas (Dent)
The Small Business Casebook, Sue Birley (MacMillan Press)
Small Firms Centres Publications 1–20 by various authors (Small Firms
Centres)

* A more extensive bibliography, divided by area of interest, is available from the
Small Firms Service. Many of the pamphlets produced by the Department of
Industry, the Department of Health and Social Security, the Inland Revenue, the
Department of Employment and the Department of the Environment will also be of
value.

Success in Bookkeeping for the Small Business, by G Whitehead (John Murray)
Success In Principles of Accounting, by G Whitehead (John Murray)
Understand Your Accounts, by A St John Price (Kogan Page)
VAT Made Easy, by A St John Price (Kogan Page)

Parts 2 and 3

Buying a Shop, E A Jensen (available from the author, 39 Withdean Crescent, Brighton)
Buying A Shop, A St John Price (Kogan Page)
A Catering Business of Your Own, by E M Turner, revised R H Johnson (Barrie & Jenkins)
Chaffer's Handbook to Hall Marks on Gold and Silver Plate (William Reeves)
Choice of Careers Booklets (HMSO)
The Fruit Garden Displayed (Royal Horticultural Society)
Gems Magazine (Lapidary Publications)
A Guide to the Building Regulations, by A J Elder (Architectural Press)
How To Become a Photographic Model, by Jean Campbell Dallas (Pelham Books)
How To Form a Playgroup (BBC Publications)
How to Write a Story and Sell It, by S Johns (Kennikat Press)
Jewellery Making and Design, by Augustus F Rose and Antonio Cirino (Dover Publications)
Money and Your Retirement, by E V Eves (Pre-Retirement Association)
Mother's Help, for Busy Mothers and Playgroup Leaders, (ed) Susan Dickinson (Collins)
Pottery, by Emmanuel Cooper (Macdonald Educational)
The Other Careers — Earning a Living in the Arts and Media, by Mike Bygrave, Joan Goodman and John Fordham (Wildwood House)
Restoring Old Junk, by Michele Brown (Lutterworth Press)
Running Your Own Hotel, by Arthur Neil (Barrie and Jenkins)
Simple Pottery, by Kenneth Drake (Studio Vista)
Soft Furnishing — A Practical Manual for the Home Upholsterer, by A V White (Routledge & Kegan Paul)
Technical Translator's Manual, (ed) J B Sykes (Aslib)
The Vegetable Garden Displayed (Royal Horticultural Society)
'Vogue' Guide to Knitting, Crochet and Macrame (Collins)
'Vogue' Sewing Book (Butterrick Pub Co)
Working with Gemstones, by V A Firsoff (David & Charles)
Working with Languages (Institute of Linguists)
Writers' and Artists' Yearbook (A & C Black)
Writing for the BBC (BBC Publications)
Writing for Television in the Seventies, by M Hulke (A & C Black)
You Too Can Write for Money, by Harvey Day (A Thomas)

Important Trade and Retail Journals

Antiques Trade Gazette
Metropress Ltd
116 Long Acre
London WC2

Autotrade
Morgan-Grampian Ltd
Morgan-Grampian House
Calderwood Street
London SE18

Bakers' Review
(Official Journal of the National Association of Master
    Bakers, Confectioners and Caterers)
Turret Press Ltd
886 High Road
Finchley
London N12 9SB

The Bookseller
12 Dyott Street
London WC1A 1DF

British Clothing Manufacturer
Textile Trade Publications Ltd
Knightsway House
20 Soho Square
London W1V 6DT

British Food Journal
Peterson House
North Bank
Berryhill Industrial Estate
Droitwich
Worcs WR9 9BL

The Builder's Journal
Hamerville Ltd
Vale House
32 Vale Road
Bushey
Watford
Herts

Building Trades Journal
Northwood Publications Ltd
Elm House
10-16 Elm Street
London WC1

Cabinet Maker and Retail Furnisher
Benn Brothers Ltd
25 New Street Square
London EC4A 3JA

Carpet Review Weekly
Haymarket Publishing Ltd
54-62 Regent Street
London W1

Caterer and Hotelkeeper
IPC Consumer Industries Press Ltd
40 Bowling Green Lane
London EC1

Catering Times
Northwood Publications Ltd
Elm House
10-16 Elm Street
London WC1X 0BP

Catering and Hotel Management
Link House
9 Dingwall Avenue
Croydon CR9 2TA

Chemist and Druggist
Benn Publications Ltd
Sovereign Way
Tonbridge
Kent TN9 1RW

Clothing and Footwear Journal
The Old School
Cogenhoe
Northampton NN7 1LT

Confectioner, Tobacconist, Newsagent
IPC Consumer Industries Press Ltd
40 Bowling Green Lane
London EC1

Craft and Hobby Dealer
Elliott Publications Ltd
9 Queen Victoria Street
Reading RG1 1SY

Do It Yourself Retailing
The Link House Group
Dingwall Avenue
Croydon CR9 2TA

Drapers' Record
Textile Trade Publications Ltd
Knightway House
20 Soho Square
London W1V 6DT

Electrial and Radio Trading
IPC Electrical-Electronic Press Ltd
Dorset House
Stamford Street
London SE1 9LU

Fashion Weekly
IPC Consumer Industries Ltd
40 Bowling Green Lane
London EC1

Fish Friers' Review
(National Federation of Fish Friers)
Federation House
289 Dewsbury Road
Leeds LS11 5HW

Fish Trader
(Official Journal of the National Federation of Fishmongers)
Retail Journals Ltd
Queensway House
Redhill
Surrey RH1 1QS

Franchise World
James House
37 Nottingham Road
London SW17

Frozen Foods
Retail Journals Ltd
Queensway House
Redhill
Surrey RH1 1QS

Retail Fruit Trade Review
Retail Fruit Trade Federation Ltd
108-10 Market Towers
No 1 Nine Elms Lane
London SW8

Fur Weekly News
122 Lea Bridge Road
London E5 9RB

Garage and Transport
Hulton Technical Press
Warwick House
Azalea Drive
Swanley
Kent

The Grocer
5-7 Southwark Street
London SE1 1RQ

Hairdressers' Journal
IPC Consumer Industries Press Ltd
40 Bowling Green Lane
London EC1

Hardware Today
(The British Hardware Federation Journal)
20 Harborne Road
Edgbaston
Birmingham B15 3AB

Hardware Trade Journal
Benn Publications Ltd
Sovereign Way
Tonbridge
Kent TN9 1RW

Hi-Fi Dealer News
Dalbeattie (Printers) Ltd
21-23 Balham Hill
London SW12 2DY

Hi-Fi Trade Journal
Kingsacre
Crown Hill
Llantwit Fardre
Pontypridd
Mid-Glamorgan

Hospitality
(Official Magazine of the Hotel, Catering and
Institutional Management Association)
D A Goodall Ltd
New Bridge Street House
30-4 New Bridge Street
London EC4

Meat Trader
(Official Journal of the National Federation of Meat Traders)
Wheatland Journals Ltd
157 Hagden Lane
Watford WD1 8LW

Meat Trades' Journal
49-50 Hatton Garden
London EC1

Men's Wear
Textile Trade Publications Ltd
Knightway House
20 Soho Square
London W1V 6DT

Motor Trader
IPC Transport Press Ltd
Dorset House
Stamford Street
London SE1 9LU

Music Week
Music Week Ltd
40 Long Acre
London WC2E 9JT

National Hairdresser
(Official Journal of the National Federation of Hairdressers)
T G Scott & Son Ltd
30-32 Southampton Street
London WC2E 7HR

Newsagent and Bookshop
Haymarket Publishing Ltd
Craven House
34 Fouberts Place
London W1A 2HG

Nurseryman and Garden Centre
Benn Publications Ltd
Sovereign Way
Tonbridge
Kent TN9 1RW

Off Licence News
5-7 Southwark Street
London SE1 1RQ

Pet Store Trader
Old Colony House
South King Street
Manchester M2 2DA

Pharmaceutical Journal
1 Lambeth High Street
London SE1 7JN

Retail Chemist
Benn Publications Ltd
Sovereign Way
Tonbridge
Kent TN9 1RW

Retail Confectioner Tobacconist
(Journal of the Retail Confectioners and Tobacconists Association)
CTN Enterprises Ltd
53 Christchurch Avenue
London N12 0DH

Retail Fruit Trade Review
(Retail Fruit Trade Federation)
8-15 Russell Chambers
Covent Garden
London WC2

Retail Jeweller
Northwood Publications Ltd
Northwood House
93-99 Goswell Road
London EC1

Retail Newsagent, Tobacconist and Confectioner
(Official Journal of the National Federation of Retail Newsagents)
News and Book Trade Review & Stationer's Gazette Limited
21-25 Earl Street
London EC2

Scottish Grocer
36 North Frederick Street
Glasgow G1

Sports Trader
Benn Publications Ltd
Sovereign Way
Tonbridge
Kent TN9 1RW

The Sub-Postmaster
The National Federation of Sub-Postmasters
Scan Publishing Co Ltd
Scan House
4-8 Church Street
Shoreham-by-Sea
West Sussex

Toy Trader
Wheatland Journals Ltd
157 Hagden Lane
Watford WD1 8LW

Travel Agency
Maclean-Hunter Ltd
30 Old Burlington Street
London W1X 2AE

Note: This is not a complete list of trade journals, and traders in more specialised areas, or those seeking alternatives to those listed here, should consult *British Rate & Date (Brad)*, Maclean-Hunter Ltd, 30 Old Burlington Street, London W1.

Members of the British Franchise Association (BFA)*

Company (name of franchise in bold)	Contact	Area of activity
Apollo Window Blinds Ltd Johnstone Avenue Cardonald Industrial Estate Glasgow G52	James Watson Tel: 041-810 3021	Supply of all types of blinds: provision of estimating, installation, and after sales service
Autopro Swift Tools Ltd Badminton Road Trading Estate Yate Bristol BS17 5JS	S B Parkin or N Brayshaw Tel: 0454-314971	Sale of tools to the garage trade through van sale distribution
British School of Motoring Ltd 102 Sydney Street Chelsea London SW3 6NJ	David Acheson Tel: 01-351 2377	Driving tuition
Budget Rent-a-Car International Inc International House 85 Gt North Road Hatfield Herts AL9 5EF	Max McHardy Tel: Hatfield 68266	National and international self-drive car, van and truck rental service
City Link Transport Holdings Ltd 13-14 Ascot Road Clockhouse Lane Feltham Middlesex TW14 8QF	Robert Thomas Tel: Ashford 43721	Same day and overnight parcel delivery service
The **Coca Cola** Export Corporation Pemberton House Wright's Lane London W8 5SN	John Marwood Tel: 01-938 2131	Soft drinks
Cookmate Reject Kitchen Shop Cookshop Supplies Ltd Unit 5, Southern Road Aylesbury Bucks	Brian Howlett Tel 0296-20695	Kitchen gadgets, equipment, accessories and furniture in glass, china, metal, plastic and wood (retail)

* The BFA was formed in 1977 by a number of leading British and international companies engaged in the distribution of goods and services through independent outlets under franchise and licensee agreements. The aims of the BFA include establishing a clear definition of the ethical franchising standards to assist members of the public, press, potential investors and government bodies in differentiating between sound business opportunities and any suspect investment offers. However, we wish to stress that non-membership of the BFA does not imply any criticism of a franchisor.

Company *(name of franchise in bold)*	*Contact*	*Area of activity*
Dinol (Car Care) UK Ltd Commerce House Stuart Street Luton Beds LU1 5BY	Sigurd Wilberg Tel 0582-413071	Vehicle rust-proofing and other car care services
Dyno-Rod Ltd The Zockoll Group Zockoll House 143 Maple Road Surbiton Surrey KT6 4BJ	Vaughan Thursby- Pelham Tel: 01-549 9711	Drain and pipe cleaning service
Halford's Franchise Halfords Ltd George House 121 High Street Henley in Arden Solihull West Midlands B95 5AU	Albert Lee Tel: 05642-3378	Retailing motor accessories, cycles, camping, caravanning and leisure goods (Isle of Man, Channel Islands and Ireland)
Holiday Inns (UK) Inc Windmill House Windmill Road Brentford Middlesex TW8 0QH	John Duncan Tel: 01-568 8800	Hotels
Home Tune Ltd Home Tune House Guildford Road Effingham nr Leatherhead Surrey KT24 5QS	Duncan Whitfield Tel: Bookham 56656	Car-tuning service
Kall-Kwik Printing Ltd K K Printing (UK) Ltd Kall-Kwik House, Tennyson Road Hanwell Middlesex W7 1LH	M Gerstenhaber Tel: 01-840 3222	Quick printing centres offering comprehensive design, printing, finishing and photocopying services
Kardomah Restaurants & Coffee Houses Trust Houses Forte Catering Ltd Quadrant House 1 Wardour Street London W1	David Merry Tel: 01-734 2704	Kardomah restaurants
Kentucky Fried Chicken (GB) Ltd Hawley Lane Farnborough Hants	Julien Fletcher Tel: 0252-516251	Fast food
Ladyline (Holdings) Ltd Bank Chambers 3 Cheshire Street Market Drayton Shropshire TF9 1JN	J Riordan Tel: 0630-2217	Retailing of marine and outdoor leisure products

Company (name of franchise in bold)	Contact	Area of activity
Pizza Express Ltd 29 Wardour Street London W1V 3HB	Ian Neill Tel: 01-437 7215	Pizzeria restaurants
Pizza Hut Inc (UK branch), 149 Earl's Court Road Kensington London SW5	Peter Bassi Tel: 01-370 6443	Family-orientated restaurants
Power-Rod Ltd Lidgra House 250 Kingsbury Road London NW9	David Wheeler Tel:01-204 9018	Drain and pipe-cleaning contractors
Prontaprint Ltd Executive Offices Coniscliffe House Darlington DL3 7EX	Martin Richmond Tel: 0325-55391	Printing shops
Pronuptia & Youngs (Franchise) Ltd 70-8 York Way Kings Cross London N1	Edward Young Tel: 01-278 7722	Bridal attire retail shops: formal wear hire service for men
Safeclean International D G Cook Ltd Pound House Upton Didcot Oxon OX11 9JG	Desmond Cook Tel: 0235-850387	Hand-cleaning of carpets and upholstery: curtain cleaning on site
Scottish & Newcastle Inns Ltd Abbey Brewery 111 Holyrood Road Edinburgh	Andrew James Tel: 031-556 2591 ext 2887	Public houses, restaurants and off-licence shops
ServiceMaster Ltd 50 Commercial Square Freeman's Common Leicester LE2 7SR	Brian Smith Tel: 0533-548620	Carpet and curtain cleaning, etc
Servowarm Servotomic Ltd 199 The Vale Acton London W3 7YY	Ted Brammer Tel: 01-743 1244	Central heating and central heating products
Silver Shield Screens Ltd 38-42 Holbrook Lane Coventry West Midlands	John Oliver Tel: 0203-661311	Twenty-four hour windscreen replacement service
Steiner Products Ltd The Broadway Cottages Stanmore Middlesex HA7 4DU	J G Macaulay Tel: 01-954 6121	Ladies' and men's hairdressing and beauty

Company (name of franchise in bold)	Contact	Area of activity
Thorntons J W Thornton Ltd Derwent Street Belper Derbyshire DE5 1WP	R E Smith Tel: 077382-4181	Specialist chocolate and sugar confectionery retail
Thuro-Clean Ltd 55 Bondway London SW8 1SJ	Ralph James Tel: 01-582 6033	'In home' cleaning of carpets, upholstery and curtains: carpet dyeing and soft furnishings service after flood/fire
TI/Midas Ltd 332-6 Goldhawk Road Hammersmith London W6 0XF	Nicholas Greville Tel: 01-741 1156	Retail exhaust system replacement
Uticolor (Great Britain) Ltd Sheraton House 35 North Street York YO1 1JD	Eric Bottomley Tel: 0904-37798	Repair, recolouring and restoration of vinyl coverings
Willie Wurst Inns Cloverbest Restaurant Associates Ltd Ingleside House Hawarden Avenue Douglas Isle of Man	J Stephen Murray Tel: 0624-21121	Retail sales of traditional German sausages
Wimpy International Ltd 214 Chiswick High Road London W4 1PH	Tony Dutfield Tel: 01-994 6454	Fast food
Ziebart GB Envirogarde Group Ltd Ziebart House Dominion Way Worthing Sussex	Keith Tarry Tel: 0903-204171	Vehicle rustproofing and other vehicle services

Glossary of Key Business Terms

It is too often assumed that the new or recently established small businessman will be conversant with all the technical jargon used in the fields of business and management. To counter this, we have included a short glossary of key terms and a list of more detailed practical reference works you may wish to consult. We acknowledge the assistance of John Blundell in the compilation of this glossary.

account(s)
1. **annual accounts** financial records of your business prepared by your accountant for the Inland Revenue.
2. **credit account** agreement whereby a valued and trusted customer is allowed to buy goods/obtain services for which he pays later (say monthly or quarterly).
3. **current account** bank account on which the bank does not pay *interest*, and from which the customer can make immediate cash or cheque withdrawals.
4. **profit and loss account** record of profits before tax, the tax due and profits after tax. Depending on your business it will also show other factors, allowances and amounts brought forward from the last financial year and to be carried forward to the next financial year.
5. **statement of account** record sent to you by your bank or a company with which you are dealing showing all transactions over a given period and concluding with the amount due from you or to you on a certain date.
6. **trading account** record showing *gross* profit only.

Articles of Association the rules which establish how a company must be run. They are drawn up when the company is formed and represent a contract between the company and its shareholders. Standard Articles of Association are now used by most new small companies.

asset piece of property owned by a company or one of its directors; see *liquid assets*.

audit process of checking the accuracy of company financial records by a third party (auditor) which is independent of both you and your accountant. He checks your financial records, states whether in his view they are accurate and may make recommendations on the future keeping of books/*accounts* by you or your accountant.

balance sheet record of your *assets* and *liabilities* at a particular date, normally the end of the financial year.

bankruptcy situation 1. where an individual cannot meet his bills 2. where a debtor (individual or company) is declared *insolvent* and his property thereafter administered for the benefit of his proven creditors.

black economy that part of the economy which does not appear in official statistics and which thus illegally avoids tax and *National Insurance* payments.

broker person who acts as an agent for others; usually used to describe 1. a person who acts for one or more insurance companies 2. a person who buys and sells stocks for members of the public on the Stock Exchange.

budgetary control system of monitoring and controlling expenditure to keep it in line with income and company financial projections.

capital total resources (of a company, etc) including property, cash, equipment and other goods.

capital gains tax tax on the profits resulting from the sale of *capital* interests and assets.

cash book day-to-day notebook in which are recorded payments and receipts.

cash discount deduction of a given amount from the price of an article or service, usually in return for cash payment, early purchase, etc.

cash flow flow of cash required to finance a business for a given period.

cash flow chart record of all payments and receipts over a specified period which establishes the *cash flow* position of a firm.

casual an employee who does not work for you on a regular basis. He/she is normally paid *net* but can be paid *gross* by prior arrangement with the Inland Revenue. It is essential to keep a complete and accurate record of all payments made to casual *employees* including their names and addresses.

chartered accountant fully qualified account who is a member of the Institute of Chartered Accountants and qualified to *audit* public company *accounts.*

clearing bank bank which is a member of the London Bankers' Clearing House, which settles inter-bank accounts at the end of each day's trading.

commission percentage of sale price paid as a fee to an agent for arranging that sale.

company corporate body established under the Companies Act.

credit 1. period allowed for repayment of loan or payment for goods or service 2. borrowing limit imposed by bank or other creditor 3. addition to financial records made on the right-hand side of the books; cf *debit.*

Customs and Excise body responsible for the collection of customs duty, excise duty and *VAT.*

debenture legal document specifying the terms of a loan.

debit deduction recorded on the left-hand side of an account.

dividend share of profits paid by a company to its shareholders.

education visit visit by a *Customs and Excise* officer to a business soon after it has registered for *VAT* or a request to educate the trader in keeping VAT records, etc.

employee person working for you either on a regular or casual basis. Unless he is working for you temporarily he will have a contract specifying the conditions of work, level of remuneration, etc. You must in most cases deduct Class 1 *National Insurance* and Schedule E tax (*PAYE*).

finance company corporate body which lends larger amounts and for longer periods than clearing banks.

financial year period covered by your profit and loss account; ie a company's accounting year.

fixed cost expense or *overhead* which does not vary with the level of production.

franchise the right to sell the product or service of a franchising company or to carry on a business using a name belonging to, or associated with, a franchisor.

freehold land or property owned (rather than leased or rented) by an individual, company, etc.

gilt-edged (refers to) investment where there is effectively no risk of loss or default.

goodwill *asset* consisting of the good reputation and established clientele of a retail or other business. It is difficult to determine the cash value of goodwill and its subjective nature is likely to cause difficulties if the person selling a business claims goodwill as a major factor in setting the sale price.

gratuity tip; taxable.

gross total before deductions; cf *net*.

income tax tax on an individual's income. The flat rate is currently 30 per cent and the tax is graduated so that higher income earners pay a larger percentage of their salary to the Inland Revenue. Most employees are taxed at source (*PAYE*), but most self-employed people make annual income tax declarations and pay a lump sum to the Inland Revenue.

indirect tax tax levied on expenditure rather than income (eg *VAT*).

inflation 1. annual increase in the supply of currency 2. (more commonly) the rate at which prices are increasing (usually judged by the retail price index).

insolvency situation in which a person, company, etc, is not able to pay his/its bills. Insolvency does not constitute *bankruptcy* however, as the insolvent may have assets which can eventually be realised to pay his bills while the bankrupt is deemed not to have such assets.

inspection visit visit by the *Customs and Excise* officer to a business every three or four years to inspect the financial records for *VAT* purposes.

interest money paid (usually as a monthly or annual percentage) for the use of *capital*. Rates of interest vary according to the nature and length of a loan, prevailing economic conditions and the government's fiscal policy.

internal audit *audit* of a company's books and appraisal of company efficiency conducted by an *employee* of that company.

invoice document issued by a business to a client giving full details of a transaction or series of transactions and indicating terms of payment. If they are registered for *VAT*, there is a legal minimum of information you must provide.

liability a debt.

limited company business association in which the liability of the directors in the event of *bankruptcy* is limited to the loss of business (ie not personal) *assets;* cf *partnership.*

liquid asset asset which can be realised into cash very quickly.

liquidation legal process of closing down a *bankrupt* company and selling off its *assets* to pay debts.

liquidity extent of the cash *assets* of a company or its ability to realise other assets into cash.

loan capital finance lent to a company for a specified period at a fixed rate of *interest* and normally secured against, say, the business premises of that company. It differs from share capital in that the provider of loan capital has no 'share' of the profits or control in the running of the company.

loss leader goods/services deliberately provided at a loss in the hope that it will attract customers who will buy other goods/services from which the provider of those goods/services will profit.

market research process of identifying and assessing the market for goods and services. It attempts to break down the market into segments and identifies motives for buying a particular good, trade-offs between price and quality, likelihood of repurchase, frequency of purchase, etc.

minimum lending rate rate of interest at which the Bank of England will lend money to other banks. If affects all other interest rates which tend to other banks. It affects all other interest rates which tend to rise or fall in line with it, and is a major tool of government fiscal policy.

National Insurance state-run scheme by which all employees, employers and self-employed people pay a percentage of their earnings to the government in return for payments in periods of unemployment and/or sickness.

net total after deductions, cf *gross.*

opportunity cost the amount of money which would have been earned if you had used your time and money elsewhere. If you are spending £20,000 on buying and stocking a shop, remember that over a year, with interest rates of 16 per cent, that would have earned an additional £3200. This is the opportunity cost of using your *capital* to set up a retail business.

overdraft 1. amount owed to a bank 2. ceiling to which a business creditor can borrow, an overdraft, unlike a loan, can be recalled by the bank at any time.

overhead cost which does not vary according to the level of production; see *fixed cost.*

overtrading situation in which a company is unable to support its high level of trading activity with sufficient capital, causing *liquidity* and *cash flow* problems.

partnership business association in which the partners are formally and personally responsible for the debts they incur. Certain professions (eg lawyers and architects) must engage in this form of association (ie are not allowed to form a *limited company*).

patent exclusive privilege, protected by law, to make and sell an invention or new product for a specified period.

PAYE pay as you earn; method of collecting tax from employees at source. Employers must *debit* the necessary amount of *income tax* and *National Insurance* from their *employees'* salaries and forward it to the Inland Revenue.

registered office the office which is registered with the Registrar of the Companies.

Schedule D — cases 1 and 2 Inland Revenue Schedule which defines the tax allowances available to *self-employed persons.*

Schedule E Inland Revenue Schedule which defines the tax allowances available to employed persons.

secured creditor person whose debt is guaranteed, for example, by using his business premises as collateral in any transaction.

self-employed person one working on his own, in a freelance capacity or in his own business. He is not under the control, direction or supervision of an employer, will supply his own equipment and organises his own work, hours, etc. He pays tax under Schedule D and pays Class 2 and 4 *National Insurance.*

shop premises where goods or services are provided to the public on cash or credit terms. If your premises meet these criteria, you should understand and comply with the regulations stated in the Shop Act 1950 and the Shops and Railways Premises Act 1963.

stock finished goods, goods in the middle of production and raw materials in store which count towards the *capital* resources of a business.

tax exemption certificate photo identity card issued to builders by the Inland Revenue which allows main contractors to pay them *gross* (ie without having deducted 30 per cent of the contract price minus the cost of materials and *VAT*). Without this certificate a main contractor will deduct this sum automatically and forward it to the Inland Revenue.

trade discount percentage reduction in price offered by one trader to another in an allied area of business (eg standard 33⅓ per cent discount on the price of books given by a publisher to a bookseller).

value added tax (VAT) percentage tax imposed at all stages of production. The trader forwards (usually quarterly) to *Customs and Excise* the amount of tax he has collected and the amount he has paid out. The rate of VAT is currently 15 per cent and is levied on all businesses with a turnover (or self-employed people with an income) greater than £15,000 per annum (not excluding goods which are exempt from VAT).

variable cost cost which varies according to the level of production; cf *fixed cost, overhead.*

wholesaler person or company, between the producer and the retailer who buys in large quantities from the former and sells in smaller quantities to the latter.

working capital proportion of a company's capital which is tied up in the normal day-to-day business of the company.

OTHER REFERENCE WORKS

Company Auditing: Concepts and Practices T A Lee (The Institute of Chartered Accountants in Scotland)
Handbook of Industrial Relations Practice Kevin Hawkins (Kogan Page)
Handbook of Management edited by Thomas Kempner (Penguin)
International Dictionary of Management edited by Hano Johannsen and G Terry Page (Kogan Page)
Operations Management T E Vollmann (Addison-Wesley, USA)
Penguin Dictionary of Commerce edited by Michael Green (Penguin)

Index

Index of Advertisers

285